# THE SUPREME COURT
## OF THE UNITED KINGDOM

HISTORY · ART · ARCHITECTURE

# THE SUPREME COURT
## OF THE UNITED KINGDOM
### HISTORY · ART · ARCHITECTURE

*Edited by Chris Miele*

**MERRELL**
LONDON · NEW YORK

FOREWORD ......................................... 7

LORD PHILLIPS

PROLOGUE ......................................... 8

JACK STRAW

FROM COUNTY HALL TO
SUPREME COURT ........................... 12

BRENDA HALE

LAW LORDS AND JUSTICES ............ 36

TOM BINGHAM

THE PLACE:
PARLIAMENT SQUARE .................... 46

CHRIS MIELE

'A DAINTY PIECE OF ORNAMENT':
THE ARCHITECTURE OF THE
FORMER MIDDLESEX GUILDHALL .... 72

JEREMY MUSSON

GOTHIC 'WITH A DIFFERENCE':
SCULPTURE AND DECORATIVE
ARTS AT THE SUPREME COURT OF
THE UNITED KINGDOM ................. 98

PETER CORMACK

THE DESIGN OF THE SUPREME
COURT OF THE UNITED
KINGDOM ...................................... 138

HUGH FEILDEN

SUPREME AND HIGH COURT
ARCHITECTURE IN THE
COMMON-LAW TRADITION: AN
INTERNATIONAL PERSPECTIVE ...... 174

G.A. BREMNER

EPILOGUE: MEMORIES OF THE
MIDDLESEX GUILDHALL AS A
CRIMINAL COURT, 1968–2007 ......... 198

FABYAN EVANS

ENDNOTES ...................................... 209

SELECTED SOURCES ......................... 212

CONTRIBUTORS' BIOGRAPHIES .............. 213

CREDITS ........................................ 214

INDEX ........................................... 217

PICTURE CREDITS ............................ 221

*Pages 6–7:* Her Majesty Queen Elizabeth II and His Royal Highness The Duke of Edinburgh arriving to open the Supreme Court of the United Kingdom on 16 October 2009. Lord Phillips, President of the Supreme Court, showed the Queen and the Duke round the building.

# FOREWORD

The creation of a Supreme Court is a great event in the history of the constitution of the United Kingdom, and it is right that it should be marked by the publication of this book.

No better location could have been found for the court than opposite the United Kingdom Parliament and next to Westminster Abbey in Parliament Square. These buildings are famous around the world. The same has not been true of the Middlesex Guildhall, but that will now change. The grime of a century has been cleaned away to reveal a handsome building of gleaming white stone. Inside, the careful adaptation and renovation will surely make a lasting impression on those who come to take part in appeals, or just to look.

Compared to some of its neighbours, the present building is not old. It first opened its doors as the Middlesex Guildhall in 1913. But the Guildhall was built on a site that has been associated with the administration of justice for more than two hundred years and one that has been subject to continual development as part of the precinct of the Abbey since the Middle Ages.

Within this book, distinguished contributors have brought to life the history both of the highest court in the United Kingdom and of the building and its contents. The authors explain the sensitive approach taken to the important task of converting the Guildhall to a Supreme Court, and have much to say about the site on which it stands and its surroundings. I am delighted that these contributors include my predecessor Lord Bingham of Cornhill, whose enthusiastic support for the creation of a Supreme Court is but one facet of the unique contribution that he has made to the administration of justice in this country.

I hope that, like the building, this is a book that you will take delight in visiting and revisiting.

*The Right Hon. Lord Phillips of Worth Matravers,*
*President of the Supreme Court*

# PROLOGUE

On 1 October 2009 the new Supreme Court took its place at the pinnacle of the United Kingdom's system of justice. Its opening was a constitutional landmark and an exciting moment in our history.

The Law Lords have served the United Kingdom and many Commonwealth jurisdictions with great distinction over many decades. But while they were based in the House of Lords, the highest court in the land appeared beyond the reach of a great number of the British public, and people were misled into thinking that judges also act as legislators. As Walter Bagehot argued nearly a century and a half ago, a Supreme Court should be 'a great conspicuous tribunal' and 'ought not to be hidden beneath the robes of a legislative assembly'. The creation of the United Kingdom Supreme Court (UKSC) marks the culmination of a long process of separation of the judiciary from the legislature and executive.

Institutions have to adapt and change to survive and maintain their legitimacy. The ability of the British Constitution to do this is, as Bagehot noted, 'its genius'. The Supreme Court is a perfect example of this. It maintains the historic balance between Parliament, government and the judiciary – the bedrock of the British constitutional settlement. But the judges are in a new environment, a refurbished building with modern facilities and technology and all the benefits these bring. As former Poet Laureate Sir Andrew Motion's fine poem, 'Lines for the Supreme Court', expresses it: 'New structures but an old foundation stone'.

It was a condition of the permission granted to the Ministry of Justice to convert the former Middlesex Guildhall into a home for the new Supreme Court that a book be produced to record the old building and document the transition to the new. This book not only fulfils that condition but also completes the process of establishing the Supreme Court as an institution separate from both Parliament and government. I am enormously grateful to Chris Miele and his team, and to Merrell Publishers, for enabling this to happen, and, of course, to the many people who played a part in creating a Supreme Court of which the United Kingdom can be proud.

*The Right Hon. Jack Straw, MP,*
*Lord Chancellor and Secretary of State for Justice*

## Lines for the Supreme Court

*Andrew Motion, Poet Laureate 1999–2009*

Tides tumbled sand through seas long-lost to earth;
Sand hardened into stone – stone cut, then brought
To frame the letter of four nations' laws
And square the circle of a single court.

Here Justice sits and lifts her steady scales
Within the Abbey's sight and Parliament's
But independent of them both. And bound
By truth of principle and argument.

A thousand years of judgment stretch behind –
The weight of rights and freedoms balancing
With fairness and with duty to the world:
The clarity time-honoured thinking brings.

New structures but an old foundation stone:
The mind of Justice still at liberty
Four nations separate but linked as one:
The light of reason falling equally.

The principal elevation of the former
Middlesex Guildhall, shortly after the
restoration and refurbishment that
have transformed it into the United
Kingdom Supreme Court.

# FROM COUNTY HALL TO SUPREME COURT

BRENDA HALE

*The closure of the Crown Court at the Middlesex Guildhall in March 2007 was an occasion of great sadness for many ... For others, the closure ... was also an occasion of great excitement. The third phase in the life of the Guildhall was about to begin.*

MIDDLESEX

*Previous page:* 1. The coat of arms of the County of Middlesex.

*Below:* 2. Map of the County of Middlesex, 1616.

*Opposite, top left:* 3. Interior of the old Middlesex Sessions House on Clerkenwell Green, 1809.

*Opposite, bottom left:* 4. Exterior of the old Middlesex Sessions House on Clerkenwell Green, 1796.

*Opposite, top right:* 5. Sir Baptist Hicks, Middlesex Magistrate and philanthropist; portrait attributed to Paul van Somer, and now hanging outside Courtroom 3 in the United Kingdom Supreme Court building.

*Opposite, bottom right:* 6. Hugh Percy, 1st Duke of Northumberland, Lord Lieutenant of the County of Middlesex; portrait by Thomas Gainsborough. It now hangs in the Supreme Court Library.

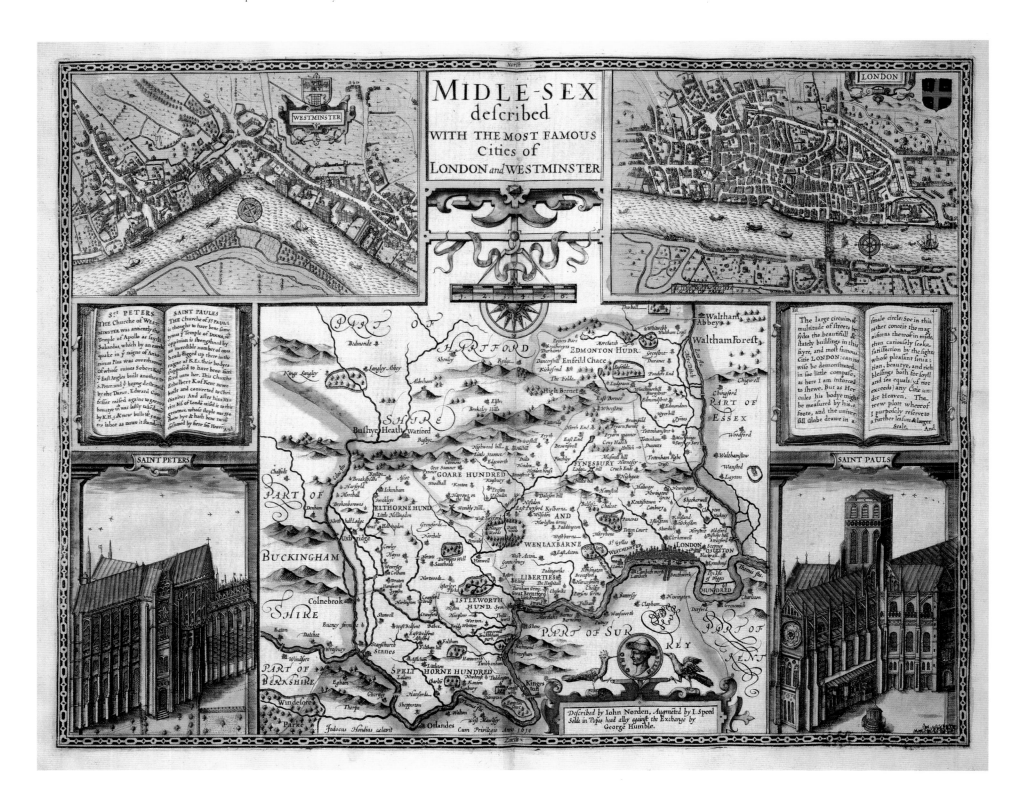

The Supreme Court building on Parliament Square has been home to three different institutions since first opening its doors in 1913: the Middlesex County Council, the Crown Court at the Middlesex Guildhall, and the Supreme Court of the United Kingdom. It is also the third guildhall to have been built on this site.

## The Middlesex County Council

The Middlesex Guildhall was built to house the Middlesex County Council and the Middlesex Justices, despite no longer being in the county.[1] Middlesex (fig. 1), the ancient county of the middle Saxons, had included within its boundaries both the self-governing City of London and the largely autonomous 'Liberty' originally granted to the abbots of Westminster (fig. 2). There was no established county town, indeed no town of any real importance elsewhere in the county. The county Assizes, where the most serious crimes were tried 'on indictment' before judge and jury, were held at the Old Bailey in the City of London. The county Quarter Sessions, where the less serious indictable crimes were tried before the county Justices of the Peace and a jury, were held in the Middlesex Sessions House on Clerkenwell Green in the county of Middlesex (fig. 3). This handsome classical building, designed by Thomas Rogers, the County Surveyor, was erected from 1779 to 1782 (fig. 4). It replaced the Sessions House in nearby St John Street. This was known as Hicks' Hall, because it had been built for the Justices in 1611 by Sir Baptist Hicks (1551–1629; fig. 5). Before that they had assembled at the Castle Tavern in St John Street. As well as their Quarter Sessions, the Justices also held general sessions of the peace, for the summary trial of petty offenders, and conducted much of the rest of the county administration, such as it was, in their Sessions House.

Local justice in the Liberty of Westminster, however, was from medieval times conducted in the Tothill Street gatehouse of the old Abbey precinct. Then, in 1766, the 1st Duke of Northumberland (fig. 6), Lord Lieutenant of the County of Middlesex, financed the purchase of some ancient buildings on the west side of King Street. King Street ran from Charing Cross to the Abbey precinct, parallel to but to the west of the present Whitehall and Parliament Street, and ended roughly opposite the north transept of the Abbey.

*Below:* 7. Map showing the precincts of the Middlesex Guildhall, *c.* 1789. + marks the spot.

*Right, top:* 8. Detail from the Bayeux Tapestry, before 1082: 'He comes before King Edward'.

*Right, bottom:* 9. Detail from the Bayeux Tapestry, before 1082: 'The body of King Edward is carried to the Church of St Peter the Apostle'.

*Opposite, top left:* 10. Conjectural reconstruction of Westminster Abbey and Westminster Hall in Norman times, showing the Sanctuary Tower in the top left-hand corner of the Abbey precinct.

*Opposite, top right:* 11. Edward the Confessor, panel from a rood screen, *c.* 1450.

*Opposite, centre:* 12. The Abbey Sanctuary before its destruction, 1775.

*Opposite, bottom:* 13. Gateway to Westminster Bridewell, near Greencoat Place. The gateway was first erected in 1655, and resited in the railings behind the Middlesex Guildhall in 1969.

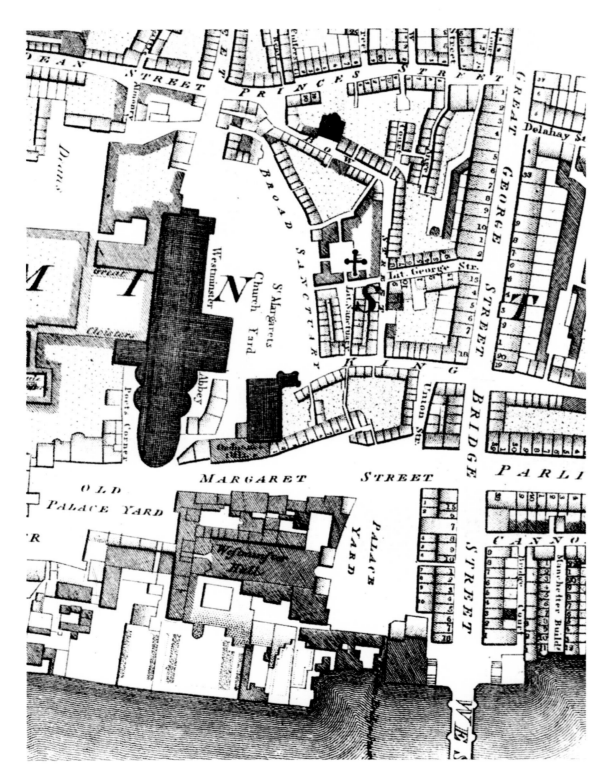

(The architect John Gwynn, who had big ideas for the improvement of London and Westminster, thought it 'a mean and obscure spot for a court house'.)[2]

An Act of 1777 authorized the building of a new courthouse or guildhall for the use of the Liberty. The site chosen for the new courthouse was just across Little George Street from the old court and at that time was occupied by the Westminster market. But the site had been built upon for a long time (fig. 7). It stood on Thorney Island, in ancient times a slightly elevated area of dry land amid the surrounding marshes, bounded by rivulets in the delta formed as the Tyburn River flowed into the Thames, which was then much wider and shallower than it is now. Some think that there was once a ford across the marshes from the bottom of ancient Watling Street (roughly where Buckingham Palace now stands) to Thorney Island and thence across the Thames to meet the end of the road to Dover.[3] This is logical, but there is no archaeological evidence to support it. There is, however, archaeological evidence of Roman settlement on the island. There are also many tales about when the first Christian church was built there, mostly put about by medieval monks at Westminster anxious to give their foundation the credentials to rival St Paul's in the City of London.

John Flete, a monk writing in the fifteenth century, dated the first church at AD 184, founded by the British king Lucius. Sulcard, a monk writing in the eleventh century, told

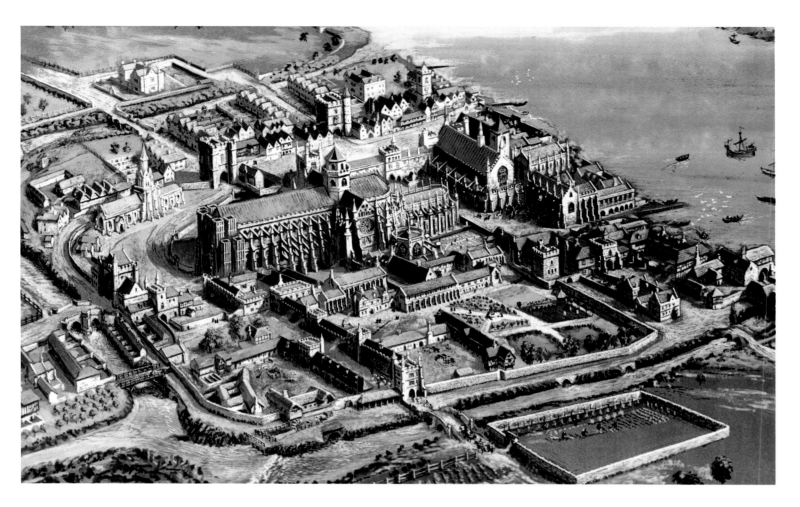

how King Aethelbert of Kent (c. 560–616), having founded a church dedicated to St Paul in London, prompted a rich Londoner and his wife to follow suit with a church dedicated to St Peter on Thorney Island. Later legend identified this couple as King Saeberht of the East Saxons (before 604–616/617) and his wife, Aethelgoda, who are thought to have founded a church, known as the West Minster, in the early seventh century. It is doubtful whether their church survived for long. Later tradition had it that the church was eventually restored by King Offa of the East Saxons (after 694–709) early in the eighth century. A little later, Offa the Great of Mercia (757–796) is said to have granted land to St Peter's, Westminster. In the middle of the tenth century, King Edgar (959–975) sold the site to St Dunstan (c. 909–988), who founded there a Benedictine monastery with monks, in place of the minster with its secular clerks. King Edgar and others gave benefactions to the monastery, which had become moderately prosperous by the early eleventh century.

The royal connections with Westminster may have begun in the early eleventh century with King Cnut (1016–1035), whose son King Harold Harefoot (1035–1040) was buried at Westminster (and then dug up again very soon after by his half-brother Harthacnut, who regarded him as a usurper). But there is no doubt that Harthacnut's brother, King Edward the Confessor (1042–1066), had the Abbey rebuilt, at great expense and on a grander scale than any

other building in England at that time, as his place of burial. It was dedicated only days before he died on 5 January 1066 (figs. 8 and 9). His successor was crowned there, establishing the tradition that has continued ever since. King Edward (fig. 11) is also credited with building the first royal palace, the West Hall, near by.[4] Before the end of the eleventh century, William Rufus (1087–1100) had built the great Westminster Hall (fig. 10). The courts set up by Henry II (1154–1189) to administer the 'common law' of the whole kingdom were originally established in the hall and remained in the Palace of Westminster until their removal to the Royal Courts of Justice in the Strand in 1882.

By Royal Charter the Abbey was also granted the peculiar right of sanctuary. Ironically enough, the Westminster Justices' new courthouse, eventually realized in 1805, was built on the site that had once been occupied by the Abbey's Sanctuary Tower and Old Belfry (fig. 12). There fugitives had for centuries sought refuge from justice, although not always with success. The area between the Guildhall and the west end of Westminster Abbey is still known as Broad Sanctuary, although the traffic now roars across it between Victoria Street and Parliament Square, and the Underground runs underneath it between St James's Park and Westminster Tube stations.

Passers-by who notice the old gateway set into the railings at the back of the building (fig. 13) might be forgiven

for thinking that the Guildhall was also the site of the old Westminster Bridewell, or House of Correction, but they would be mistaken. The Bridewell was erected in 1618 next door to the old Greencoat School, to the west of what is now Artillery Row, and enlarged in 1655. In 1834 a new Bridewell, also known as Tothill Fields prison, was built near by on the site now occupied by the Roman Catholic Westminster Cathedral. The primitive stone gateway of the old prison was preserved, with an inscription in the lintel: 'The Gateway, or Principal Entrance, to Tothill Fields Prison; erected 1655; taken down and removed to this site A.D. 1836'.[5] That gate now stands in the railings on the western side of the Guildhall, having been resited there by the London authorities in 1969.

Following the dissolution of the monasteries in the 1530s by Henry VIII (1509–1547), the Sanctuary Tower was eventually partly demolished and turned into a tavern known as the Three Tunns. The tavern was itself demolished in 1750 to make way for the market, which in turn made way for the new Westminster courthouse, the first of the three guildhalls to have stood on this site. This was an elegant single-storey building with a classical portico, built in 1805 to designs by Samuel Pepys Cockerell (1753–1827; fig. 14). Under an Act of Parliament of 1845, this Guildhall was transferred to the jurisdiction of the Middlesex Justices.

Next came the complete reorganization of local government in the English shire counties by the Local Government Act 1888. This created the new county councils, including those of London and Middlesex. By this time the built-up metropolitan area had spread far outside the City of London and the Liberty of Westminster and into parts of Middlesex on the north bank of the river and parts of Surrey and Kent to the south. These areas were combined to form the new London County Council (taking over and expanding upon the functions of the Metropolitan Board of Works), and the areas served by the new Middlesex, Kent and Surrey County Councils were correspondingly reduced. But it was not thought convenient for the Middlesex Justices to leave their central London home, and there was nowhere obvious for them to go. So it was agreed that they would retain their Guildhall in Westminster, while surrendering their Sessions House in Clerkenwell to be used for the London Quarter Sessions. The London sessions continued to be held both in

Clerkenwell and in the former Surrey Sessions House in Newington until the London County Council decided to consolidate them in a new courthouse opened on the Newington site in 1917. The last trial took place in Clerkenwell in December 1920, and the building has had several uses since then.[6]

The first Guildhall was not big enough to house the new county council as well as the county sessions, and so a second Guildhall was built around the first, and opened in 1892 (fig. 15). It was an imposing red-brick Gothic building, which would have harmonized well with the Royal Institution of Chartered Surveyors' building next door on Little George Street. But it quickly proved too small for the expanding administration, and was replaced by the third Guildhall, opened by Prince Arthur of Connaught (1883–1938) on 19 December 1913 (fig. 16). Only then was it decided to demolish the foundations of the old Sanctuary Tower, which had survived beneath the Westminster market and the first two Guildhall buildings: 'Under the crypt was a raft of rubble five feet thick and seventy two and a half feet square, built on oak piles driven into the primeval sand of Thorney Island.'[7] One of those piles was preserved and exhibited in the Guildhall. Like many such buildings up and down the country, the Guildhall contained a Council Chamber (on the second floor) in which the councillors could hold their meetings; two courtrooms (on the ground floor) in which the Justices could hold their sessions; and the administrative and other offices necessary for both functions. It also contained a collection of portraits of Lord Lieutenants and other prominent people connected with the administration of justice in Middlesex.

## The Crown Court at the Middlesex Guildhall

The seeds of the second life of the Middlesex Guildhall were sown by the Local Government Act 1963. By then the metropolitan built-up area had spread with little interruption throughout almost the whole of Middlesex. The 1963 Act abolished the county councils of both Middlesex and London and established the Greater London Council. Almost the whole of Middlesex was swallowed up by Greater London, although a few outlying areas were transferred to Hertfordshire and Surrey. The Middlesex lieutenancy and magistracy were abolished by the Administration of Justice

### THE NEW MIDDLESEX GUILDHALL, WESTMINSTER
#### OPENED THIS WEEK BY PRINCE ARTHUR OF CONNAUGHT

THE OLD MIDDLESEX GUILDHALL AND ITS RE-ERECTION ON AN INCREASING SCALE ON THE SAME SITE

The New Middlesex Guildhall, which is to be opened to-day (December 19) by Prince Arthur of Connaught, has been described by a famous art critic as one of the most striking and amusing architectural features of modern London, the exuberant decorative trimmings being essentially modern in their coarseness, and not performing any structural function, while the squat appearance of the ground floor is further accentuated by a deep and heavy frieze representing historical incidents in a fussy, unsculpturesque manner.

Act 1964. Thus Middlesex ceased to exist as either an administrative or a judicial area, although it lived on as a postal address and in the much-loved bodies that continue to bear its name. The Middlesex County Cricket Club, for example, plays on the Lord's ground of the Marylebone Cricket Club in St John's Wood.

Quarter Sessions continued to be held in the Middlesex Guildhall. But shortly after the abolition of Middlesex, county Quarter Sessions and Assizes were themselves abolished by the Courts Act 1971. This created a single Crown Court for England and Wales, where all crimes serious enough to be tried 'on indictment' could be heard before a single judge sitting with a jury. The former Middlesex Guildhall thus became a Crown Court, sitting permanently to try the ever-increasing volume of serious crime in inner London.[8] With the departure of the Middlesex County Council there was room to develop more courtrooms within the building. A major refit and refurbishment took place between 1982 and 1988, converting the former Council Chamber into a proper courtroom and creating four new ones, all with their attendant jury rooms and cells to hold the prisoners awaiting trial or sentence. This obscured a good deal of the original shape of the building, although the former Council Chamber and historic courtrooms remained much as they had always been (figs. 17 and 18). All the courts were traditional criminal courts, with a witness box, a jury box, a dock and an elevated bench. Their appearance was full of character, but the atmosphere was dark and severe, designed to impress everyone appearing there with the authority and solemnity of the law.

The closure of the Crown Court at the Middlesex Guildhall in March 2007 was an occasion of great sadness for many of the court staff as well as for the judges who had sat there and the counsel who had appeared there over the years. The epilogue to this book, by His Honour Fabyan Evans, who retired as Resident Judge at the Guildhall in 2005, is ample testimony to this.

**The Supreme Court of the United Kingdom**
For others, the closure of the Crown Court was also an occasion of great excitement. The third phase in the life of the Guildhall was about to begin. It had been chosen as the home for the new Supreme Court of the United Kingdom,

set up by the Constitutional Reform Act 2005. The Supreme Court has taken over the role of 'apex court' for the whole of the United Kingdom, a role formerly performed by the Lords of Appeal in Ordinary (the 'Law Lords') sitting as the appellate committee of the House of Lords. As Lord Bingham of Cornhill explains in the next chapter, 'The exercise of judicial authority by the House of Lords was the product of historical happenstance.' The senior judiciary had been independent of the government from at least the beginning of the eighteenth century: by the Act of Settlement of 1701, Her Majesty's judges hold office *quamdiu se bene gesserint*, rather than at Her Majesty's pleasure.[9] Nowhere else in the world was the judiciary part of the upper house of the legislature. In principle, at least, it was time to demonstrate our independence of Parliament as well as of government.

The Law Lords' presence in the House of Lords had also become increasingly inconvenient. For purely practical reasons, we were unable to play much part in the legislative work of the House. The timing of our judicial work overlapped with the Parliamentary sittings, so that we could

not always be in the House when we might otherwise want to take part. There were also principled reasons for us not to do so. As Lord Bingham explained to the House in June 2000, the Law Lords did not think it proper to contribute to debates on matters of party-political controversy; they had also to bear in mind that if they did take part in any legislative debate or vote, they might disqualify themselves from sitting on a case in which that legislation was an issue.[10]

Thus, for example, two of the Law Lords voted against the bill that eventually became the Hunting Act 2004 (fig. 19). This did not fall foul of the first principle. Although the bill was intensely controversial, and took up more time in Parliament than any other passed since 1997, it was not party political. All parties allowed a free vote on it; prominent Labour members opposed it, just as prominent Conservative members supported it. But it did mean that the two Law Lords who voted were unable to sit on any of the three fascinating and important cases about the Act that came before the Law Lords.[11] The first of these challenged the validity of the Act as an Act of Parliament; the second challenged its compatibility with the fundamental rights and freedoms protected by the European Convention on Human Rights 1950, made part of UK law by the Human Rights Act 1998; and the third challenged its compatibility with the rights to free movement of goods and services protected by European Community law. The first case showed only too clearly how important it might be to establish a Supreme Court separately from the House of Lords. At issue were the circumstances in which an Act of Parliament might become law with the consent only of the House of Commons and the monarch, and without the consent of the House of Lords. How could a court consisting of members of the House of Lords be considered independent and impartial on such a subject? Only if, in practice, they played no part in the legislative business of the House.

Thus it was difficult to justify our continued presence in an institution to the core function of which we could make so little contribution. The twelve Law Lords, our office manager and the four research assistants and four secretaries whom we shared among us, together with the judicial clerk and officers who managed the casework, all took up a considerable amount of space in the Palace of Westminster (fig. 20). We were better accommodated than most of the working peers who conducted the parliamentary business of the House. These working peers had become a great deal busier since the departure of most of the hereditary peers following the House of Lords Act 1999. The busier the working peers became, the greater the pressure on the space and facilities there. Yet the Law Lords were also badly served in comparison with the space, the staff and the facilities that are taken for granted in Supreme Courts around the world. Each Associate Justice of the Supreme Court of the United States, for example, has his or her own suite of rooms and several secretaries, as well as four law clerks to help him or her to research opinions.

The move to the Supreme Court of the United Kingdom housed in the former Middlesex Guildhall was a golden opportunity for everyone to think about what was wanted from our 'apex court' and how it could best serve the people, the law and the legal systems of the United Kingdom. What sort of cases should it hear? How should it hear them? And how should it communicate its work to the people on whose behalf it is all done?

On the surface nothing much was to change, apart from the place in which the work was done. The work itself would stay the same. An 'apex court', as the term suggests, sits at the top of the legal pyramid (fig. 21). At the bottom are all the courts and tribunals that do the hard work of administering both criminal and civil justice. In England and Wales, these begin with the magistrates' courts, staffed by the lay Justices of the Peace and some professional district judges. They try the less serious criminal cases, enforce some debts to the public purse and hear some family cases. Next

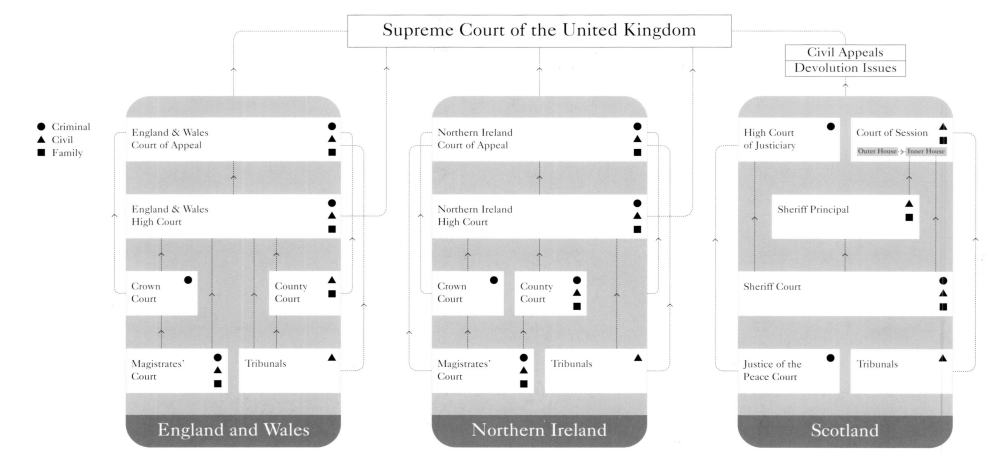

come the county courts, staffed by professional judges. They try most civil and family disputes between individuals or businesses, husbands and wives, mothers and fathers. The Crown Court has taken over from the old Assizes and Quarter Sessions, trying the more serious criminal cases before judge and jury. The High Court tries the most serious civil and family disputes and most of the serious disputes between citizens and the state. The legal system of Northern Ireland is the same as that of England and Wales, except that it makes less use of lay Justices. The legal system of Scotland is completely different, but has a similar three-tier structure. In all three jurisdictions, there is also a host of specialist tribunals, many now brought within a unified tribunal structure. Some of these deal with private disputes, between employers and employees, or between landlords and tenants of residential property. Most deal with appeals by claimants who have been denied various kinds of state benefits or services, including social security benefits and the right to enter or remain in this country.

In the middle of the pyramid are the various avenues of appeal from the trial courts or tribunals. Sometimes there is only one layer of appeal, from the High Court or the Crown Court to the Court of Appeal. Sometimes there is more than one, from the county court to the High Court and then to the Court of Appeal, or from the lower-tier tribunal to the upper-tier tribunal and then to the Court of Appeal.

On top of them all sits the Supreme Court, almost always a second or third tier of appeal, from the Court of Appeal in England and Wales, the Court of Appeal in Northern Ireland, and the Court of Session in Scotland. The Supreme Court hears both civil and criminal appeals from England, Wales and Northern Ireland, but only civil appeals from Scotland. This is a consequence of the Acts of Union of 1706 and 1707 (respectively passed by the English and Scottish Parliaments on the same day; but England still kept to the old Julian calendar, in which the New Year started on 25 March, while Scotland had adopted the Gregorian calendar, in which the New Year began on 1 January).[12] Article XIX guaranteed the independence of the Scottish civil and criminal courts. It provided that no causes in Scotland should be subject to review by the English courts, which then sat in Westminster Hall. Westminster Hall had a sinister reputation north of the border, as William Wallace,

the Scottish patriot, had been tried for treason there in 1305 (fig. 22). His plea, that he could not be guilty of treason as he had never been a subject of the English king, was disregarded. But the Acts of Union did not mention the House of Lords, which was not a court and did not sit in Westminster Hall. Doubts about whether an appeal lay to the House of Lords in civil matters were soon resolved on the ground that it had succeeded to the jurisdiction of the Scottish Parliament.[13] But this was held not to extend to criminal cases, because no precedent could be found for the Scottish Parliament having entertained any appeal from the High Court of Justiciary, the supreme criminal court in Scotland.[14]

The Supreme Court also hears 'devolution cases' from Scotland, Wales and Northern Ireland. Here the issue is whether their devolved governments and legislatures[15] have acted within the powers that have been granted to them by the Westminster Parliament. This is an obvious matter for a Supreme Court in any federal constitution to adjudicate. But for as long as the apex court of the United Kingdom was a committee of the Westminster Parliament, it might not be seen as an independent and impartial judge of a dispute between that Parliament and the devolved institutions. So at first the task of hearing devolution cases was given to the Judicial Committee of the Privy Council. Under the 2005 Act, it has now been assigned to its rightful place, in the Supreme Court for the whole United Kingdom.

*Opposite:* 21. Diagram showing the structure of courts in England and Wales, Northern Ireland and Scotland.

22. The trial of William Wallace in Westminster Hall, 1305, as depicted by William Bell Scott in the nineteenth century.

The Judicial Committee of the Privy Council has also moved into the former Guildhall, leaving its premises at 9 Downing Street. These were purpose-built for the Privy Council from 1823 to 1827 to designs by Sir John Soane (1753–1837; fig. 23). They still retain many of their original features, although others have been lost. The chamber originally had a spectacular 'starfish' vault ceiling, but this was removed in 1845 by Sir Charles Barry on the orders of the Clerk to the Privy Council.[16] The chamber remains a remarkably handsome room, with elaborate panelling designed by Soane (fig. 24). The oak chairs that he designed for spectators have been preserved in the lawyers' suite in the Supreme Court.

The Judicial Committee is a survival of the British Empire. It was placed on a statutory footing in 1833. Appeals lay to the sovereign from all over the empire, and the role of the Judicial Committee was to advise the monarch how they should be decided. Some Commonwealth countries, such as Canada, Australia, South Africa, Sri Lanka and New Zealand, retained the right of appeal to the Privy Council for some time after they became entirely self-governing Dominions.

But one by one, and for a variety of reasons, they have now dispensed with it.[17] Other countries, such as the United States of America, India, Pakistan and the new African countries, abandoned the right of appeal immediately they became independent. A few, however, have kept it, for the time being at least. So the Privy Council still hears appeals from a number of independent countries in the Caribbean[18] and from Mauritius, as well as from the Crown dependencies in the Channel Islands and the Isle of Man; the few remaining British Overseas Territories;[19] and also, by special arrangement with the Sultan, from the Kingdom of Brunei. It is also still concerned with some United Kingdom cases, mainly in the areas of ecclesiastical and professional discipline.[20]

In practice, the same Law Lords who sat in the House of Lords and have now become the Supreme Court Justices also sit as the Judicial Committee of the Privy Council. Other judges, from the Courts of Appeal in the United Kingdom and the other countries from which the appeals come, may also sit if they are members of the Privy Council. But the Privy Council and the Supreme Court are two quite separate institutions. The separation used to be underlined by the short but stately car journey from the House of Lords to Downing Street, latterly in an elderly Daimler limousine kept in service for this purpose (fig. 25). Now that the Judicial Committee shares the same building as the Supreme Court, care is taken to avoid confusion between them. The Judicial Committee usually sits in one of the two historic courtrooms on the ground floor. The portraits that used to hang in the Downing Street chamber are now hanging there, along with some of the best from the Middlesex Guildhall Collection. The symbol of the Privy Council is woven into the carpet between the judges' and counsel's benches. The flag of the country from which the appeal has come is prominently displayed. Counsel address the committee wearing the same court dress as they wear at home; some countries have abandoned the traditional barrister's wig, and some have not.

The Privy Council work adds greatly to the variety of life for the judges. Not only do they hear counsel from faraway places discussing events in what, often, are exotic locations, but they also hear a wider range of cases. At one extreme are the capital cases coming from those Caribbean

countries that still impose the death penalty for murder. At the other are ordinary civil disputes in which there is an automatic right of appeal if the sum of money involved is more than what is now a comparatively small amount.[21] In between there may be cases involving an important point of law, where in practice the decision will be followed in the United Kingdom as well as in the place from which the appeal came. In December 2008, for example, the Privy Council decided a case from the Isle of Man concerning the legal effect of ante- and postnuptial agreements providing for a future separation or divorce between husband and wife.[22] The law in the Isle of Man is virtually identical to the law in England and Wales, and so the decision should also be followed here. Other Privy Council cases can involve intriguing points of constitutional law. In February 2009, for example, the Privy Council decided whether Her Majesty The Queen could still grant letters patent setting up an honours system for Trinidad and Tobago, after its independence in 1962 but before it became a republic in 1976 (fig. 26).[23]

The Supreme Court of the United Kingdom, on the other hand, hears only cases involving 'points of law of general public importance'. The case has already been heard and decided, usually by two lower courts, sometimes by three, and only occasionally by one. It is not the task of the Supreme Court to give the parties a third bite at the cherry in disputes that matter only to them. Its task is to settle points of law that matter to a great many other people as well, or that have ramifications well beyond the particular facts of the case. Sometimes such points arise in disputes between businesses and/or private individuals. For example, does a landlord have a duty to protect a neighbour from harm inflicted by a disruptive tenant?[24] What are the principles governing the distribution of property on divorce?[25]

Increasingly, however, these points arise in disputes between private individuals or businesses and some organ of government. There have always been cases about the interpretation of the tax laws. Now there are more and more claims that a public authority has acted unfairly, unlawfully or unreasonably. One recent case in the House of Lords concerned the design of a local authority's scheme for choosing who should be allocated council or other social housing.[26] Another concerned whether it was lawful for the

director of the Serious Fraud Office to stop investigating whether BAE Systems Ltd had been involved in bribing a Saudi Arabian official in order to obtain an arms contract, when the Saudi government threatened to withdraw security co-operation if he continued.[27] Since the Human Rights Act 1998 came into force, there have also been many claims that a public authority has acted in breach of a person's fundamental rights. Examples are the claims by a Muslim schoolgirl that school-uniform rules that prohibited her from wearing a jilbab (a long black dress covering arms and legs) constituted an unjustified interference with her right to manifest her religion; or by a bereaved family that a hospital had failed properly to protect the life of a mental patient who had been allowed to leave the hospital and had then thrown herself under a train.[28]

Claims against the government and public officials are nothing new. The courts have been upholding the rule of law by checking the abuse, misuse or excess of power by public authorities for centuries. But such claims have increased greatly in number and scope with the advent of new rights against the state, derived either from European Community law or from the European Convention on Human Rights. These European treaties have also added another dimension to the courts' powers. For the first time, a court may disregard an Act of Parliament if it is contrary to the rights protected by European Community law; and it may declare

*Below:* 25. The stately Daimler limousine in which the Law Lords used to travel the short distance from the House of Lords to the Privy Council in Downing Street.

*Above:* 26. The coat of arms of the Republic of Trinidad and Tobago. In 2008 there were more appeals to the Privy Council from Trinidad and Tobago than from any other country.

an Act of Parliament incompatible with the rights protected by the European Convention on Human Rights (although it may not disregard it). That is why it was possible to challenge the Hunting Act 2004 on the grounds that it unjustifiably infringed the right to free movement of goods across European borders, or unjustifiably infringed the rights to freedom of assembly and respect for private life, or interfered with the use of property under the European Convention. Other cases have argued (unsuccessfully) that the ban on corporal punishment in all schools was an unjustifiable restriction on the rights of parents and teachers to manifest their religious belief in 'spare the rod and spoil the child', or (successfully) that the procedure for provisionally blacklisting care workers under the Care Standards Act 2000 was an unjustifiable interference with their rights to a fair hearing and to respect for their private lives.[29] These recently acquired powers to challenge not only the acts of government but also the Acts of Parliament represent another reason why it was right in principle to set up a Supreme Court separate from the United Kingdom Parliament.

This does not mean that the Supreme Court of the United Kingdom has any general power to strike down Acts of Parliament on the ground that they are 'unconstitutional'. It is not like the Supreme Court of the United States (and many other countries), which has power to hold invalid an Act of Congress if it is contrary to the United States Constitution (fig. 27). The United Kingdom does not have a written constitution. Its governing constitutional principle is that Parliament is sovereign and may do what it likes. The powers that the courts now possess to challenge Acts of Parliament have been given to them by Parliament itself. What Parliament has given, Parliament may take away. In the meantime, however, the courts must decide cases according to law. In the glass screen that marks the entrance to the new Supreme Court is etched an extract from the oath taken by the Supreme Court Justices: 'I will do right to all manner of people, after the laws and usages of this realm, without fear or favour, affection or ill will' (fig. 28).

While the work of the court may stay much the same, the move to our own building makes it possible for the highest court in the land to become more open and accessible to all. Many people did not know that the committee rooms in the House of Lords were open to the general public; nor were they easy to find. Members of the public had first to go through the visitors' entrance to the Houses of Parliament and then somehow to make their way to the committee corridor. Many were also mystified by the way in which the Law Lords gave their judgments. This was done in the chamber of the House of Lords, in a formal debate and vote upon the motion that 'the report of the appellate committee be agreed to' (fig. 29). Each of the Law Lords who had taken part in the appeal would make a formulaic speech saying what order he would make, allowing or dismissing the appeal. But the reasons would be given separately in writing, and spectators who did not have copies of these 'speeches' would not know what the Lords had said. Still less would the spectators know what it was all about. The lawyers might understand what the decision meant, but there was no machinery for explaining this to the onlookers, let alone to the wider public.

In contrast, the refurbished Guildhall has a friendly, welcoming entrance, opening directly from Parliament Square. A semicircle of stone benches, echoing the designs

29. The Law Lords giving judgment in the Chamber of the House of Lords, 'debating' the motion that 'the report of the appellate committee be agreed to'.

of George Grey Wornum (1888–1957) for the square, faces the entrance door. Carved into the benches is the poem by the then Poet Laureate, Andrew Motion, commissioned to mark the foundation of the Supreme Court. Inside, the security screening is tucked discreetly to one side of the front door. There is an information point just beyond that, and helpful signage throughout the public areas of the building. There is not far to go. The simplicity of the original layout has been restored. As Hugh Feilden explains in his chapter in this book, a great deal of thought has been given to making the building a brighter and more cheerful place, while preserving much of what was there before.

There are now three courtrooms. The smaller of the two original historic courts on the ground floor has been retained and will generally be used by the Judicial Committee of the Privy Council. A new double-height courtroom, Courtroom 2, has been created on the first floor, overlooking Broad Sanctuary and Westminster Abbey. This will generally be used by the Supreme Court. The Council Chamber on the second floor has been transformed into a courtroom, Courtroom 1, large enough to accommodate a panel of at least nine judges. This will be used for the most important cases heard either by the Supreme Court or by the Privy Council. At present both usually sit in panels of five judges, but in more important cases they have sat in panels of seven or nine. The larger of the two historic courts (previously Court 1), which could not be converted into a courtroom suitable for the work of the Supreme Court, has become a magnificent triple-height library at the heart of the building (fig. 30). This is not only a beautiful space in which to work, but also a symbol of the evolution of the common law through centuries of decided cases; the Justices are not making it up as they go along. On the doors leading into the Library is etched a facsimile of Magna Carta (fig. 31), echoing the portion of the frieze on the outside of the building that records the barons presenting their charter to King John in 1215 (fig. 32).

The three courtrooms are designed very differently from courts trying criminal cases. They have therefore had to lose some of their original furniture, and this has been controversial. They are now designed to suit the work that the Supreme Court does – hearing only the legal arguments. The court does not hear the witnesses, so it does not need a witness box. It does not decide the facts, so it does not need

*Opposite:* 30. The new Supreme Court Library, created out of Court 1 in the Middlesex Guildhall.

*Left:* 31. The facsimile of Magna Carta etched into the doors leading into the new Supreme Court Library.

*Below:* 32. The stone frieze over the entrance to the building, showing the barons presenting Magna Carta to King John.

a jury box. In the few criminal cases it decides, it does not impose punishment upon the offender: that has already been done. If the offender is in custody, his attendance is not required, so the Supreme Court does not need a dock. It does not need to impress the world with the majesty of the law: its authority can be taken for granted. It needs a dignified but attractive environment in which the most difficult issues can be debated between counsel and the bench in a structured but informal way. At its best, it has been said, the atmosphere is that of a learned seminar.

In the House of Lords, the Law Lords sat in a committee room arranged in much the same way as those used by the Parliamentarians. There was a semicircular table for the judges and a central podium from which the barristers spoke, all on the same level (fig. 33). There are similar podiums in other Supreme Courts, for example in the United States and Canada. The Supreme Court has kept to the House of Lords' model, with benches for judges and barristers on the same

*Opposite, top:* 33. The Law Lords sitting in Committee Room 1 in the Houses of Parliament: 'a learned seminar'.

*Opposite, bottom:* 34. The Justices of the Supreme Court hearing their first case in Courtroom 1, October 2009.

35. Bench-ends from the councillors' benches in the former Council Chamber incorporated into the public benches in Courtroom 1.

level and close enough for the lawyers to engage one another in debate. The only change is that the bench is curved rather than semicircular and the barristers' bench mirrors that of the judges (figs. 34 and 36 (a) and (c)). There is no podium, and the barristers can stand to address the bench from the place where they sit. Behind them are the usual benches for their solicitors and clients, and behind those are rows of seats for the interested public. The carved bench-ends and armrests from the former Council Chamber have been incorporated into the public benches in the largest courtroom, Courtroom 1 (fig. 35). But there is not the usual courtroom drama. The debate can be somewhat mystifying, tedious even, for people who are not directly involved. Now, however, there are much better facilities to explain what is going on.

The proceedings in the Supreme Court may eventually be televised. They are already broadcast within the building, and these broadcasts may be made available to the media. The court is seeking to reach out to the public in many ways.

The Law Lords always published very detailed and learned reasons for their decisions, and this continues. But now the Supreme Court issues a press notice with every decision as well, explaining what it means for a general audience. The court is also developing an education programme for schools and colleges. This will consist not only of guided visits to the building, but also of educational materials to enable students to understand the issues and consider the arguments in some of the more eye-catching cases (such as the school-uniform case mentioned earlier). The court has a friendly and welcoming website,[30] where interested users can gain access to the written arguments lodged by the parties, as well as to the decisions and press notices, and a great deal more helpful information about the court and its work.

In the building are a cafe, a souvenir shop and an exhibition space at lower-ground-floor level. The exhibition explains the history and the work of the Supreme Court and the Judicial Committee of the Privy Council, and where they

36 (a), (b) and (c). Courtroom 2 in the United Kingdom Supreme Court, showing how the furniture is laid out: the 'learned seminar' continues.

37. The badge of the United Kingdom Supreme Court, comprising the rose for England, the thistle for Scotland, the leek for Wales and the flax for Northern Ireland, encased within Libra for justice and Omega for finality, designed by Yvonne Holton, the Scottish herald painter.

fit into the legal systems of the countries that they serve, as well as the history and development of the building in which they sit. The memory of Middlesex is well preserved throughout the building, not least in the memorial to the Middlesex Regiment in the entrance hall, in the coats of arms that recur throughout, and in the Middlesex Guildhall Collection, which has been restored and rehung to its best advantage. Also recurring throughout the building is the new badge of the United Kingdom Supreme Court, with four plants to represent the four nations making up the Union: the rose for England, the thistle for Scotland, the leek for Wales and the flax for Northern Ireland, encased within a frame that is not only the sign of Libra, the scales, but also of Omega, the last letter of the Greek alphabet (fig. 37), symbolizing the final court of justice for the whole country.

There could not be a better place than the former Guildhall in which to begin this exciting new phase in our constitutional history. By a happy accident, it sits on one side of Parliament Square, which Chris Miele explores in his chapter. The legislature, in the shape of the Houses of Parliament, sits on the opposite side of the square. The government, represented by its most powerful department, the Treasury, is to the left. The Crown and the established Church – of which the monarch is head – are represented by Westminster Abbey to the right. The object of this book is to celebrate the Guildhall in all its glory, its place on Parliament Square, its past, its present and its future.

# LAW LORDS AND JUSTICES

TOM BINGHAM

*The Middlesex Guildhall, extensively and sensitively altered to meet the needs of an independent, self-contained twenty-first-century Supreme Court, ... will be a fitting home for one of the world's oldest and best-known courts. This country, the birthplace of those robust and fertile twins – the common law and the rule of law – deserves no less.*

On 12 June 2003 the government announced that the ancient office of Lord Chancellor (fig. 1) was to be abolished and a new Supreme Court of the United Kingdom, separate from the House of Lords, established. The announcement came as a surprise to the public, the legal profession and some senior ministers. There had been no Royal Commission or select committee, as in 1867–76 when the last major change to the structure of the judiciary had been made. There had been no manifesto pledge to make such changes. There had been no public consultation. Nor was there any substantial groundswell of public opinion demanding change. Early indications were that the proposals had not been very fully thought out. Yet viewed in a wider historical perspective, the changes were not perhaps as surprising as they seemed to many at the time, and the sky out of which they came was not entirely blue.

The exercise of judicial authority by the House of Lords was the product of historical happenstance. In early medieval times all power – legislative, executive and judicial – was concentrated in the monarch (fig. 2), but by the end of the medieval period this power had been largely devolved:

legislative power to the Crown in Parliament (fig. 3), executive power to the king's (or queen's) ministers, judicial power to a body of appointed, professional, royal Justices. There was no obvious reason why the residual judicial power of the king in Council should have been exercised by the House of Lords, but by Tudor times this arrangement had come to be accepted. In relation to impeachment and the trial of peers for felony, the Lords were the court of trial (fig. 5), but their jurisdiction was very largely appellate.[1]

During the eighteenth and nineteenth centuries it became clear that the House of Lords was failing as a judicial tribunal. There were a number of reasons for this. One was a flood of appeals from Scotland following the Act of Union in 1707 (fig. 4), attributable partly to the reluctance of the Court of Session in Edinburgh to give reasons for its decisions, partly to a rule that suspended a debtor's obligation to pay until an appeal had been finally resolved.[2] These Scottish appeals, often raising very trivial issues, exacerbated an existing problem of workload. In 1811, for instance, the House of Lords heard 23 appeals, while 266 awaited hearing: 203 from Scotland, 36 from Ireland, and 27 from England and Wales (Stevens, *Law and Politics*, p. 16). By contrast, in 2005 the Law Lords decided 94 appeals: 82 from England and Wales, 10 from Scotland and 2 from Northern Ireland. Only by the middle of the nineteenth century did the number of English and Welsh appeals exceed the number of Scottish (Stevens, p. 69). A further problem related to the Lord Chancellor, an office originally held by churchmen, but since Tudor times by lawyers. The burden of presiding over the judicial business of the House of Lords lay on him, but he was also until 1813 the only, and then the principal, judge of the Court of Chancery – and even Lord Chancellors cannot sit in two places at the same time.[3]

In the House of Lords, unlike the lower courts, there was no corps of appointed professional judges. The only professionally qualified peers were the Lord Chancellor, any former Lord Chancellor and any ennobled judge:[4] hence the practice by which the House of Lords would seek the opinion of the common law judges on the law, something that was done as late as 1897 in *Allen* v. *Flood*.[5] To overcome the shortage of professional legal talent in the House, lay peers (not legally qualified) were permitted to participate fully in legal hearings, and did so, sometimes to decisive

effect. One case, against a bishop, was resolved by the narrowest majority, on a bloc vote of the Bench of Bishops. An appeal by the Princess of Wales, against a decision of Lord Eldon, was upheld on a vote of lay peers mustered by the Prince of Wales.[6] But the lay peers were an uncertain quantity. Willing enough to sit in high-profile and apparently interesting cases, they showed less eagerness to sit in more mundane appeals. So it came about that lay peers were rostered to attend, on pain of a fine for non-attendance. They were, however, rostered only for a day at a time, so if a case lasted longer there would be different peers hearing different parts of the case.[7] The orthodox view at the time was that judicial business was House business, in which all peers could take part.[8] As late as 1834, an appeal to the House was decided by lay peers alone (Stevens, p. 29).

All these problems were compounded by the pressure on the Judicial Committee of the Privy Council, a pressure that inevitably increased as the British Empire expanded, making demands on very much the same judges as sat in the House of Lords. In 1828 the Privy Council sat, as was usual, on nine feast days; there were 517 cases waiting to be heard (Stevens, p. 27). The backlog of pending cases remained large: 157 in 1865, 329 in 1869 (Stevens, pp. 45, 49). By contrast, in 2005 the Judicial Committee took in 71 appeals, and disposed of 57, leaving 83 pending at the end of the year.

Speaking of the House of Lords, the Solicitor General in 1855 said that 'judicial business was conducted before the Supreme Court of Appeal in a manner which would disgrace the lowest court of justice in the kingdom' (Stevens, p. 40). Not surprisingly, there were proposals for reform. Select committees were appointed in 1811, 1812, 1823 and 1856. Bills were introduced in 1834, 1842, 1856 and 1869.[9] In 1834 it was proposed to transfer the business of the House of Lords to the Privy Council, in 1842 to transfer the business of the Privy Council to the House of Lords.[10] All attempts failed, as did a proposal to merge the two bodies in 1856 (Stevens, p. 43). In the same year an attempt to professionalize the membership of the House by conferring a life peerage on Baron Parke was defeated, because there was held to be no prerogative power to confer life peerages. The problem was solved in his case by conferring a hereditary peerage. But Dr Lushington, also earmarked for a life peerage, was not similarly favoured.[11] Eventually, in 1871,

a proposal to appoint professional judges to sit in the Privy Council was adopted, and proved an immediate success (Stevens, p. 27). After 1844, lay peers no longer participated in judicial business.[12] This was no doubt regretted by some. When the Duke of Buccleuch questioned his fitness to sit on a nine-day Indian appeal he was assured that 'the natives of India would much rather have this appeal decided by a great Scotch Duke than by lawyers alone'.[13] When, in 1883, the son of a former Lord Chief Justice tried to vote on an appeal (perhaps believing that judicial authority, like legislative, was hereditary), his vote was discounted.[14]

A Judicature Commission was appointed in 1867 to report on the superior courts of England and Wales and appeals therefrom. After it had reported, a select committee was appointed. The upshot was the establishment of a new Court of Appeal, which, together with the High Court, became the Supreme Court of England and Wales (renamed the Senior Courts of England and Wales by the Constitutional Reform Act 2005 to avoid confusion with the new Supreme Court of the United Kingdom). As provided by section 20 of the Supreme Court of Judicature Act 1873, the

4. The Act of Union 1707, uniting the Parliaments of Scotland and England and Wales.

5. *The Trial of Queen Caroline*, 1820, painting by George Haytor.

right of appeal to the House of Lords from England and Wales was to be abolished. It was expected that appeals from Scotland and Ireland would also be brought to an end, but they were not covered by the Act. For England and Wales, the Court of Appeal was to be the last stop. The change was to take effect in November 1874.

But by then the government of William Gladstone (1809–1898) had fallen and a government led by Benjamin Disraeli (1804–1881) had come into power. There was a virtual identity of view between the leading legal authorities of both parties on the future shape of the judicature, but the impending abolition of the right of appeal to the Lords led to a strong Conservative backlash, fuelled less by admiration for the judicial achievements of the House than by a feeling that the House would be diminished if its appellate jurisdiction were removed (Stevens, p. 61). As a result, the operation of section 20 (abolishing the right of appeal) was first suspended, then repealed and replaced by the Appellate Jurisdiction Act 1876. This provided for the appointment of paid, full-time, professional judges (Lords of Appeal in Ordinary or, colloquially, Law Lords) to exercise the judicial

authority of the House. The first appointee came from the English bench, the second from the Scottish bar, the fourth (in 1882) from the Irish bench. The Law Lords, like the bishops, were to be members of the House only while holding office, but when the first appointee (Lord Blackburn) came to retire, his contribution to the non-judicial business of the House was judged to be too valuable to lose, and the rule was changed so that the Law Lords remained peers for life.[15] Between 1876 and 2009, a total of 111 men and 1 woman held office as Lords of Appeal in Ordinary.

Since 1876 there have been a number of important changes. The first is that the Law Lords have been (there is no more elegant word for it) depoliticized. Some of the early appointments, and some of the early decisions, were, or appeared to be, political: in 1905 the outgoing government encouraged Lord Lindley, apolitical and highly respected, to retire in order that a Conservative nominee could take his place; such decisions as those in *Taff Vale Railway Co* v. *Amalgamated Society of Railway Servants*[16] and *Roberts* v. *Hopwood*[17] seemed to be politically motivated. Of the first thirty appointees, a majority had sat in the House of Commons. Such experience is, or appears to be, a thing of the past.

Secondly, the number of Law Lords increased from the original two to the eventual twelve (although that number was depleted by secondments to conduct inquiries or sit in the Final Court of Appeal of Hong Kong). Since very early on, there have by convention been two Scottish Law Lords, and for most of the time there has been one from Ireland or Northern Ireland, although this has become a requirement only in the United Kingdom Supreme Court.

A third change was the establishment of an appellate committee of the House to deal with its judicial business. Until 1945 the Law Lords sat judicially in the chamber of the House (save when it was occupied, during the Second World War, by the Commons, whose chamber had been bombed), rising before the House sat at 4.15 or 4.30 pm (fig. 6). But building works close to the King's Robing Room (temporarily used by the House of Lords as their chamber) made it an uncongenial place to sit judicially, and the pressure of post-war legislation required the House to sit earlier.[18] Since the Law Lords could not then sit for a full court day in the chamber, except during the recess, an appellate committee was formed as a temporary measure, which quickly became permanent. Henceforward the appellate committee routinely sat in an upstairs committee room, which led to a change of ambience in favour of much greater informality (figs. 7 and 8). Gone was the ornate Gothic of the chamber, with leading counsel in full-bottomed wigs. Counsel and judges were now close together, and on the same level, encouraging reasoned debate rather than gladiatorial rhetoric. Indeed, at its best, the atmosphere became more like a learned seminar than an adversarial contest.

The half-century following the Second World War saw another significant change: a huge increase in the political responsibilities of the Lord Chancellor. Formerly the head of a small office with important but limited functions as head of the judiciary, the Lord Chancellor became the political chief of a sizeable public department with thousands of civil servants and responsibility for, among many other things, the Court Service and the (politically sensitive) legal-aid budget. One consequence of this development was a reduction in the time that Lord Chancellors could devote to judicial work, a reduction more marked – because of the numerical inferiority of Labour peers – during Labour than during Conservative administrations. On average (an average that conceals considerable variations), Lord Chancellors sat judicially for eight days a year between 1945 and 2001, since when no Lord Chancellor has sat judicially at all.[19] At the outset of the period, Lord Chancellors decided which Law Lords should sit on which cases, a function gradually abandoned and taken over by the senior professional judges.

When sitting judicially in the House of Lords or the Privy Council, the Lord Chancellor presided. The Law Lords took precedence according to their seniority of appointment, but so long as the Lord Chancellor was in the chair (and, until Lord Gardiner forswore the privilege in 1969, former Lord Chancellors had precedence over the professional Law Lords[20]) the rank of the Law Lords among themselves was of relatively minor importance. As the judicial role of the Lord Chancellor shrank, however, a recognizable office of Senior Law Lord began to emerge. Initially, the Senior Law Lord was simply the most senior by date of appointment, a convention observed (with one very minor deviation in the 1980s) until 2000, when the Lord Chief Justice of England and Wales was appointed Senior

9. Alexander Hamilton, Founding Father, economist, constitutional lawyer and political philosopher. Portrait by Alonzo Chappel.

10. Walter Bagehot, political economist and journalist, editor of *The Economist* and author of *The English Constitution* (1867).

*Opposite, top:* 11. Richard Haldane, 1st Viscount Haldane, statesman, Lord Chancellor 1912–1915, and in the first Labour government of 1924. This portrait by Arthur Stockdale Cope moved with the Judicial Committee of the Privy Council from Downing Street to the Guildhall, 2009.

Law Lord, a practice repeated in 2008 with the intention that Lord Phillips of Worth Matravers should become the first president of the Supreme Court of the United Kingdom.

The contribution of the Law Lords to the non-judicial business of the House, valuable in the past,[21] has sharply declined in recent years, almost to the point of disappearance. The reasons for this change are various: the Law Lords have perhaps inclined to regard the dispensing of justice at the highest level as a task calling for their undivided attention, a function to be put first, not second; their judicial work may perhaps – but this is speculative – have become more demanding; and there is a greater sensitivity (among the Law Lords and the public) to the conflict that may arise if a judge deals judicially with a matter that he or she has addressed legislatively or for which he or she has been collectively responsible.[22] In June 2000, responding to the Report of a Royal Commission on the Reform of the House of Lords chaired by Lord Wakeham, the Law Lords asserted their right to participate in the business of the House, but accepted that they would not engage in matters of party-political controversy nor where participation might disqualify them from sitting.[23] In practice, the contribution of the Law Lords since that date has been minimal.

The shrinking of the Law Lords' legislative role has, it would seem, been matched by an enhancement of their judicial role. Partly this is attributable to the exponential growth, over the last thirty years, of applications for judicial review, holding the government and public authorities to account. Partly it is attributable to the impact of European Community law, a body of law that Parliament cannot simply legislate to reverse in the wake of an adverse court decision. It may also be partly attributable to the mandate given by Parliament to the courts to interpret and apply the central provisions of the European Convention on Human Rights. Partly again it may derive from the inevitable tension between the aim of the government to protect the public against acts of terrorist violence and the role of the judges as auditors of legality. Whatever the reason, there is little room for doubt about the result.

One last change in the judicial role is worthy of mention. By a questionable decision made in 1898, the House of Lords held itself bound to follow the reasoning of its earlier decisions.[24] Thus a rule, once laid down, could not be altered. By a Practice Statement issued by Lord Gardiner as Lord Chancellor in 1966, adherence to precedent was to continue to be the rule, but the House was henceforward to be free to depart from an earlier precedent if justice were held to require it. This is a power that the House has exercised sparingly, but the change effectively destroyed the old and unconvincing fiction that the judges did not make law but simply declared what the law had always been. From now on their role in developing the law would be more clearly defined, and also more important.

The exercise of judicial authority by one branch of the legislature did not escape criticism down the years. Montesquieu wrote: 'Nor is there liberty if the power of judging is not separate from legislative power and from executive power'.[25] During the debates on the United States Constitution, Alexander Hamilton (fig. 9) agreed: 'These considerations teach us to applaud the wisdom of those States who have committed the judicial power, in the last resort, not to a part of the legislature, but to distinct and independent bodies of men.'[26] The American colonies that had borrowed the British model rejected it on independence, and it was not adopted on a federal level. Closer to home, Walter Bagehot (fig. 10) in *The English Constitution* (1867) wrote:

*I do not reckon the judicial function of the House of Lords as one of its true subsidiary functions, first because it does not in fact exercise it, next because I wish to see it in appearance deprived of it. The supreme court of the English people ought to be a great conspicuous tribunal, ought to rule all other courts, ought to have no competitor, ought to bring our law into unity, ought not to be hidden beneath the robes of a legislative assembly.*[27]

Central to the role of the House of Lords as a judicial institution was the office of Lord Chancellor, but this also attracted criticism. Jeremy Bentham, in language strong even for him, attacked the office as a 'monster'.[28] Lord Brougham harboured ill-defined ambitions to divide the Lord Chancellor's functions and establish a Ministry of Justice, a scheme favoured by Lord Westbury.[29] Lord Langdale, MR, a disciple of Bentham, echoed his master's criticisms in 1836 and favoured a recasting of the Lord

Chancellor's role, confining his judicial function to the Court of Chancery.[30] He referred to the 'utter impossibility of [the Lord Chancellor's] great and important duties being satisfactorily performed by one man, however great his abilities'.[31] Eighty years later, in 1918, the Machinery of Government Committee, chaired by Lord Haldane (fig. 11), proposed in its report that there should be a Ministry of Justice, with the Lord Chancellor's judicial duties separated from responsibility for administration. It was envisaged that the minister for justice would probably sit in the House of Commons.[32] Haldane was willing to return to the Woolsack in 1924 only on condition that he exercised no judicial function.[33]

In more recent years the volume of criticism of the Lord Chancellor's role has intensified. Sir Nicolas Browne-Wilkinson, then the Vice-Chancellor, suggested in 1988 that the administrative and financial constraints on the Lord Chancellor made it 'more and more difficult' for him to protect judicial independence.[34] The judicial contribution of the Lord Chancellor has also been disparaged.[35] In March 1998 an early day motion in the House of Commons, calling for abolition of the office and establishment of a justice department under a minister accountable to the Commons, attracted one hundred signatures.[36] In written evidence to the Royal Commission on Reform of the House of Lords, a strong working party of JUSTICE (a rights-based law-reform group), comprising members across the political spectrum and outside it, recommended that the Lord Chancellor should cease to be head of the judiciary of England and Wales and should no longer sit as a judge in the House of Lords.[37] A detailed study of the office, funded by the Economic and Social Research Council (ESRC), concluded in 2001 that in its present form it was 'untenable', that the Lord Chancellor's multiple roles were no longer sustainable, that he should relinquish his role as a judge and that it was unacceptable for him to sit as one.[38]

So long as the Lord Chancellor was recognized as the head of the judiciary, entitled to preside in the appellate committee, it made a measure of sense to retain the highest court in the House of Lords, since that was the place where, until 2003, he discharged his administrative, legislative and judicial functions. But as his role was challenged, so arguments were again advanced in favour of

a Supreme Court institutionally and functionally separate from the House of Lords. At the front of the field was the Constitution Unit, under whose auspices Andrew Le Sueur and Richard Cornes began to address the function of top courts in June 2000.[39] Lectures and publications followed.[40] Thus the government's proposals of 12 June 2003 were not wholly unheralded, even though inconsistent with previous ministerial statements on the subject.

The proposals were not well received in some quarters. Partly the opposition was procedural, provoked by the manner of their presentation and the lack of consultation. But there was also strong opposition to the merits of the proposals. It was seen as an act of vandalism to destroy the old and respected office of Lord Chancellor, and after much debate that office was preserved, although in an emasculated form, with its holder deprived of judicial status and recognition as head of the judiciary, and with primary responsibility for judicial appointments and discipline allocated elsewhere. This much-reduced office was held, jointly with their existing offices, first by the Secretary of State for Constitutional Affairs (Lord Falconer of Thoroton), and then by the Secretary of State for Justice (Mr Jack Straw, MP; figs. 12 and 13).

The creation of a new Supreme Court was also criticized, notably by a large majority of serving and former Law Lords, not on party-political grounds but because they saw it as an expensive and unnecessary attempt to mend something that was not broken. Anomalous the appellate committee might be, but there was in practice no conflict between the Law Lords' roles as judges and as members of the House. The general respect that House of Lords' judgments commanded around the world was convincing evidence that the system worked, whether it was anomalous or not. So, it was argued, there was no need to change it. But the practising profession was generally in favour of a separate Supreme Court, independent of the legislature, and the issue was not one about which most members of the public felt strongly one way or another.

In many respects the new Supreme Court of the United Kingdom resembles the old appellate committee. It will continue to hear civil and criminal appeals from England and Wales and Northern Ireland, and civil appeals from Scotland, but with the addition of appeals arising under the

*Above, centre:* 12. Lord Falconer of Thoroton, Lord Chancellor and Secretary of State for Constitutional Affairs, promoter of the Constitutional Reform Act 2005.

*Above, bottom:* 13. Jack Straw, MP, Secretary of State for Justice and the first Lord Chancellor to sit in the House of Commons.

Scots, Welsh and Northern Irish devolution legislation of
1998, formerly heard by the Privy Council. It will exercise
the same powers, and will have no new power (like most
Supreme Courts) to annul or strike down statutes. It will
continue, very largely, to select the cases it will hear. Its
procedures, although modernized, will much more closely
resemble those of its predecessor than those of, say, the top
courts of European countries or the Supreme Court of the
United States. The Law Lords holding office on the formal
establishment of the Supreme Court are automatically
transmuted into Justices of the Supreme Court, drawn
from the three UK jurisdictions.

But the formal establishment of the Supreme Court,
provided for by the Constitutional Reform Act 2005, was
delayed for four years for one very obvious reason: that while,
under the Act, the Law Lords were to leave the Palace of
Westminster, the Act identified no alternative home. That
home is to be found in the building, formerly known as the
Middlesex Guildhall, that is the subject of this book. As
Lady Hale points out in the previous chapter, the building –
flanked by the Treasury on one side and Westminster Abbey
on the other, looking eastwards across Parliament Square
towards Big Ben and the Houses of Parliament – is ideally
placed to reflect the centrality of the law in the British state
(fig. 14). The brief given in 1929 to the architect of the
world's best-known Supreme Court was to provide 'a
building of dignity and importance suitable for its use as
the Supreme Court of the United States'. The Middlesex
Guildhall, extensively and sensitively altered to meet the
needs of an independent, self-contained twenty-first-century
Supreme Court, has a similar purpose. It will be a fitting
home for one of the world's oldest and best-known courts.
This country, the birthplace of those robust and fertile twins
– the common law and the rule of law – deserves no less.

# THE PLACE: PARLIAMENT SQUARE

CHRIS MIELE

*The lack of any obvious designed relationships around the square is evidence of disputes that have not so much been resolved as allowed to happen. Notwithstanding the absence of a masterplan, the whole makes perfect sense.*

*Page 47:* 1. Aerial view of Parliament Square, *c.* 1990.

*Opposite and left:* 2 (a) and (b). Westminster Abbey and the Houses of Parliament as seen from the statue of Churchill, 2009.

*Below:* 3. *The Burning of the Houses of Lords and Commons, October 16, 1834,* painting by J.M.W. Turner.

Entering the phrase 'London, United Kingdom' into Google Earth takes you straight to Parliament Square (fig. 1), to a point very near the bronze of Winston Churchill (1874–1965) that dates from 1973, the work of Ivor Roberts-Jones (1913–1996). On foot this spot is harder to reach: fast-moving traffic makes for slow progress. This is not ideal, but neither is it inappropriate. Victorian engineers and architects formed the square as the linking space between new roads, making one large space out of several ancient ones. Concerns about traffic congestion and safety led to the installation of the world's first set of traffic lights there in 1868. In 1926 the square became London's first traffic gyratory.

Difficult though he may be to reach, the view from Churchill is worth the effort (figs. 2 (a) and (b)). To the south is Westminster Abbey, founded during the reign of the Saxon King Edgar (959–975). The north transept facing you was the main front in Henry III's time (1216–1272), a perfect example of thirteenth-century style thanks to the Victorian architects who improved it. To the left, or east, are the Houses of Parliament, a masterpiece of revived Gothic including a few real medieval elements that survived a massive fire in 1834 (fig. 3). Most notable is Westminster Hall, constructed in the eleventh century and enlarged between 1397 and 1401. The architect of the Victorian palace, Sir Charles Barry (1795–1860), had wanted to build office ranges right up to the corner finishing the square, but the cost was too great.

If the visitor looks to the left of the palace from the foot of Churchill, there is a winding view up Parliament Street, another Victorian improvement, towards the older line of Whitehall and Sir Edwin Lutyens's (1869–1944) Cenotaph (1920), where each year, on Remembrance Sunday in November, the United Kingdom and Commonwealth nations gather to honour the war dead. What visitors on a typical day may not realize is the important role the square plays in official ceremonies, from the opening of Parliament to royal weddings and state funerals (fig. 4).

Forming the north side of the square are the former Government Buildings, now HM Treasury, designed by J.M. Brydon (1840–1901) as civil service offices (1899–1915). It was restored and refurbished in 2002–2004 by Foster+Partners working with Feilden+Mawson, the architects for the Supreme Court. Its symmetrical stone façade does not align with any feature in the square. In fact, no building has any axial relationship with any other (fig. 5). The square itself is a self-contained design.

The lack of any obvious designed relationships around the square is evidence of disputes that have not so much been resolved as allowed to happen. Notwithstanding the absence of a masterplan, the whole makes perfect sense. Here are monumental expressions of the law and the will of the people. Between them is the established Church, which, because of its association with the monarchy, enjoys a special position in the English constitutional settlement. These three important buildings – Abbey, Parliament and Supreme Court – are all recognizably Gothic. Government and the civil service are represented by HM Treasury, grandiose Edwardian Baroque, setting a classical theme that continues north along Whitehall.

It is too easy to dismiss the square as a failure of urban planning. Its story should, instead, be read as a lesson in Victorian notions of the role of the state – notions that are with us still. At no point in this history has any government had the political will to impose a coherent vision on a space that more than a century and a half ago came to be regarded as the centre of the largest empire the world had yet seen. Neither has any Parliament, which does have the potential power, sought to impose a single solution. Centralized authority worried the Victorian political classes. In 1847 Benjamin Disraeli (1804–1881) observed that centralization

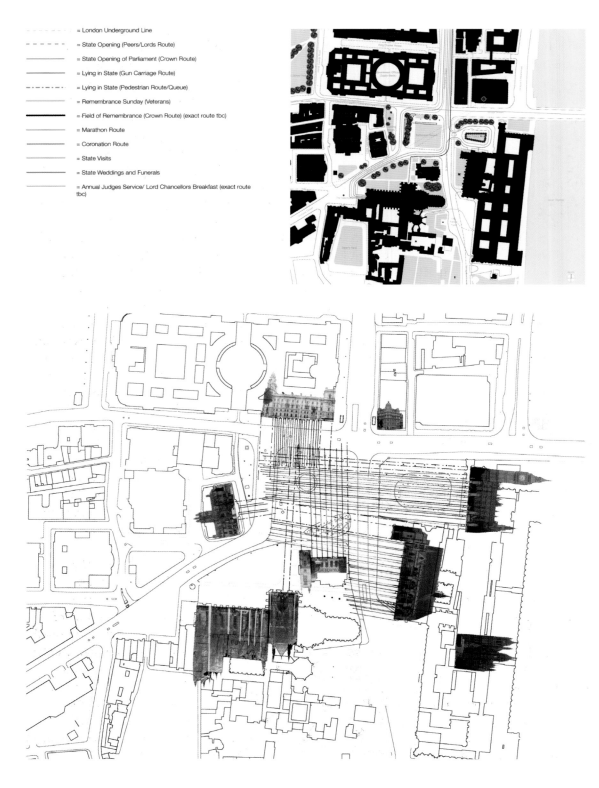

= London Underground Line
= State Opening (Peers/Lords Route)
= State Opening of Parliament (Crown Route)
= Lying in State (Gun Carriage Route)
= Lying in State (Pedestrian Route/Queue)
= Remembrance Sunday (Veterans)
= Field of Remembrance (Crown Route) (exact route tbc)
= Marathon Route
= Coronation Route
= State Visits
= State Weddings and Funerals
= Annual Judges Service/ Lord Chancellors Breakfast (exact route tbc)

'if left unchecked will prove fatal to the national character'.[1] Victorian Tories and Liberals alike (even many Radicals besides) did not see the state as a single entity requiring a singular physical expression. As one earlier critic of the operation of the new Poor Law put it in 1841, this approach was the 'Saxon system' of governance, and desirable precisely because it called the 'energies of all … into play'.[2]

For many political thinkers in the nineteenth century, central government was the enemy of personal liberty, which, so the argument went, could be traced back to Anglo-Saxon institutions – and this is where the style of some of the buildings that line the square becomes significant. In the eighteenth century, Gothic came to be seen as the expression of a free people whose liberty was preserved by a common law seen then as an inheritance of Saxon institutions (the common law is now understood to be an Angevin creation).[3] Gothic had no strict canon of style. Flexible and organic, it embodied the same evolutionary principles that had shaped the law and the British constitution. And so, looked at in one way, the square is an unintended monument; and as for the whole, so for the part. The new UK Supreme Court (UKSC), the highest court in the land, has – as Lord Bingham explains in the previous chapter – emerged out of an adjudicative function that happened to be performed by the House of Lords and that had reached the point where it made sense for this function to take on an independent character. In so doing, the court has found a home in a suitable location, making use of a historic building that happened to be available on the day.

**Beginnings**

The longer story of the place begins, though, with the geology of London and the Thames Valley. The land in and around the square was the product of the alluvial landscape created by the river and its tributaries tens of thousands of years ago. This historic core of the City of Westminster (one of thirty-three public authorities comprising Greater London) is formed on a gravel eyot, known as Thorney Island, deposited over millennia. The River Tyburn near by – now culverted – helped to define this feature, one of many that emerged in the early Holocene period (*c.* 9000 BC) to become the focus for settlement during the Late Neolithic and Early Bronze ages (*c.* 4500–3500 BC).[4]

6. The constituent parts of what would become Parliament Square in the early sixteenth century, as shown on a plan prepared by the Museum of London Archaeological Service.

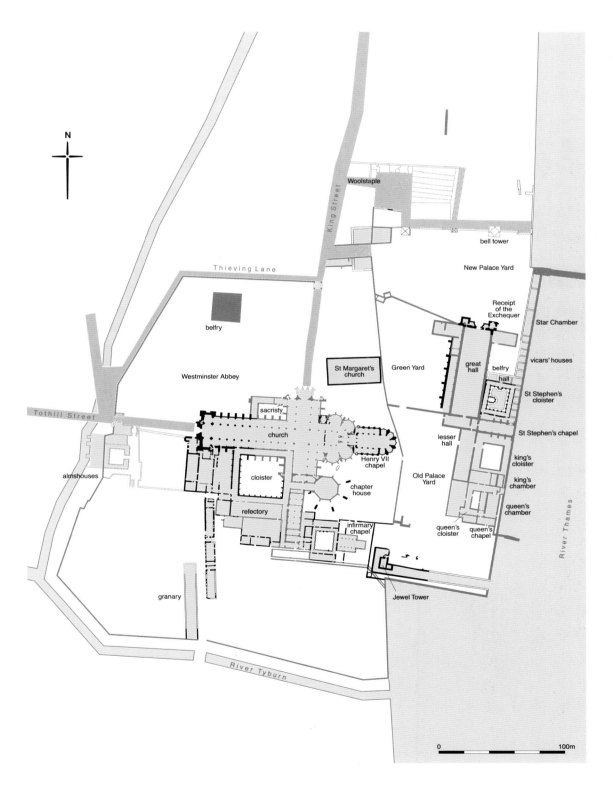

Thanks to excavations undertaken in association with the Jubilee line extension to the London Underground, archaeologists have had the opportunity to document the historical geography of the area produced by the constant movement of the boundary between land and water. By the middle of the eleventh century AD, shortly before the Norman Conquest, Edward the Confessor (1042–1066) made Thorney Island a principal royal residence. He rebuilt the older abbey to a design resembling the abbey at Jumièges, as a private church equivalent to Saint-Denis in Paris. In the last decade of the century William Rufus (later King William II of England, 1087–1100) built a great hall of gigantic proportions in this residence. The lower parts of the walls of Westminster Hall are survivals of it. By about 1100 two routes ran out from Edward's new abbey. King Street started at the north transept; it was stopped up in the 1860s with the construction of the new Foreign and Commonwealth Office, or Government Offices as they were formerly known. Tothill Street ran from the west front, on an axis with the nave of the Abbey. A street of the same name survives beside Methodist Central Hall, but its alignment was affected by the cutting of Victoria Street from 1845 to 1851.

By the early sixteenth century the component parts of the Abbey precinct and palace were fully developed, and understanding these elements helps to explain the street names that today mystify even native Londoners. St Margaret's Street, Old Palace Yard and Abingdon Street are one road over no more than 100 metres (328 feet); their names reflect a now lost sequence of distinct spaces.

A plan prepared by the Museum of London Archaeological Service shows two large complexes (fig. 6). One is the Royal Palace. It was organized around the reconstructed hall, its cloisters and courtyards. On the 'land side' are three walled yards: Green Yard (a statue of Cromwell by Hamo Thornycroft, 1850–1925, was positioned here in 1899); Old Palace Yard, which survives in name only; and New Palace Yard, which is an open area enclosed by E.M. Barry's (1830–1880) heavy iron railings in the 1860s. What is today Parliament Square fell mostly within the Abbey's precincts, and was entered by a gate near the junction of Great Smith and Victoria streets. There was then no bridge across the Thames at this point.

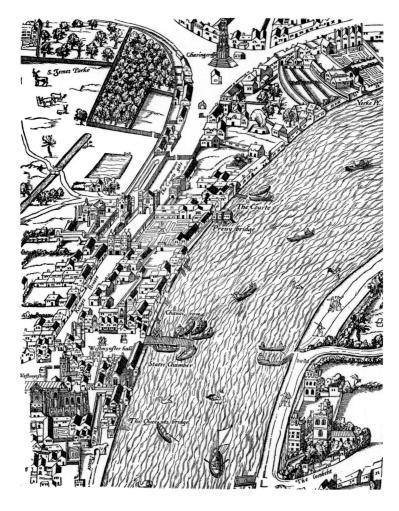

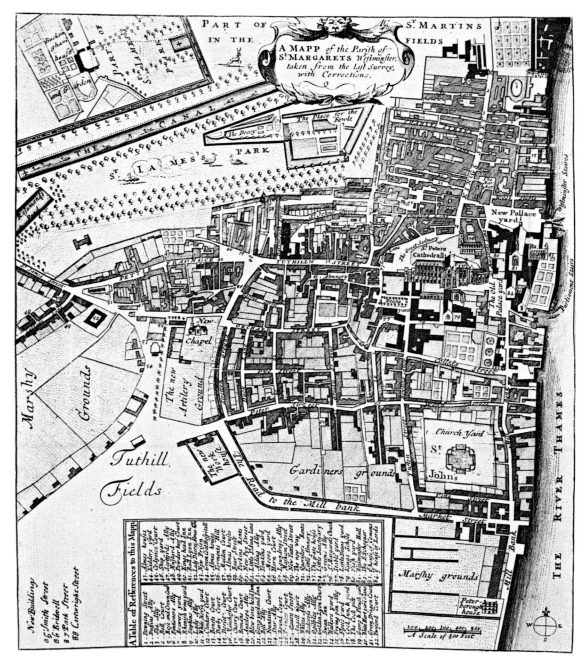

The first map evidence (fig. 7) dates from the time of Elizabeth I (1558–1603). Then comes a plan by John Norden and finally one by Stow (fig. 8), the most reliable of this early sequence. Here New Palace Yard, Old Palace Yard and Broad Sanctuary stand out as separate areas. The most formal of the three was New Palace Yard, recorded in an engraving by Wenceslaus Hollar (1607–1677; fig. 9).

The building of Westminster Bridge in the 1740s increased traffic through the area, and specially appointed Bridge Commissioners widened streets to deal with the congestion.[5] In the 1750s the first major public building – new law courts designed by John Vardy (1718–1765) and built up against the side of Westminster Hall – was added to the palace (fig. 10).[6]

By the 1750s Londoners had started to take in the views from the new Westminster Bridge (a modern engineering wonder; see fig. 11). This was demolished in the 1850s to make way for the current iron one. Canaletto (1697–1768), who came to England in 1746 on the heels of potential patrons, made a painting of the west front of the Abbey and Broad Sanctuary, with St Margaret's Church and tower closing the view to the rear (fig. 12). Just above St Margaret's is the long roof of Westminster Hall.[7] This Canaletto is the best historic view we have that records how the area corresponding to Parliament Square looked before its

*Opposite, top left:* 7. An extract from Agas's *Civitatis Londinium…*, c. 1560, the earliest map evidence for the capital, rendered as a city view after the manner of Italian city plans.

*Opposite, top right:* 8. From John Stow's *Survey of the Cities of London and Westminster* (London: 1720), the most reliable of the early map sequence for central London.

*Opposite, bottom:* 9. Wenceslaus Hollar's mid-seventeenth-century view of New Palace Yard as seen from the river side. The large gable end of Westminster Hall is on the left.

*Below:* 10. Old Palace Yard in the late eighteenth century, showing John Vardy's law courts with the roof of Westminster Hall rising behind them.

*Right:* 11. Canaletto's *Westminster Bridge from the North with the Lord Mayor's Procession, 25 May 1750*. Then newly constructed, this was the second permanent crossing of the Thames.

*Right, bottom:* 12. Canaletto's *Westminster Abbey with the Knights Companion of the Order of the Bath in Procession, 26 June 1749*. The outer precinct of the Abbey, visible left, corresponds to the area now occupied by Parliament Square.

Victorian improvement. The whole outer Abbey precinct was bounded by railings, and outside were buildings on a domestic scale. It is hard to think of a similar sort of space in England today. It is not a cathedral close, similar to Salisbury. Instead, the proximity of city to great church would have had a more Continental feel to it.

**The New Sessions House and 'Garden Square'**

Only in the early nineteenth century was there any interest in designing the space or the buildings around the Abbey and Parliament. The opportunity came from a local initiative, the rebuilding of the Middlesex Sessions House. In 1804 a new site within the old precinct was found, one occupied by the remains of the old Sanctuary Tower (and the future site of the Supreme Court). Completed in 1805, the new courthouse was the work of architect Samuel Pepys Cockerell (1753–1827), whose Neoclassical building was arranged on a Greek-cross plan (see fig. 14, p. 54, and fig. 6, p. 77).

The proposals for a new public building persuaded Parliament to set up another commission with powers to purchase land. Private Acts of 1806, 1808 and 1814 enabled the acquisition of sites for clearances to improve the movement of traffic. All this was on the understanding that the freeholds acquired would be vested in the Crown, which

*Below:* 13. St Margaret's is the parish church of Westminster and commonly called the parish church of Parliament.

*Right:* 14. This plan shows the location of the new Sessions House (below the Abbey and on the opposite side of Broad Sanctuary). The lots tinted yellow were proposed for redevelopment with grand commercial terraces. The blue area shows the extent of clearances enabled by Private Acts of Parliament in order to improve the setting of the Abbey.

*Right, centre:* 15. Leverton and Chawner's proposals for a new commercial parade flanking the Sessions House.

*Right, bottom:* 16. James Wyatt's proposals of about 1806 for a Gothic terrace, including the rehandling of the then newly completed Sessions House. The style reflects the period's growing interest in medieval buildings and was chosen to harmonize with the Abbey.

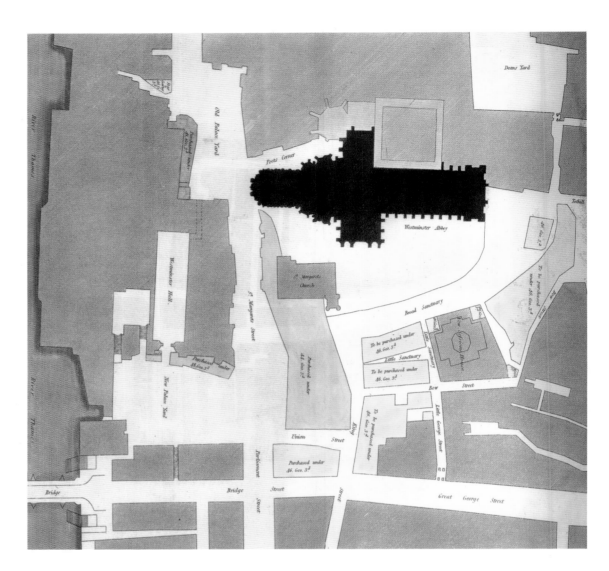

as a result to this day owns Parliament Square. (The Greater London Authority manages it on the Crown's behalf.)

The commissioners did have powers to provide footways and ornamental gardens associated with them, although the Treasury was there to keep costs down. First, land to the north and east of St Margaret's – Westminster's parish church (fig. 13) – was cleared to give an uninterrupted view of the courthouse. Cockerell, the Sessions House architect, repaired and tidied up the outside of St Margaret's (he had previously, in 1801, restored the church).

In 1806 the commissioners invited proposals to create a new terrace of buildings on the line of the medieval enclosure, flanking Cockerell's Sessions House. This included the creation of a new 'Garden Square'. A plan (fig. 14) shows the position of the new court, the block of houses to be demolished to link the Abbey precinct to New Palace Yard, and the new plots that the commissioners envisaged to complete the square.[8] A handful of proposals for this scheme survive in The National Archives at Kew.[9] One is for matching terraces in the Palladian style (fig. 15). James Wyatt (1746–1813) also proposed building terraces in a medieval style and recladding the then newly completed court to match (fig. 16).

No terraces were built, but the commissioners did form a park to the north of St Margaret's. This Wyatt design had curving paths and ponds, and probably also ornamental beds,

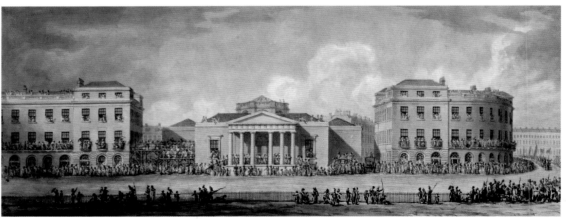

*Right:* 17. An early nineteenth-century plan showing the layout of the new Garden Square to the north of St Margaret's Church. This layout survived until the late 1860s.

*Right, bottom:* 18. A plan dating from the 1860s, showing the early nineteenth-century landscape scheme comprising Garden Square, including Canning Green, which appears to the right of the Sessions House at the top of the drawing.

*Below:* 19. View of the Palace of Westminster in the late 1820s, before the fire, illustrating Sir John Soane's Gothic ranges to the old law courts.

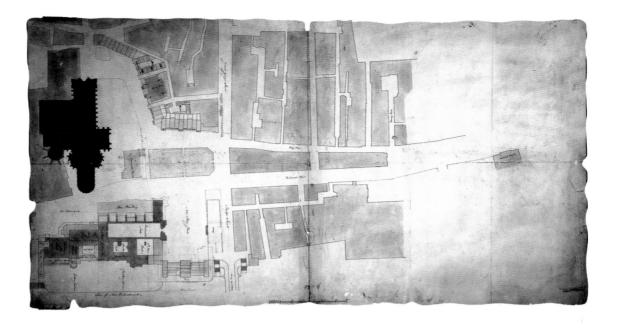

in a layout typical of the period.[10] Another garden enclosure was later created to the north of the Sessions House. This space eventually came to be known as 'Canning Green' after Richard Westmacott's (1775–1856) bronze of the Tory prime minister (completed in 1832) was positioned here (figs. 17 and 18).

Within the palace, the architect Sir John Soane (1753–1837) was in 1824 asked to rehandle Vardy's earlier court buildings beside Westminster Hall in a modern version of English Gothic, an exercise not to his liking.[11] These ranges were most visible from within the new Garden Square (fig. 19). Thus before the great fire of 1834 destroyed the ancient Palace of Westminster, the Gothic style was understood to be appropriate here, at the symbolic centre of the United Kingdom. As for the Soane–Vardy courts, they survived the fire only to be demolished in 1882, when the High Court decamped to another new Gothic building, the Royal Courts of Justice in the Strand.[12]

## Barry's Parliament Square

When, in 1855, the new parliament was nearing completion, its architect, Sir Charles Barry (fig. 20 – he turned more than once to A.W.N. Pugin, 1812–1852, for help with the medieval detail) proposed enclosing New Palace Yard with a range of buildings entered on the corner by an elaborate Gothic-style lantern.[13] This would have entailed moving the law courts and St Margaret's (the latter stone by stone) to a site between

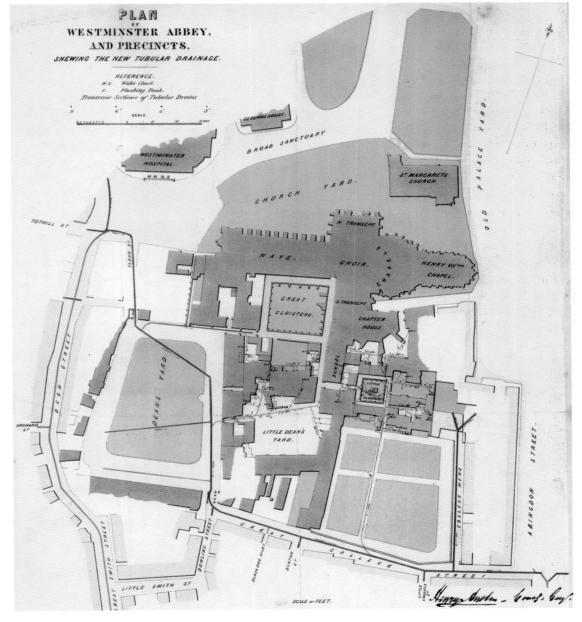

Princes and Tothill streets. Barry planned another green square for Old Palace Yard, which would have provided a fine setting for the chapel of Henry VII.[14] These plans – which would have properly enclosed the square on one side (fig. 21) – were costed at a staggering £651,285, and failed for that reason.

This scheme was soon eclipsed by Barry's more ambitious set of proposals for the complete replanning of the area (fig. 22). At the centre was a new Palace of Administration on the north side of Whitehall, facing the Thames across a public park, answering the 'Palace of Legislature' or Parliament. Just as the new palace for civil servants was be given an appropriate setting, so too did Barry envisage Parliament and Westminster Abbey with a generous new public open space, a 3.6-hectare (9-acre) park composed of three lawns occupying the area that today corresponds to Parliament Square. This was to have been bounded by wide roads on regular alignments continuing along Victoria Street. A more private ornamental garden, New Abbey Gardens, would be on land just west of Old Palace Yard. From this garden the Chapter House (later to be restored by Sir George Gilbert Scott, 1811–1878) and Henry VII's Chapel could be contemplated alongside a new range of buildings for the Abbey School. This plan envisaged a new river crossing next

to Waterloo Bridge. On the opposite side of the Thames, Barry showed new monumental buildings along a new road (beside an embanked river), with public squares at the bridge heads.[15] This was grand planning in a European context, equivalent in its ambition to contemporary proposals for a new Ringstrasse in Vienna.

This plan may seem fantastic now, but at the time, there was reason to hope that something very significant might happen to give London an administrative centre commensurate with the country's expanding empire. A new Office of Works had been created in 1855, and its First Commissioner, Sir Benjamin Hall, hoped to use his powers to improve London. A select committee was appointed to look into consolidating all government activities around Parliament. The first project to emerge from this was a massive, single structure, housing the Foreign, Colonial and India Offices, which was built to the designs of Scott (and known generally as Government Offices – not to be confused with J.M. Brydon's later Government Buildings, now HM Treasury).[16] And in that same year, 1855, Parliament legislated a new London-wide authority, the Metropolitan Board of Works, to deal with roads and public health matters. Its first great plan was to construct huge intercepting sewers to deposit the capital's filth far downstream, and then to embank the Thames in the central area. There followed a series of new roads, which some hoped might be developed with terraces in a grand, Parisian manner. In the end, though, there was no body with the powers to control the appearance of new buildings realized through these clearances. The new streets – Southwark Street, Charing Cross Road, Shaftesbury Avenue – were architecturally disappointing and remain so.

When Barry died, his son Edward took over the job of completing the palace. With it fell to him the problem of what to do with the surrounding area, which had been a construction site for nearly thirty years and was still being dug up to create the first underground railway. Whatever he might have thought of his father's aspirations, E.M. Barry's plan of May 1861 for the new 'Parliament Square' – the earliest use of that term – was more pragmatic. He was also charged with finding 'suitable positions for statues of public men, and securing as much uniformity in the treatment of their pedestals, and accessories, as may be consonant with the dictates of architectural propriety and good taste'. This

gathering of statesmen was seen as an extension of the commemorative burials that had colonized the Abbey. It also reflected the creation of a new National Portrait Gallery. Established in 1857, this collection was housed from 1859 to 1869 on the very edge of the square, overlooking the Houses of Parliament, in a terraced house that stood at 29 Great George Street.

Barry's design was for a carriageway ringing a railed enclosure to a simple greensward. It was bisected by a viewing axis that framed Canning's memorial at the far or north end (fig. 23). The railings incorporated gas standards on granite piers, all in the Gothic manner similar to heavy cast-iron railings Barry designed for New Palace Yard. Instead of linking the park back to the Abbey precinct, as the existing Garden Square did, Barry proposed for convenience a road or 'short street between [Victoria Street] and St Margaret's Church. 55 feet wide and 150 feet long, it would', he wrote, 'cut the distance [for] carriages travelling from St Stephen's Tower to Victoria Street by 200 yards'. Therein lies the source of the pedestrian troubles today.[17] Until then, the

22. Barry's grand plan for the replanning of the wider area to create distinct administrative and legislative quarters, from the Reverend Alfred Barry's memoir of Sir Charles.

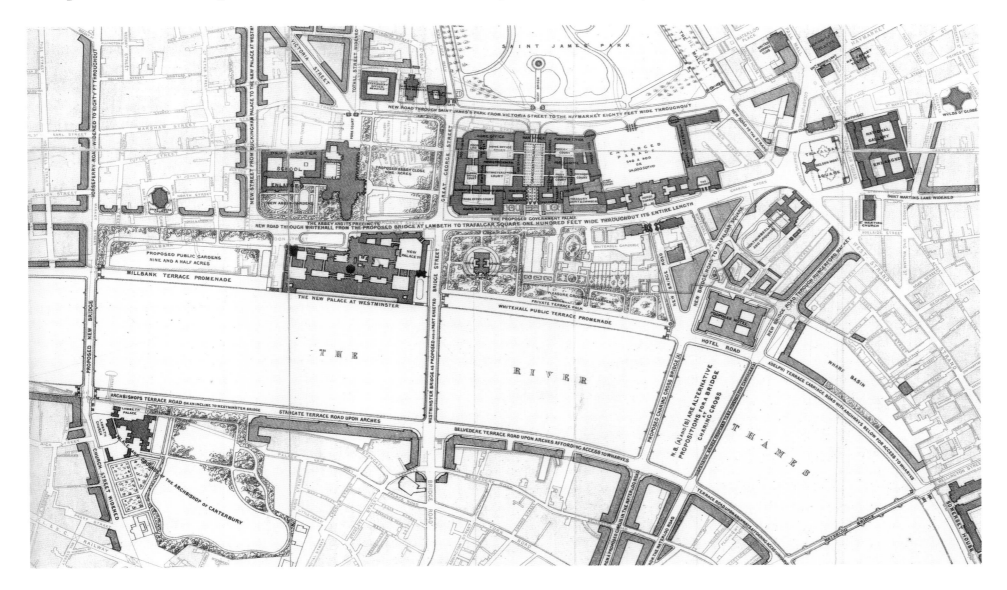

*Below:* 23. E.M. Barry's design of 1861 for Parliament Square, recorded in a later drawing prepared when the London County Council was contemplating a new alignment for Parliament Street.

*Right:* 24. A woodcut engraving from the *Illustrated London News* from 1861 shows the mature planting of Wyatt's Garden Square, shortly to be replaced by Barry's traffic island. Contemporaries admired the picturesque qualities of this approach from Victoria Street. Westminster Hospital is to the left. Built in the 1830s, it is another early nineteenth-century building designed in the Gothic manner out of respect for the setting of the Abbey.

green area around St Margaret's had at least kept the traffic away from the Abbey and provided a picturesque and green setting for the ancient and modern Gothic buildings (fig. 24).

E.M. Barry's new piece of greenery had no footpaths, planted beds or benches from which to admire the monuments all around. It was a traffic island laid out to display sculpture. In 1851 a statue of the Tory Sir Robert Peel (1788–1850) had been placed in Wyatt's Garden Square (Matthew Noble, 1818–1876, was the sculptor). It was the first to take up a place near Canning in the new Barry layout. Later came Edward Stanley, the 14th Earl of Derby (1799–1868, a Whig turned Tory, the statue again by Matthew Noble and completed in 1874). After Stanley was Henry Temple, 3rd Viscount Palmerston (1784–1865, whose politics defy easy classification; the sculpture once more by Noble, in 1876). The great Conservative politician Benjamin Disraeli had to wait more than a decade to take up his place (in 1883; his likeness executed, appropriately, by a sculptor who was, like the Earl of Beaconsfield, of Italian extraction – Mario Raggi, 1821–1907). Students of Victorian politics may be surprised to find Gladstone nowhere in sight, but there was no iconographic programme being methodically worked out here.

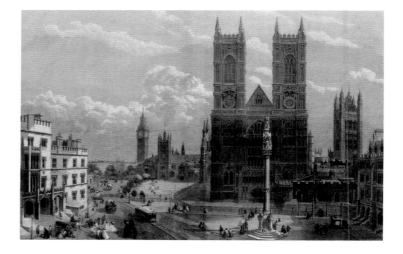

After the square was redesigned in 1951, and the Victorian statesmen assigned their present positions, the next commemorative sculpture was of the South African politician Jan Christiaan Smuts (1870–1950, depicted in what is perhaps the finest work of art in the square – by Jacob Epstein, 1880–1959, and dating from 1956). Smuts actually fought against the British in the Boer War, but he was later a loyal ally through two world wars, and played an important role in forming the United Nations, which met for the first time near by, in Methodist Central Hall. The bronze of Nelson Mandela by Ian Walters (1930–2006) was unveiled in August 2007 after a lengthy planning process. It will probably be the last statue to be erected in the square.

A notable feature of the Barry plan was the alignment of a north–south roadway between the square proper and Canning Green on axis with the north door of the Abbey, providing a fine view to people in carriages (and later motor cars) of that medieval monument, Scott's restoration of which was by this time (the 1860s) well under way. There is no suggestion that Barry was trying to reflect the line of King Street that had emanated from the precinct along the lines of the north transept. The position of this road was instead set by the distance needed at either end for the 'weaving' of vehicles across lanes as they wheeled around the junctions.

The roundabout as built was bisected by an east–west path extending the line of the carriageway entrance to New Palace Yard. The statue of Canning was repositioned on this axis and in this position provoked a (brief) debate in the

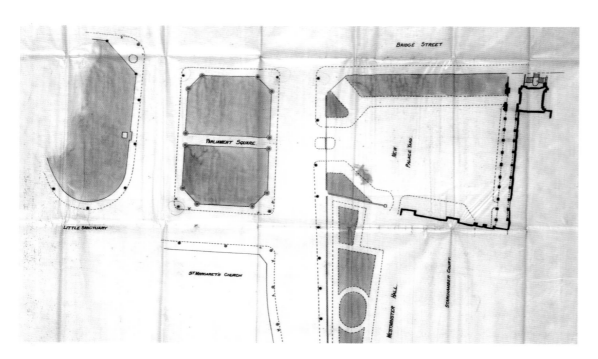

Commons at the end of the session of 1867.[18] Then the Tory MP Alexander Beresford-Hope took the opportunity to canvas support for Barry's scheme as an improvement over existing conditions, commenting that it provided a suitable position as well for the anticipated commemorative statue of Palmerston.[19] It is not surprising that Barry's scheme pleased Beresford-Hope and the MPs on hand that day and led them to support his motion, since it was laid out for their appreciation, orientated on axis with the carriageway approach they used to enter and leave New Palace Yard. The layout did not direct itself to the wider public at all; it was an extension of Parliament into the square.

### The Next Instalment: Public Outcry and Traffic Again

Even on its own terms, as an ornament to Parliament, the Barry layout was far from perfect. The greensward to the west, Canning Green, was bounded on one side by an imposing Victorian block, Westminster House, a commercial building in multiple tenancies. In 1933 Middlesex County Council learned that the Westminster Real Property Company had acquired the leases on this site from the Ecclesiastical Commissioners and was intending a much larger speculative office block. The proposed building, which would have towered over the Guildhall, caused a minor public outcry (fig. 25).[20] In response the company instructed Giles Gilbert Scott (1880–1960; the grandson of Sir George, the Abbey surveyor, and himself the designer of the familiar red phone box) to improve and 'Gothicize' the first proposals.[21]

Indeed, the project came quite close to being a reality. The developer tendered for the work, which prompted Middlesex – not the Office of Works, not Parliament, not the London County Council (LCC) – to campaign against the proposals, which it claimed would be out of keeping with the historical surroundings of the square. The council's Clerk tried to purchase a lease from the property company. Talks stalled, and Middlesex sought a private member's bill for the compulsory purchase of the land. Negotiations eased and the developer agreed to sell for £375,000 the 999-year lease that it had acquired from the Ecclesiastical Commissioners.

There is a very interesting pair of drawings from this time that illustrates the existing layout of the square, one showing Westminster House and the other with it removed (figs. 26 and 27). Middlesex wished to gift the plot it had

25. The public outcry caused by this proposed speculative office block led Middlesex County Council to purchase the land that formed the basis of the modern square.

26. An aerial perspective prepared by London County Council shows the Barry layout and Westminster House, the office block on Canning Green.

27. The same viewpoint as in fig. 26, altered to show the benefit of removing Westminster House, and a proposed new layout for the square.

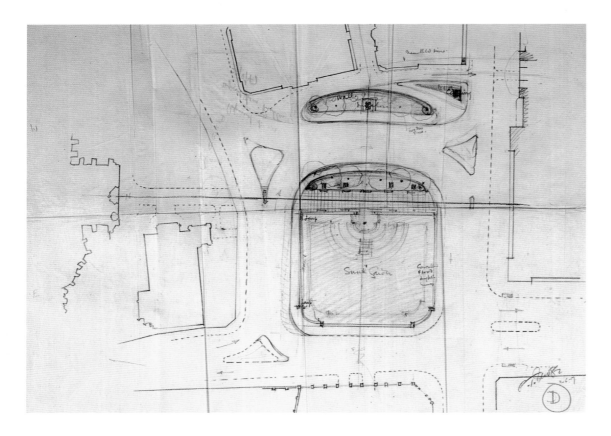

acquired in perpetuity as public open space to preserve the setting of the square. The London County Council agreed to contribute some funds to purchase the site from Middlesex, but only if the Treasury bore most of the costs. Despite public petitions, the First Commissioner of Works – the government's agent in such land transactions – was not supportive. 'Normally', one of his civil servants wrote, 'the responsibility for civic improvements falls upon the local authorities concerned. The proposed improvement of the amenities of Parliament Square is not, in the opinion of His Majesty's Government, of sufficient importance from a national point of view to justify a departure from the general rule.' If not here, one might ask where.

The desire to commemorate George V (1910–1936) offered a way out, perhaps. The parties promoting the expansion of the square suggested a national memorial to the king on Canning Green in order to force the government's hand. The prime minister, Stanley Baldwin, embraced the idea of a monument, but – and here was the fatal snag – he favoured a site in Abingdon Street, which the government conveniently owned already. William Reid Dick's (1879–1961) stone monument, with a base by Giles Gilbert Scott, was erected there near Old Palace Yard in 1947. At this point entered an improbable hero, the Ministry of Transport (MoT), which had long wanted to acquire the square for traffic improvements. In 1935 it came to the table with a plan for the rehandling of the square (fig. 28). This entailed doubling the area of Barry's roundabout and forming a new road obliterating half of Canning Green; all the memorials would have to be relocated.

This plan would speed the flow of traffic and reduce pedestrian accidents, and it is essentially the one that came to be realized in 1950–51. The MoT's engineers understood that this was no simple piece of traffic engineering, and their plan indicates how the space in the roundabout might be designed: there is a paved walk on axis of the north transept, an open greensward, and what appears to be a hemicycle (perhaps for a sculptural group).[22]

So, finally, with necessary traffic improvements leading the way, the MoT was able to persuade a previously unwilling Office of Works to commit funds to the project, but still the Treasury drove a hard bargain. The estimate for the works was £400,000, in addition to the cost of the land. The transport minister agreed to meet some of this, and looked to other sources for the rest. Eventually Middlesex County Council offered £50,000, the LCC £100,000 and Westminster City Council £50,000. On that basis, in 1939, the Treasury agreed to buy the land provided that the LCC, Westminster and poor old Middlesex itself would also bear some more of the cost. They all agreed, with the help of the Pilgrim Trust (£50,000) and the Royal Institution of Chartered Surveyors (RICS; £10,000). Years of deal-making came to nothing, however, when war was declared later that year. And so the site remained as it had been, with a run-down office block bounding one side.

The cause of beautifying Parliament Square was, however, taken up in the ambitious County of London Plan of 1943. This proposed diverting traffic from the area by turning Great George Street into a dual carriageway on the basis that this 'noble group of buildings around the nation's ancient shrine [the Abbey] calls for a more tranquil setting … It demands too, for ceremonial occasions, a dignified and reasonably spacious environment.' An aerial perspective showed how this proposal would solve, as the authors put it, 'the whole traffic problem in Westminster' (fig. 29).

The editors of the *Architectural Review* took up the cause in their issue of November 1947, which published Gordon Cullen's proposals for a new, pedestrianized precinct (figs. 30–32). Although he did not turn Great George Street into a dual carriageway, Cullen closed the whole area south of it, including Broad Sanctuary. He assumed vehicular access to the palace would be by means of an underpass and roundabout excavated in New Palace Yard (possibly not the most preservation-friendly solution; a massive underground car park for MPs was, however, eventually constructed there). Parliament Square was to be hard-paved, and the statues of Victorian statesmen moved to the north edge lining Great George Street and facing Whitehall. Old Palace Yard would be turfed in the manner of an English cathedral close. It might seem now pie in the sky, but in 1947 many things seemed possible. The LCC was still confident it could transform Parliament Square, but 'as a long-term project, say 40–50 years'.

Meanwhile, the LCC was busy reworking the MoT plan of 1935 specifically to allow 'a more adequate weaving length on the north side of the roundabout'. This new version allowed the retention of mature London plane trees planted in the nineteenth century. There remained, though, a few points at issue between the newly created Ministry of Works and the LCC. One was whether the 'roundabout' – the word used at the time – should be enclosed as Barry's had been, to keep pedestrians out; or, if not, whether people should be allowed, even encouraged, to cross to the square and so interrupt traffic. Once there, assuming this was the outcome, how were pedestrians to be protected from the traffic raging on all sides?

The Metropolitan Police did not want any access on road-safety grounds. The Ministry of Works took a different view. Its deputy secretary, Sir Eric de Normann, set out his concerns in an internal memorandum: 'I get the impression that this plan has been prepared by the LCC … entirely from the point of view of improving traffic facilities in Parliament Square. This may be very right and proper but from our point of view we must consider the matter from a wider aspect and amenities must certainly come into the picture.' He worried, too, about how the Victorian statues could be given a meaningful setting. Recalling the County of London Plan of 1943, he continued: 'Moreover, I am doubtful whether this increase in traffic facilities is in line with planning policy. Surely … Abercrombie [the author of the County of London Plan] … intended to divert traffic away from the Abbey? Though this plan may not be realizable for a good many years, I see no reason why in the interval we should go so completely against the spirit of it.'[23]

De Normann encouraged an open debate, and that is just what he got over the following three years. At the heart of it were questions concerning what sort of place the square should be. Was it to be a small park, an ornamental roundabout or both? That was not the only problem. Other colleagues in the ministry disliked the winnowing away of Canning Green 'to a small pointed strip on which it will be difficult, if not impossible, to site either the Canning or Lincoln statues'. The latter had been a gift from the US government in 1920 (the work of Augustus Saint-Gaudens, 1848–1907, it is a copy of an earlier casting in Chicago). Finally, the chief architect at the Works tried to wrest control of the design from the MoT by proposing to buy the site from Middlesex County Council, which, it will be remembered, had been looking for someone to take it off its

*Right:* 30. Gordon Cullen proposed the pedestrianization of the wider area in the November 1947 issue of the *Architectural Review* (vol. 102, pp. 159–70). This image shows a view west along Great George Street, with the Victorian statesmen looking up Whitehall.

*Below:* 31. Cullen's general layout for Parliament Square.

*Opposite:* 32. Cullen envisaged reinstating the old Abbey boundary railing shown in the painting by Canaletto of 1749, illustrated earlier in this chapter (p. 53). This would have required diverting the traffic in Victoria Street north.

books for some time. One compromise idea offered was to form a subway to the centre of the square, surround it with a high wall to screen out traffic noise, and arrange the statues in a circle round a garden. A Ministry of Works civil servant remarked that 'this would look pretty queer'.

By summer of 1947 the ministry had persuaded the LCC to adopt a compromise design that allowed for a pedestrian crossing to a walkway on the line of the north transept of the Abbey, a feature of particular importance to civil servants. The view of the north transept that Barry's arrangements afforded was just about the only thing admired in the Victorian layout. The Works also hoped that this walkway would be part of the normal route for people making their way on foot from Whitehall to Parliament (although that seems strange, since this alignment is far from the line of Whitehall, and negotiating it involved crossing twice over large roads).

The MoT officials now lost their patience. If the LCC wanted something architectural, it should pay for it or accept an expedient, short-term solution for dealing with the traffic. Otherwise, congestion across the wider area would become unacceptable. MoT staff also pointed out that a solid block of vehicles harmed the setting of the Abbey and Parliament far more than the steady movement of traffic – a fair point. Congestion had been bad before 1939, had eased during the war, but by early 1948 was getting serious again despite petrol rationing. No agreement seemed possible. In February 1948 de Normann complained, 'Every time I go through Parliament Square I reflect on its bedraggled appearance.' Maybe, he conjectured, the Victorian arrangement could be smartened up by fresh planting. He asked the Royal Parks, which suggested rhododendrons, but pointed out that these would have to be rotated seasonally to recover from the effects of air pollution. It is a mark of the austerity of the time that the modest sum of £4600 a year could not be found even for this window dressing.

The Ministry of Works decided finally to intervene and force a compromise with an aesthetic edge. Instead of leaving the design of the roundabout to an engineer, de Normann approached the Royal Town Planning Institute and the Royal Institute of British Architects (RIBA) to suggest architects capable of working with the LCC's engineers to make the roundabout attractive. George Grey Wornum

(1888–1957) won the subsequent limited competition.[24] He had previously gained an RIBA medal for 'Street Architecture'. It helped that he advised Westminster City Council on municipal projects, including social housing. His best-known work is the headquarters building of the RIBA itself, in Portland Place. He also designed a lighting standard, examples of which can still be seen around the square.

From Wornum's appointment in November 1949 the project took on a particular urgency, since everyone wanted the works finished by the opening of the Festival of Britain in 1951 – in its day an event of as much significance as the 2012 Olympics. Parliament Square was not, however, one of those linked Festival projects, such as Churchill Gardens in Pimlico or the Lansbury Estate in Poplar, where the design was deliberately Modern to echo the spirit of the event. If that had been the intention, then Wornum was the wrong choice. His sensibility was that of a previous generation, and he was a safe pair of hands. Today his design certainly appears attractive, but it looks similar to something Lutyens could have done for a country house in the 1920s.

Wornum definitely wanted pavements on each side of the roundabout so that his new space could become part of the pattern of pedestrian circulation in the area. The Metropolitan Police disagreed. Westminster City Council, along with the MoT, weighed in against Wornum's best intentions. Now that the proposals were achieving architectural form, the Royal Fine Arts Commission became involved. It particularly approved the handling of the west side of the square by means of a low terrace that retained the trees and provided a platform for the statues, which Wornum repositioned there. Middlesex County Council was disgruntled because the MoT plan brought traffic too close to its front door at the Guildhall (as it still does). The irony of this would not have been lost on the county, without the far-sighted intervention of which there would have been no new plan to debate in the first place.

But the talk could go on only for so long. The Ministry of Works put a bill before Parliament seeking authorization for the plans. Middlesex, Westminster and the Metropolitan Police all threatened formal objections because Wornum's paved area round the edge continued to look as though it might accommodate pedestrians. The Works got all parties together to broker a compromise at a meeting with the architect, who suggested that if the path on the north side were extended farther east, to meet the corner, the space would become more inviting for pedestrians. And so the favoured Google Earth 'hit spot' with which this essay began arose out of a last-minute compromise. Wornum agreed to remove the wide pavements on the south and east edges of the square for which he had previously been fighting. These became instead the rough paved strips we have today, which were retained to provide areas for the public to view official processions (grass on its own presented practical difficulties). At last the matter was settled, and the work completed in time for the opening of the Festival of Britain. Wornum was rewarded with the RIBA's highest accolade, its Gold Medal, although it is tempting to think that this may well have been in recognition of his sheer dogged determination (figs. 33–35).

Although Wornum, the Ministry of Works and the Royal Fine Arts Commission had all wanted the square to be what we today would call 'accessible', the documents give no indication of just what this meant. Wornum must have realized that only a few people would get into the square. He decided to pave it with Portland stone, which is a beautiful, quintessentially London stone, but not hard-wearing and therefore never specified for well-used footways or public spaces.

Today certain features of Wornum's vision are admirable. The large greensward provides visual relief from the traffic and, with that light Portland stone, creates a calm foreground setting to the Abbey and Parliament. The scheme turns its back to the rest, but to dwell on this would

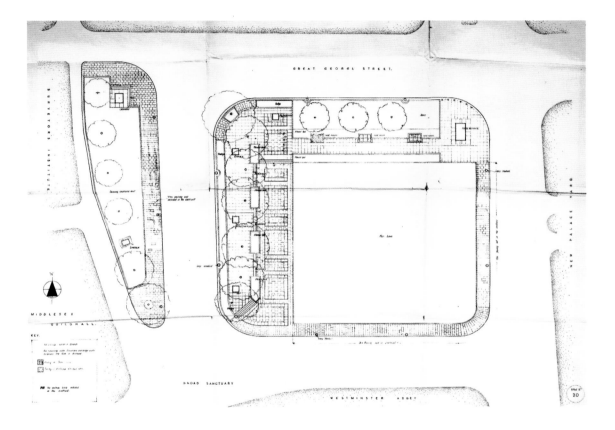

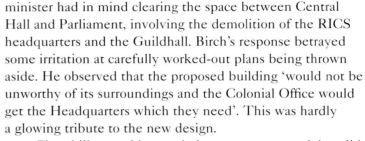

be to criticize it for failing to do something that was never in Wornum's brief. The subtle level change across the site is well handled, too. All this can be appreciated, however, only by the brave, the fleet of foot, the patient, or the determined protester. There are roughly 40 million pedestrian movements along the pavements lining the square each year. Of these, only 500,000 actually get into the centre, and about half of them do so on events days, when the roads are closed to traffic (these figures come from Transport for London Surveys of *c.* 2005).

## A Greater Parliament Square?

Proposals to redevelop the site to the west of the Guildhall, occupied by the Stationery Office and Westminster Hospital, were revived in 1947, when the government purchased the site for £412,000 and commissioned designs for a new Foreign and Colonial Office (fig. 36). This was seen as an opportunity to set back the old building line and create a larger space in front of Methodist Central Hall on one side of Broad Sanctuary. Churchill himself, however, seriously questioned whether there should be any building at all there. On 22 October 1954 he wrote to Nigel Birch, Minister of Works: 'Pray give your early consideration to the question of building the Colonial Office on the site opposite to Westminster Abbey. It seems a great pity to fill this unique space. What alternatives could be proposed?' The prime

minister had in mind clearing the space between Central Hall and Parliament, involving the demolition of the RICS headquarters and the Guildhall. Birch's response betrayed some irritation at carefully worked-out plans being thrown aside. He observed that the proposed building 'would not be unworthy of its surroundings and the Colonial Office would get the Headquarters which they need'. This was hardly a glowing tribute to the new design.

Churchill sensed he was being outmanoeuvred, but did not let go. In November he prepared a letter (which was never sent) to answer Birch. In it he outlined his vision of a greater Parliament Square:

*It might one day be possible for the whole of this site, from the [Methodist] Central Hall to the Houses of Parliament, to be cleared of buildings and laid out as a great square. The cost no doubt would be heavy, but it would be spread over many years, perhaps even generations. I am not convinced that we should prejudice this magnificent prospect now by erecting an obstacle to it [a new Colonial Office] which might last for centuries.*

*I remember there was a lot of public criticism of the proposal when the Labour Government announced it, and that there was opposition from all Parties in the House. One alternative which has been suggested to me … is Somerset House. There are few buildings which would be more impressive to Colonials, and I should not think it is beyond human ingenuity to move the Inland Revenue and Wills to less grand premises.*

*I am not proposing that the final decision should be taken now, but I do consider that building [the Colonial Office] should be postponed for a few years. Meanwhile, the palisade [around the cleared site] should be pulled down so that the public could see for the first time what possibilities the site presents.*[25]

In the final version to the Chancellor of the Exchequer, Churchill wrote, 'I believe we should take a long-term view and go for what Birch describes as a "truly noble conception", i.e., aim at eventually (possibly not in our lifetime) getting the whole site … cleared and laid out as a great square … Once they [the public] have seen it there would, I think, be a spontaneous demand that it should not be built over.' The chancellor replied: 'I do not see how I could defend in Parliament the big unproductive expenditure, to say nothing of the destruction, involved in such a scheme.'

The public criticism to which Churchill referred was that of the Royal Fine Arts Commission, which was unhappy with the bulk and height of the proposed Colonial Office in relation to the Abbey. Wornum suggested a compromise in a massing diagram of that year (and the eventual redevelopment of the site with the Queen Elizabeth II Conference Centre follows his sketch almost exactly; see figs. 37 and 38). The Hospital and Stationery sites were then cleared, and, regrettably, there was no 'spontaneous demand it should not be built over'.

In April 1955 Churchill's son-in-law Duncan Sandys, Minister of Housing and Local Government, held off redevelopment and arranged for the site to be used temporarily as a surface car park. In 1958 the Colonial Office proposals were abandoned; the whole notion of a Colonial Office was coming into question, and the UK was then beginning to reformulate its relationship with its overseas dominions. The question of what to do with the vacant site was set aside to avoid prejudicing Leslie Martin's (1908–2000) proposals for replanning Whitehall. He proposed a traffic-free precinct around Parliament Square, and on the hospital site a building of 'international significance', but not for governmental use. The proposals involved considerable demolition, were contentious and so led to a public inquiry. They were dismissed, but out of them came the decision that the cleared site to the rear of the Guildhall should be a government conference centre. Although a brief for this was issued in 1969, architects were not selected until ten years later, and construction on Powell and Moya's Queen Elizabeth II Conference Centre began in 1982.

By this point Westminster City Council, as the local planning authority, was promoting its own proposals to pedestrianize Parliament Square, and published formal guidance on this in 1984. Political intent did not focus on the knotty problem of whether it was right for traffic to take a back seat to people on foot, however, until the more recent major reorientation in thinking about our towns and cities that has occurred as planning policy has moved towards concepts of sustainable development. So it was that in 1996 agencies and public authorities with an interest in central London came together to form the 'World Squares for All' Steering Group to improve pedestrian provision and reduce the impact of traffic in London's two most important public spaces, Trafalgar Square and Parliament Square. From 2001 this group was

*Above:* 39. A visualization of the proposed Foster+Partners' masterplan of 1998 for Parliament Square, part of the World Squares for All initiative.

*Right:* 40. A visualization of Foster's scheme of 1998, made from just north of Westminster Abbey.

*Opposite, right:* 41. A plan of the first World Squares for All proposals, which would have increased the tree planting along existing footways of Wornum's scheme.

chaired by the newly created Greater London Authority (GLA), working closely with its strategic traffic and highway authority, Transport for London (TfL). 'Partnership working' was by this point de rigueur, and the steering group was packed with agencies, government departments and public authorities with an interest in these two spaces: English Heritage, the government's adviser on the historic environment; the Department for Culture, Media and Sport; the Parliamentary Works Directorate; Westminster Abbey; Westminster City Council; the Metropolitan Police; and the Royal Parks Agency. A masterplan by Foster+Partners was completed in 1998, and the first phase, the closure of one arm of the Trafalgar Square gyratory, was realized in 2003.

The second part of World Squares for All was Parliament Square, the implementation of which was also integral to the delivery of the Westminster World Heritage Site Management Plan (figs. 39, 40 and 41). This not

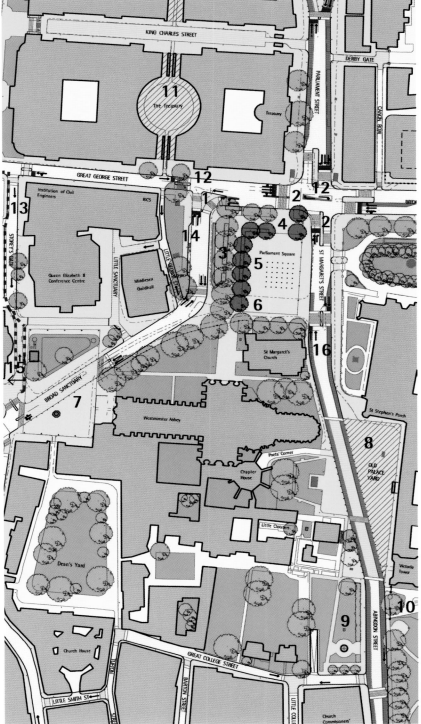

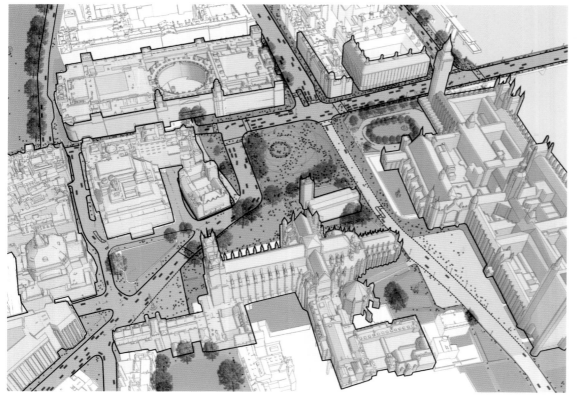

surprisingly identified high traffic levels as the single largest threat to the 'outstanding universal significance' reflected in the UNESCO-approved designation. Detailed work on the redesign began in 2006, and by early 2007 a team of landscape designers, conservation experts and traffic engineers was appointed under the direction of masterplan architect Hawkins\Brown, which was charged with implementing the closure of the road separating the Abbey from the roundabout that Barry had created to ease traffic congestion, and with downgrading St Margaret's Street to the east so that it would take much lower volumes of traffic.

A Zurich-based landscape practice, Vogt Landschaftsarchitekten, proposed to replace Wornum's work with a new paved scheme and associated planting around St Margaret's, the latter deliberately echoing Wyatt's first Garden Square (figs. 42 and 43). The architects proposed using natural building stones from across the UK and laying these in a rhythmic mesh pattern that was seen as organic and also redolent of Gothic rib vaulting. A knoll was to be created at the north-west corner to give views of the World Heritage Site. Vogt also retained the raised platform on the western edge to preserve the trees, and maintained the sculptures in their current positions.

In some quarters the proposed removal of Wornum's landscape of 1951 was contentious. In 2001 English Heritage had added Parliament Square to its non-statutory Register of Historic Parks and Gardens, a list reserved for landscapes of national significance. Nevertheless, the design team believed it was necessary to undo Wornum's scheme. The proposed road closures undermined the logic of his design. Portland stone and turf are not durable enough to cope with the tens of millions of people who were anticipated to use the new space. The scheme of 1951 also relied on steps to deal with level changes, and so required extensive adaptation to meet inclusive design standards. While English Heritage supported the closure of the south side and the remodelling of the square to improve accessibility, it wished to retain elements of the Wornum scheme that it considered provided a simple, elegant setting for the World Heritage Site. The GLA, led by the then mayor, Ken Livingstone, was strongly supportive of a contemporary, fully inclusive scheme, emblematic of the twenty-first century, and so instructed TfL to prepare the necessary planning application.

Then Livingstone lost the mayoral election of May 2008 to the Conservative candidate, Boris Johnson. Johnson reviewed all capital projects under TfL's control and on

6 August 2008 announced that Parliament Square would not proceed. He was concerned that the potential cumulative effects on traffic in central London, arising from significant developments at Victoria and Elephant and Castle, would be simply too great. In reaching this view the new mayor took into account the congestion that would arise from traffic diverted by the construction of Crossrail (the most important public transport project in the capital and now under way). All in all, the TfL project would, the official press release went on, make congestion in London even worse, since traffic, as TfL itself had just revealed, was returning to pre-Congestion Charging levels. Additionally, Johnson's administration was opposed to losing the turfed area in the square. And so the last word on this latest instalment in the history of this small, politically charged piece of land must belong to the current mayor (as recorded on the GLA website): 'There is absolutely no sense in Londoners paying £18 million from their stretched transport budget in order to reduce capacity on London's roads. This scheme would have turned a green glade of heroes into a vast, blasted, chewing-gummed piazza.'

42. The Vogt–Hawkins\Brown proposals for the redesigned Parliament Square, 2008, as visualized by GMJ.

43. The Vogt–Hawkins\Brown masterplan of 2008 developed the Foster concept design on the basis of pedestrian and visitor studies that demonstrated that axial routes would not support real pedestrian desire-lines. For this reason a more open design, with no hierarchy of movement, was adopted.

# 'A DAINTY PIECE OF ORNAMENT': THE ARCHITECTURE OF THE FORMER MIDDLESEX GUILDHALL

JEREMY MUSSON

*'That spirit and form of Gothic giving a picturesque variety of features and delicacy of detail was felt to be the most appropriate treatment, and the building should be considered a dainty piece of ornament set amongst the austere and formal buildings of the neighbourhood.'*

James Gibson, architect of the Middlesex Guildhall

*Previous page:* 1. The United Kingdom Supreme Court building, formerly the Middlesex Guildhall, in 2009.

2. Parliament Square: the Palace of Westminster, the church of St Margaret's, and Westminster Abbey. In the foreground stands Sir George Gilbert Scott's monument of 1859–61 to those from Westminster School who fell in the Crimean War.

As an ensemble of ancient and modern buildings, Parliament Square vividly reflects the story of a nation. Within the changing story of any state, there are always numerous conflicting values, hopes and dreams, and the great and small buildings erected at different times at the centre of a nation's life and governance inevitably reflect different values. Not only do such buildings speak of the needs and ideals of the age in which they are built, but also, in later times, new ideas, ambitions and desires may be projected on to them.

The new home of the recently formed UK Supreme Court (UKSC) is one such building (fig. 1). Designed in 1911, it was built on Little George Street, in the very heart of ancient Westminster, in 1912–13, to serve then as the Middlesex Guildhall, framing the south-west corner of Parliament Square. It still catches the eye today, much as it was intended to when first built. Pale – built in an almost creamy Portland stone – and elegant, it is a distinctive and well-modelled element in the overall topography of this historically rich square.[1]

The building's harmonization with the rest of the square is hardly surprising. The Middlesex Guildhall was deliberately designed to do honour to its setting and to the sense of history – of monarchy, of the established Church, of national (and then imperial) government and of the rule of law – that attends on that setting (fig. 2). On one side is the Palace of Westminster, royal palace turned seat of government – admired by some as a home to a model of democracy, but also once the hub of an empire. Next to that is Westminster Abbey, founded by Edward the Confessor (1042–1066), and the burial place of the kings and queens of England. As mentioned in the previous chapter, the Abbey is the setting for many state occasions. Opposite the new Supreme Court is St Margaret's, Westminster, sometimes called (incorrectly, as it is just an ordinary parish church) the 'parish church of Parliament'.

The Middlesex Guildhall was built in the years just before the massive cultural and political upheavals of the First World War, but even then the political world was already changing fast – both on a national and a local level. This building is, in its form and character, a vivid demonstration of the skilful fusion of contemporary construction techniques and planning, and of an architecture deliberately rooted in history – a combination typical of Late Victorian and Edwardian public architecture. By this date, however, the choice of a Gothic style was unusual.[2]

3. Portrait of James Gibson, architect of the Middlesex Guildhall.

4. The Middlesex Guildhall in 1913, shortly before the unveiling. Image from the *Illustrated London News*.

For the former Guildhall was certainly designed with a broadly Late Gothic flavour, a self-conscious nod to the great Gothic and Gothic Revival buildings around Parliament Square. Each elevation of the Guildhall is somewhat distinct in character, too. It is true that, as many critics, including the great Nikolaus Pevsner (1902–1983), have noted, this is a very free interpretation of Gothic, with an almost art nouveau flavour, and references to sixteenth-century French and Flemish sources are also apparent; but it is certainly Gothic in overall effect.

James Gibson (1861–1951), the Scottish-born architect of the Middlesex Guildhall, was deeply conscious of the challenge of the site itself (fig. 3). He had tried in his design, he said, to 'keep it quite distinct in scale and style so as to preserve its own individuality and act as a foil to the larger buildings near [by]; somewhat in the same way as St Margaret's Church enhances the scale of Westminster Abbey'. He was not, therefore, interested just in style or detail, but in how the volumes of the buildings work with and against one another – itself a rather modern approach to design.[3]

Gibson justifiably felt that this site was 'one of the finest in London … surrounded as it is by historical and great public buildings'. This made the challenge of the design, he said, 'a very difficult one, it being quite impossible to compete with the big scale of buildings like Westminster Abbey or the Houses of Parliament, and a classic treatment which would vie with the huge blocks of Government Offices [Government Buildings, or HM Treasury] would have invited failure'. He continued, 'No attempt, therefore, was made to design the building on a big scale.' This may also have been for reasons of expediency, in that there were discussions about the effect of the new building on light to the neighbouring Royal Institution of Chartered Surveyors, and there may have been discussions about its effect on the Abbey. But it must have been tempting to build on a scale to match the growing imperial character of nearby Whitehall.

The other buildings that contributed then (and some still do now) to the ensemble around Parliament Square included not only the great national treasures already mentioned, but also near-contemporary buildings of widely divergent architectural styles, such as the Royal Institution of Chartered Surveyors in a red-brick, Flemish-Gothic-with-Jacobean style designed by Alfred Waterhouse (1830–1905) and completed in 1898, and the vast Government Buildings beyond that, designed in a typically grandiose Edwardian Baroque by another Scottish architect, J.M. Brydon (1840–1901), and built between 1899 and 1915. Other buildings, such as the Westminster Hospital, have been replaced; in that case, the site is now occupied by the landmark modern Queen Elizabeth II Conference Centre (1982–86), by architects Powell and Moya.[4]

The Middlesex Guildhall is now newly adapted to house the UKSC and the Judicial Committee of the Privy Council, discussed in the first two chapters. To understand the development and execution of the original design, however, it should be remembered that when it was formally opened by HRH Prince Arthur of Connaught (1883–1938) on 19 December 1913 (fig. 4), it was not strictly a building of national significance – at least in terms of its function. For it was built to house the local government of the relatively newly reformed Middlesex County Council (MCC; although Middlesex was an ancient county, such councils were an innovation of the late 1880s), and included in its provision a stately Council Chamber, like a mini-Parliament, and two dignified courtrooms for the Middlesex Quarter Sessions. These were courts held by the Middlesex Justices of the Peace sitting with a jury, with a history going back to the fourteenth century, ending in 1971. During its history the Guildhall has also contained numerous council and other offices, cells for prisoners and space to store records.[5]

Gibson clearly wanted his design to stand confidently, but respectfully, alongside two of the most important buildings in the capital (fig. 5). Thus it had to express, through its architecture, detail and decoration, the dignity of an ancient English county. Middlesex had just had to hand over a substantial part of its jurisdiction, population and wealth to the newly formed London County Council, and so the historical associations of the Guildhall's architecture may also be seen as something of a political salve. In some ways, then, this building embodies the sometimes tense relationship between local and national government; their interaction is itself a long-standing feature of British democracy. This is of particular relevance to the Guildhall's newest function as home to the Supreme Court, as the majesty of the law is vividly evoked in both its architecture and its decoration – and law is defined at heart in this country by the tradition of precedent.[6]

There were two purpose-built predecessors to the present building. The early nineteenth-century Guildhall was designed in an unadorned Neoclassical style, as a handsome single-storey yellow-brick octagonal building constructed over the foundations of the earlier Abbey belfry (fig. 6). It contained a central double-height courtroom under a lantern, behind a distinctive Doric portico. The architect was Samuel Pepys Cockerell (1753–1827), who had held posts in the Office of the King's Works and was later Surveyor to St Paul's.[7] In 1892–93 Cockerell's building was extended and encased within a new, loosely Late Gothic-styled Guildhall, in red-brick and stone dressings (fig. 7), designed by F.H. Pownall (1832–1907), who had been Surveyor to the Justices of Middlesex and, from

1888, the County Surveyor for Middlesex. One of his drawings, illustrating an interest in the texture of the brick and stone, but perhaps not any great response to the historical setting, survives in the London Metropolitan Archives (fig. 8).

As the pamphlet that accompanied the opening of the third Guildhall in 1913 observed: 'In consequence of the great increase in the work of Quarter Sessions, and the many additional duties cast upon the County Council by Parliament, the enlarged building became, in its turn, quite inadequate for its purpose.' For these reasons, in 1905, the MCC had acquired the neighbouring building to the north, previously the home of the National Society – responsible for the promotion of Christian education in schools – thereby almost doubling the available site area. The council spent some time considering whether to extend or rebuild entirely. In fact, the new building took in only two-thirds of the additional space, as provision was made for a new road between the Guildhall and the Royal Institution of Chartered Surveyors.

Gibson was apparently first appointed as an independent consultant, with recognized experience in town-hall and court design, to help the council decide which was the best course, and the minutes of the specially convened Guildhall Committee show how he impressed the members charged with resolving this issue. He adroitly showed them the possibilities and economies of a new building, which would also do so much more to dignify its site and function. The design did not fall to the County Surveyor, although he was involved in the process, nor was it the subject of an open architectural competition, as one might have expected. At that time, architectural competitions for public buildings were very much the norm, and Gibson must have been delighted by the way such a choice commission virtually fell into his lap.[8]

Gibson wrote to the MCC's Guildhall Extension Committee on 5 February 1909 to discuss his approach: 'In dealing with the architectural treatment of the building, two courses are open to you: first, to carry on the present design in brick and stone in the new buildings. This is manifestly the cheapest method, but, if adopted, would commit you to the retention of a style of work which cannot be recommended as worthy of this important site.' At this date he was still considering an extension rather than an entire new build, but the progress of his thinking is clear:

*The second course would be to design the new buildings in a dignified and artistic style of architecture, worthy of the purposes for which the buildings are to be used. In this latter case it might be desirable to erect a central feature on the east front to emphasize the character of the buildings and to separate the new from the old part. Considering the historical and artistic buildings in the immediate vicinity I feel that the elevations will demand very careful artistic handling.[9]*

The minutes of the committee show that Gibson attended a meeting the next day and, after he had shown its members some rough sketch plans (which sadly do not appear to survive

today), the committee resolved to appoint him to advise 'upon the question of demolishing the existing Guildhall and erecting a new building on the site'. As noted – in suitably alderman-ish language – in the pamphlet that accompanied the opening in 1913, 'After protracted consideration of the matter in all its bearings, with designs to show the possibilities of various schemes of alterations and additions, the conclusion was ultimately arrived at that the interests of the County would be best served by clearing the whole site and erecting an entirely new building.'[10]

Gibson rose more courageously than Pownall had to the challenge of providing a building that could hold its own visually with the historic grandeur of the setting (fig. 9). This was a considerable challenge, not least because of changing attitudes among architectural critics and a younger generation of architects to the prevailing historicism of the late nineteenth century, especially the long dominance of the Gothic Revival, as we shall see from published criticism at the time of the Guildhall's construction. Although Gibson persuaded his committee that it would be relatively economical to build anew, the completed works incurred a final cost of over £111,000, whereas the original estimate had been £85,000.

Gibson paid very careful attention to all aspects of the building's context. While it is a novel design overall, certain details closely mirror features of buildings near by: the carved, canopied niches echo those in Henry VII's Chapel in Westminster Abbey; the parapets and dormers are reminiscent of Barry and Pugin's Palace of Westminster; the balconies are modelled on George Gilbert Scott's (1811–1878) lively terrace that faces the Middlesex Guildhall (fig. 10); and the height of the tower aspires to that of the parish church of St Margaret. A letter by Gibson to the committee referred explicitly to raising the height of the tower of the Guildhall in the design, to match more closely the height of St Margaret's.

But what seems to have been little discussed are the Continental sources for this building. This is most evident in the treatment of the dormers, which show the clear design

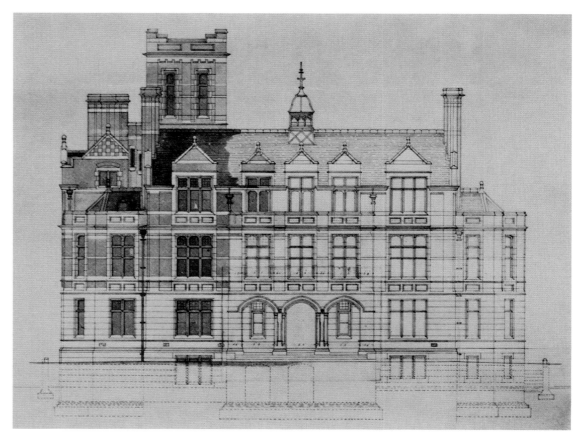

9. The south and east elevations of the Guildhall, as seen from near Westminster Abbey.

*Below:* 10. Balcony detail from the earlier terrace designed by George Gilbert Scott, opposite the Middlesex Guildhall.

*Right:* 11. James Gibson may have drawn on the examples of sixteenth-century French chateaux of the Loire, such as Amboise (illustrated here), to help bind the various Gothic and classical influences of other buildings in the square.

influence of sixteenth-century Loire chateaux (fig. 11), such as Chambord, Blois, Chenonceau or Amboise (although it would be wrong to suggest too precise a source). Gibson had travelled in France in the 1880s, and would have been aware of the interest in French precedents among his Scottish contemporaries, such as J.J. Burnet (1857–1938), who had studied in Paris. Some of the detailing, together with the overall character of the south elevation and the character of the main staircase in particular, suggest Gibson's active interest in early Renaissance architecture of France.[11]

Part of the attraction of the French chateau as a model may well have been that it provided a meeting-point, stylistically speaking, between the Gothic of the Abbey, the Gothic Revival of the Palace of Westminster and the Baroque classicism of Brydon's Government Buildings. The Baroque was increasingly the preferred style for public buildings in the early years of the twentieth century. Indeed, there are very few public buildings designed at this date in the Gothic style (Late or otherwise) outside the ancient universities and public schools. The distinctly French flavour of Gibson's Guildhall design is evident not only in the dormers and detailing of the parapet but also in the south elevation, which was additionally contrived to present an almost independent and composed façade towards the Abbey. The Middlesex councillors were clearly very conscious of the excellent view it would give them over great state events.[12]

What sort of man was Gibson? As is shown by his extensive list of executed works, and his gifts of persuasion with the committee, he was clearly a highly efficient and hardworking professional. He was more than usually successful in both commercial architecture – in the great age of the department store – and the field of public architecture, where he enjoyed particular success in competitions. He was one of a number of ambitious and well-trained Scottish architects, including J.J. Burnet, William Young, James Miller and J.J. Joass, who migrated south to London and carved out influential careers.

Gibson began his career articled to Ireland and Maclaren of Dundee. He came to London in the early 1880s,

worked in the office of T.E. Collcutt (1840–1924), architect of the Imperial Institute (now Imperial College), the Savoy Hotel and the Palace Theatre, all still important London landmarks (only the tower of the Institute survives, incorporated into later educational buildings). Gibson started his own practice in 1889. He went into partnership with S.B. Russell in 1890, and they successfully competed for a London County Council Hostel for Men – in Drury Lane in 1891 – and for the West Riding County Hall in Wakefield in 1894 (fig. 12), including a handsomely furnished council chamber with carving by the sculptor Henry Fehr (1867–1940), with whom Gibson also collaborated at the Middlesex Guildhall. In 1895 the Russell/Gibson partnership won the commission for West Ham Technological College.[13]

Gibson gradually moved from highly decorated Flemish Renaissance public architecture to a more fluid approach, and a refined and monumental style in his early twentieth-century works. Pevsner observed of his building at West Ham: 'Every conceivable motif is used which was available at that peculiar moment in the history of English architecture when the allegiance to forms of the past was at last thrown to the winds. … the turret and cupola shapes, for instance, are without any period precedent. Besides the grouping of the masses is completely free.'[14] Pevsner concluded in his inimitable style: 'Altogether the architects have certainly enjoyed being fanciful and have not minded being a little vulgar. But the whole is of a robust vitality which seems enviable today.' This perceptive analysis can also be applied in some degree to Gibson's work at the Guildhall, which combines an intelligent handling of volume with abundant carved decoration confidently applied and contrasted with large areas of plain stone surface. As Pevsner observed of the Guildhall: 'In spite of nearness to the Abbey', it had been designed in a style that was 'essentially original, even if boldly playing with Gothic motifs'.

In 1897 Gibson and Russell came second in the competition for the Cardiff City Hall and Law Courts won by Lanchester, Stewart and Rickards – who later designed the

Methodist Central Hall, built between 1905 and 1911 close to the Middlesex Guildhall, and on which Henry Fehr also worked. Gibson parted with Russell in 1899, and joined William Wallace. He had been a partner of J.M. Brydon, who had designed the new Government Buildings in 1898. These were constructed in two phases, with part of the buildings completed in 1908, and part in 1911–15.

Together, in 1900, Wallace & Gibson won the important competition to design the Walsall municipal buildings in Staffordshire, in a stately Edwardian Baroque; these were completed in 1905 (again, Fehr was involved). In 1906–1907 Wallace & Gibson secured the commission to design the Debenham and Freebody department store in Wigmore Street (fig. 13). Gibson's other well-known department store was Arding and Hobbs near Clapham Junction.

At the time of designing the Guildhall, Gibson's practice was described as Gibson, Skipwith & Gordon, as he had also been joined in partnership by his assistants. One was Walter Gordon, who had been articled to another Scot working south of the border, Robert Rowand Anderson (1834–1921), and had previously studied at the Edinburgh School of Applied Art. The other was Frank Peyton Skipwith (1881–1915), who was educated at Heidelberg and the Architectural Association. It is possible that Skipwith played a significant role in the Guildhall design.[15]

This idea would certainly accord with the reputation of Gibson as a particularly able designer, with a noted skill in the internal planning of public buildings, but who was happy to delegate some of the more detailed exterior work to such gifted, younger draughtsmen as Skipwith. There is, however, no documentary evidence yet to confirm that this sort of delegation in fact took place at the Guildhall. How Skipwith's career might have developed is impossible to say, as he was killed on active service in the First World War. The practice continued after the war as Gibson and Gordon.

As well as running a busy practice, Gibson was an influential figure in the Royal Institute of British Architects (RIBA), serving as Vice-President between 1906 and 1910. It is perhaps surprising that he was not President, given his remarkably prolific career and reputation. His obituary in the *RIBA Journal* for 1951 suggests a character of considerable strength. A former pupil, Ernest Rahbula, wrote that at the turn of the twentieth century Gibson 'was already established in one of the most promising practices in London, a practice he had himself built up without any influence, by sheer ability and force of character'.

Rahbula also recalled Gibson as a 'clever planner', and as someone who 'enjoyed life to the full and spent freely' and 'was generous to a degree … many were his unknown acts of kindness'. Some picture of how he would have handled the Guildhall Committee is given in the same obituary, in which H.V. Lanchester wrote that while Gibson was 'firm and emphatic in the expression of his opinion, he was invariably genial and courteous in his contacts with those who sometimes differed from the views and proposals he advocated'.

DEBENHAM & FREEBODY'S PREMISES, WIGMORE STREET, CAVENDISH SQUARE, LONDON, W.
*From a painting by Mortimer Menpes.*

The foundation stone for the Middlesex Guildhall was laid in 1912 by the Duke of Bedford as Lord Lieutenant of Middlesex. The building was largely completed by December 1913.[16] In March 1911, *The Builder* published, in monochrome, two elegant perspectives painted by the architect and draughtsman William Walcot (1874–1943; fig. 14). These capture the flavour of stylish modernity that the architects were trying to achieve in these principal elevations; one was published in colour as the frontispiece in *Academy Architecture* (also in 1911; fig. 15) – incidentally the only secular Gothic Revival building to be featured that year.[17]

No original presentation drawings or models can be traced, but a series of pre-contract tender drawings of March 1911, and signed contract drawings dated September 1911 (figs. 16 and 17), are preserved in the London Metropolitan Archives, as is the original contract specification between Gibson and James Carmichael, the contractor, dated August 1911.[18] These plans, if read closely with the detailed floor plans and sections published in *The Builder* on 3 March 1911 (figs. 18–20), and then on 14 November 1913, demonstrate an admirably clear layout and the sophistication of Gibson's response to a complicated brief.

The court functions were originally confined to the ground floor, and the two principal courtrooms are double-height rooms. They are interesting examples of court design, drawing on different sixteenth-century sources for their character and decorative detail. The substantial, if

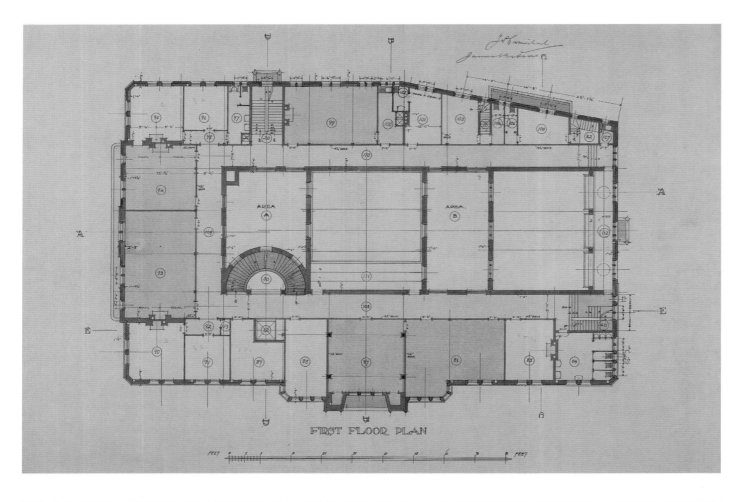

FIRST FLOOR PLAN

FEET FEET

16. The first floor in the contract drawings of 1911, showing Gibson's skill with circulation spaces.

17. The second floor in the contract drawings of 1911, showing the scale of the Council Chamber, now Courtroom 1.

*Opposite, top:* 18. A cross-section showing the Council Chamber over the original Court 1, as published in *The Builder* in 1911.

*Opposite, bottom left:* 19. The ground-floor plan, as published in *The Builder* in 1911; note the courtyards.

*Opposite, bottom right:* 20. The second-floor plan, as published in *The Builder* in 1911.

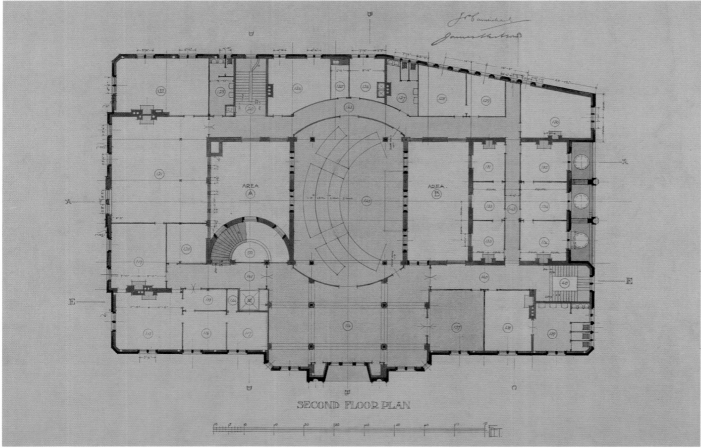

SECOND FLOOR PLAN

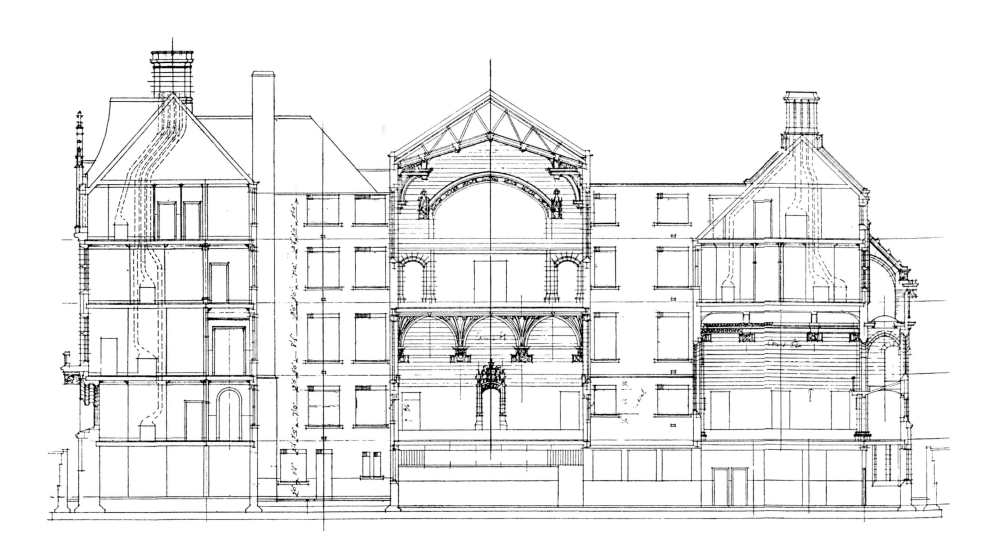

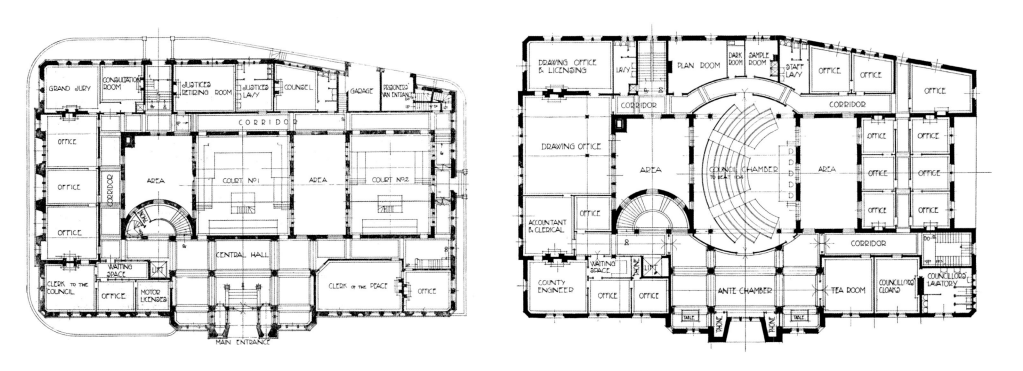

low-ceilinged entrance hall (fig. 21) led directly to what was originally described as Court 1 (fig. 22), with its impressive fan-vaulted ceiling carried out in plasterwork but painted to resemble stonework, as were all the wall treatments of the entrance and staircase halls. The royal coat of arms marks the centre of this vault, which probably takes inspiration from Henry VII's Chapel in the Abbey. This room is now the Library of the Supreme Court, with the floor opened up to include space beneath (fig. 23).

The original entrance hall might seem surprisingly modest in scale, but this would have increased the dramatic impact of entering the lofty courtrooms on this level. The magnificent marble bust of Edward VII by Percy Bryant Baker (1881–1970) originally stood in the centre of the entrance hall (it has now been relocated to the cafe area in

*Opposite, top left:* 21. The entrance hall in the 1970s, with the bust of Edward VII by Percy Bryant Baker.

*Opposite, bottom left:* 22. The original Court 1 in 1939, showing the fan-vaulted ceiling executed in plasterwork.

*Opposite, right:* 23. The new Library of the United Kingdom Supreme Court.

*Above:* 24. The ceiling of the staircase compartment.

*Right:* 25. The main staircase, possibly inspired by French chateau staircases of the sixteenth century.

the basement). To the south rises the sinuous form of the open semicircular staircase, which could be said to recall the famous one, attributed to Leonardo da Vinci, at the chateau of Chambord in the Loire Valley (figs. 24 and 25).[19] The Guildhall stair is a dramatic architectural statement, leading from the courtroom floors to the council offices on the first and second floors, and the Council Chamber on the second (now Courtroom 1), and perhaps, in its grandeur, expressing the building's duality of function.

The original Court 2 (now Courtroom 3, to be used principally by the Judicial Committee of the Privy Council) on the north side of the building has a handsome flat ceiling of moulded timber beams and tall Perpendicular-style windows, bearing armorial stained glass (figs. 26 and 27). On either side of what was Court 1 (now the Library) were

*Above:* 26. The original Court 2 in 1939.

*Right:* 27. The same room, now Courtroom 3, is used principally by the Judicial Committee of the Privy Council.

substantial open courtyards or light-wells, with white, light-reflective salt-glazed tiles, which allowed, and still allow, a good amount of natural light to all levels of the building, notwithstanding the insertion of some very fine stained-glass windows to the old courts themselves. (In the recent works of adaptation, both these light-wells have had all later accretions removed.) This ingenious arrangement meant that both ground-floor courtrooms and the second-floor Council Chamber were lit from two sides, giving them the feeling almost of free-standing buildings.[20]

The second floor was laid out with admirable clarity for the use of the county council and its officials. The central portion was occupied by the original Council Chamber, which sat directly above what was Court 1 and so lay at the heart of the whole complex (fig. 28). It was designed to seat 104 councillors, and is spanned by what appears to be a hammer-beam roof with furnishings and panelling in Austrian oak. This Council Chamber is now Courtroom 1, principal courtroom for the UKSC (fig. 29). With galleries at either end for the public and the press, it is immediately evocative of a Tudor Great Hall; it, too, has stained-glass windows, bearing armorial glass of the Lord Lieutenants of Middlesex, including the Dukes of Bedford, Newcastle and Wellington. The ceiling is more than a nod to the roof of nearby Westminster Hall, one of the greatest displays of architectural engineering of the fourteenth century (the

mason was Henry Yevele, *c.* 1320–1400, and the carpenter Hugh Herland, *c.* 1330– *c.* 1405).

The furnishings were of a very high standard. It is interesting to note that Gibson took the chairman of the Middlesex Quarter Sessions, a councillor and two aldermen to visit his work at the West Riding County Hall at Wakefield, and that ultimately he was left to approve the design of furnishings himself.[21] All the materials throughout, as the specifications of 1911 show, were of good quality. Portland stone for the exterior, Corsham Bath stone for interior details, and the grand sweep of the main staircase was in a warm grey Hopton Wood stone ('all faces showing to be polished'), which was also used for the floor of the entrance hall. Austrian oak was used for the ceiling of the Council Chamber, and most of the floors of the principal rooms were laid with American oak.[22]

There were also carved oak pieces supplied for the Council Chamber by the firm of cabinet-makers and furnishers Wylie & Lochhead. These included curved benches, the visual focus being the highly carved throne-like chair for the chairman of the council. The furniture of the two courtrooms was supplied by H.H. Martyn & Co. of Cheltenham, which also provided the clocks throughout the building. Henry Fehr, who had trained at the RA Schools, carried out internal and external stone carving and supplied models for wood carving; the plasterwork was carried out by Gilbert Seale & Son, and the stained glass by Abbott & Co.[23]

30. The original Council Committee Room.

31. The Justices' sitting-room, with original panelling moved here in the 1980s from the Committee Room.

*Opposite:* 32. The new Courtroom 2, on the south side, occupies two storeys that originally provided council offices, including the Committee Room. These were remodelled into two Crown Courts in the 1980s.

*The Builder* in March 1915 praised the craftsmanship on show: 'The lament of those publicists that to-day the artist-craftsman is dead, although possessing a substratum of truth, reveals a class of mind that is buried in the glories of the past and is unable to see the wonderful panorama of the present' – which the author ('A.F.') saw illustrated in the 'stately' new Middlesex Guildhall, with its 'fine examples of the modern craftsman's work'.[24] (Peter Cormack discusses the decorative art and furnishings in the following chapter of this book.)

The main Council Committee Room (fig. 30) was on the first floor on the south side.[25] It was handsomely finished with linen-fold panelling and had a carved overmantel; both of these were resited and reused in 1988, along with light-fittings, in the barristers' dining-room. The latter is now the private sitting-room for the Justices of the Supreme Court (fig. 31). There is also a private dining-room, still furnished with a Neoclassical marble chimney piece, which may be among those mentioned in the specifications of 1911 as reused from the earlier building.[26] The Jacobean-style plasterwork ceiling of the Committee Room no longer survives. Apart from committee rooms to the south and east, and some smaller offices, the first floor was otherwise largely taken up by the upper levels of the two original courtrooms on the ground floor.

According to the original plans, the offices of the County Engineer and his staff were on the second floor of the south side of the building. These spaces, fitted out as courtrooms in the 1980s, have now been opened up and absorbed into the entirely new Courtroom 2 of the UK Supreme Court, which is intended for most cases. This rises through two storeys (fig. 32). A spacious antechamber, facing east, provided a considerable amount of circulation space outside the Council Chamber. The walls of this antechamber are still distinctively panelled in oak, while the corridors are covered in salt-glazed ceramic tiles of a beautiful grass-green colour. There were yet more rooms on the third floor.

Gibson's skill at planning is reflected in the seamless flow of the circulation spaces around these major rooms on both principal floors, with a well-lit corridor giving access between courtrooms, offices, Justices' retiring-rooms and jury rooms. There was a separate access for prisoners, with one

hundred prison cells in the basement, and accommodation for warders, wardresses, witnesses and police.[27] By 1938 the prison cells had been reduced to 'about fifty improved cells for prisoners' (fig. 33), and in the Westminster Archives a plan for air-raid precautions records this arrangement.[28] The remainder of the basement, mostly on the south side, was divided into vaulted space for 'the safe custody of the many valuable records belonging to the County Council' (fig. 34), long since moved elsewhere.[29]

As this enumeration of the various original functions suggests, Gibson had to solve a very complex brief indeed. He had to provide all the rooms that have been listed above, as well as other related facilities, with sufficient dignity for their public purpose, and all fitted together neatly in a public building of relatively modest scale (under 6000 square metres/64,583 square feet gross internal area). As well as accomplishing this, he managed at the same time to deliver a real sense of arrival, indeed an architecture that accommodates and reflects the spirit of ceremonial appropriate to its principal functions. This was a solid

architectural achievement by Gibson, and one that has probably not been sufficiently recognized until now in academic literature.

The construction of the Guildhall building of 1913 was given a special notice in *The Builder* of that year, noting that the engineer was H.T. Wakelam, the County Surveyor, who presumably moved into the second-floor offices when it was completed. The main contractor was James Carmichael (1858–1934), the unsung hero of many major London projects of the time. Also Scottish-born, he was based in Wandsworth, and in 1901 had worked on the extension of the Strand frontage of the Hotel Cecil as well as St Thomas's Hospital and Harrods.[30]

During the excavation of the site, the builders uncovered evidence of the foundations of the ancient Sanctuary building, in the form of a 'heavy rubble concrete raft, 5 feet thick and about 80 feet by 70 feet in plan, and rested on elm and beech piles about 10 feet long, driven closely together into the subsoil. This solid and wonderfully well preserved mass of masonry and concrete undoubtedly constituted the foundation on which the Norman builders raised the ponderous structure of the sanctuary keep.' It still had to be removed.[31]

The author of the account in *The Builder* (14 November 1913) noted that the structure of the Guildhall was made up of load-bearing outer walls with an internal steel frame. The beams of this frame were supported by piers bonded into the external bearing walls. All the remaining internal structure was supported off the frame. *The Builder* carried illustrations of the concrete footings constructed by the Concrete Steel Company Ltd. The structural steelwork was by Redpath and Brown of Greenwich, and the suspended floor panels were by Diespeker & Co. The roof over the main Council Chamber, *The Builder* article observed, was carried by two steel trusses, with a span of 11.4 metres (37 feet 6 inches), supporting rolled-steel purlins (which the magazine illustrated). These homages to the massive structural timber in Westminster Hall are, then, entirely decorative.

The final comment of this article concerned the choice of material and style: 'All the elevations of the building are in Portland stone, and, having regard to the vicinity of the Abbey, the Gothic style was adopted by the architects, with results which our readers will be able to judge for themselves.' This somewhat neutral remark must be seen in the context of the

debate that was already taking place in the pages of this journal, as two months before there is a note about the style chosen:

*The adoption of a type of Gothic for the new Middlesex Guildhall raises a question in our minds, which is quite irrespective of, and apart from, any questions of the design per se. We are told that a Gothic design was decided on on account of the proximity of the new Guildhall to the Abbey. Would it not therefore follow that any new building in proximity to the Guildhall should also be designed in the Gothic manner, and what about building in proximity to the latter? Arguments as to the sustainability or otherwise of a particular style would, according to such methods of reasoning, always be decided by their relative position to some other building. Such a type of reasoning is at any rate interesting, but we are afraid the result might prejudice the future of architectural development if we are to get ahead at last. Rather, we believe, we should honestly try to work in the style which is most characteristic of our times, and depend on the general arrangement of mass and grouping to give that harmony which we all desire and should strive to attain – a harmony that does not depend on detail or type.*[32]

This commentary reflects the new architectural ideas that were emerging just before the outbreak of the First World War, and the progress towards the arrival of Modernist architecture and a more functionalist aesthetic, especially in the 1920s and 1930s. But then, as the architecture of the nineteenth century in this area alone illustrates, the detail, style and character of historically informed architecture can be very vibrant, and such buildings can in their own way be entirely representative of the time in which they were built. The work by Barry and Pugin on the Palace of Westminster, for example, reflects the preoccupations of nineteenth-century designers and their fascination with history and national identity, infused with a spirit of Romanticism as well as Gothic Revival.

But *The Builder*'s critic had a good point to make, and it could be argued that Gibson, Gordon and Skipwith answered it with confidence in the nature of the resulting building, which certainly relies on overall massing and grouping for its principal aesthetic effect. As the Late Gothic style was hardly the norm for public buildings at this date, it is possible to argue that its use here is all the more interesting, and reflects the symbolic and historic significance of the site.

Another critic, P.G. Konody, wrote in the *Daily Mail* on 23 September 1913:

*One of the most striking and amusing architectural features of modern London is now rapidly nearing completion … Its style is nondescript. It is apparently inspired by certain French buildings of the transition period from late Gothic to Renaissance, but the exuberant decorative trimmings are essentially modern in their coarseness … The squat weighed-down appearance of the ground floor in the centre of the building is still further accentuated by a very deep, heavy frieze in which some historical incidents are presented in a fussy, unsculpturesque manner.*[33]

On the other hand, there was also published praise. A note in the *British Architect*, 3 January 1913, read: 'This picturesque building is already sufficiently advanced to show that by reason of its comparatively modest height it will interfere less with the open and pleasant aspect of Parliament Square than might have been feared. Some critics will see in it a pleasant evidence that we are not entirely overrun by Classic revivals.'[34]

Gibson himself said, in the text of the pamphlet published for the opening, that the design was chosen to work with all the competing styles of the context:

*That spirit and form of Gothic giving a picturesque variety of features and delicacy of detail was felt to be the most appropriate treatment, and the building should be considered a dainty piece of ornament set amongst the austere and formal buildings of the neighbourhood. The detail employed, while preserving many of the features and mouldings of the later Gothic, has been imbued with a modern spirit of freshness in precisely the same way as the original Gothic must have been kept more virile by the introduction of more detail. If the design is sufficiently interesting to attract the attention of the passer-by, it has fulfilled one of the main objects of the designer.*[35]

Not quite the full-blooded confidence of a Pugin or a Barry, perhaps, but then think of the so-called 'battle of the styles' in mid-nineteenth-century Westminster, where the Gothic of the Houses of Parliament was succeeded symbolically by the classical Italianate of the Foreign Office and Treasury and the Edwardian Baroque of the Government Buildings (fig. 35), which tower over the north side of the square.

*Top left:* 35. The Government Buildings (now HM Treasury – on the right of the photograph), designed by J.M. Brydon and built between 1899 and 1915.

*Top right:* 36. Liverpool Cathedral, designed by Giles Gilbert Scott, and under construction from 1904.

*Above:* 37. The Rockefeller Chapel, University of Chicago, designed by Bertram Grosvenor Goodhue in 1918.

*Right:* 38. The John Rylands Library in Manchester, designed by Basil Champneys and built in the 1890s.

It is the overall fluency of composition and consistency of detail of Gibson's building that are immediately noticeable to a passer-by today, the curiously modelled flavour that has something in common with the work of Sir Edwin Lutyens (1869–1944), the designer of the Cenotaph near by, or even Charles Holden (1875–1960), the architect of the University of London's Senate House and of many interwar Underground stations. The significance of this manner, in which the sculptural decoration relates to the overall unadorned wall planes, is reminiscent in its character of another early twentieth-century masterpiece – Liverpool Cathedral (fig. 36), designed by Sir Giles Gilbert Scott (1880–1960).

At the same time, the style of the Guildhall must be linked with the late nineteenth-century efforts to enliven London's public architecture with sculpture, evident in such buildings as the hall for the Institute of Chartered Accountants in the City of London by John Belcher (1841–1913). There, the friezes by sculptor Hamo Thornycroft (1850–1925) are on a higher register than the Guildhall, but have the same effect of tying the architecture together. Belcher spoke to the RIBA of the collaboration between architect and sculptor: 'When

sculpture stands forward to illustrate a subject ... architecture should give it loving assistance and unobtrusive support, treating the work as a jewel whose beauty is to be enhanced by an appropriate setting.'[36]

Gibson's work at the Guildhall has also been compared to that of the American Gothic Revival architect Bertram Grosvenor Goodhue (1869–1924), especially in such works as the Rockefeller Chapel at the University of Chicago (fig. 37), commissioned in 1918.[37] If one is looking for non-ecclesiastical parallels, in its combination of Late Gothic style and mood and interior fittings of the finest quality, the Guildhall can also be compared to the John Rylands Library in Manchester (fig. 38), designed by Basil Champneys (1842–1935) and built in the 1890s, where the Gothic style (again in its Late Gothic or Perpendicular version) was used to add dignity and atmosphere to a secular building. Champneys had worked extensively in Oxford and Cambridge, where Gothic Revival had a longer continuity in secular use.[38]

The use of full-relief and low-relief carving of historical figures by Henry Fehr, around the entrance and indeed across the whole front of the Guildhall, is not merely historicist, as

some reviewers have sought to suggest. This relief has been considered by later critics, notably Pevsner, to be of an art nouveau type, and so entirely of its own time. These figurative friezes include King John and the barons at the signing of Magna Carta at Runnymede, and the Duke of Northumberland offering the crown of England to Lady Jane Grey.[39] Then again, the completely unadorned dignity of the west elevation, which would have been seen only by arriving and departing prisoners and their escorts, perhaps hints at the more austere modern style that might have been employed in a different context (fig. 39).

Thus the new UK Supreme Court occupies a building of considerable historic interest, designed by a master planner of public buildings in the last creative phase of the Gothic Revival, a style that has been so much part of the identity of British architecture and perhaps therefore of the British nation, too.[40] The building, with its confident grouping and fluid detailing, is in many ways a monument to the vitality of British design at a key point in Britain's history. In 1911, the year it was begun, the nature of British democracy changed, with the power of the House of Lords being dramatically reduced by an Act of Parliament of that year. In 1913, the year the Guildhall was officially opened, Britain stood on the verge of the First World War, which stimulated massive social and political change, and marked perhaps the real end of empire. The Guildhall building thus brings a resonant history and great dignity to the new function it has been adapted to fulfil – to be the UK Supreme Court, part of the continuing evolution of the British legal system, long associated with the Palace of Westminster just across the square (fig. 40).

# GOTHIC 'WITH A DIFFERENCE': SCULPTURE AND DECORATIVE ARTS AT THE SUPREME COURT OF THE UNITED KINGDOM

PETER CORMACK

*Thus one of the most prominent public buildings in London was lavishly embellished with exterior and interior sculpture without any apparent advisory input from its commissioning clients. This is all the more surprising when one considers that most of the carvings either symbolize the county of Middlesex and its history, or are emblematic of the councillors' and Justices' official duties.*

*Previous page:* 1. *Truth*, one of the allegorical figures overlooking the new Library of the Supreme Court. The miniature portrait above the sculpture's head shows Carlo Magnoni, the principal carver of the interior and exterior statuary.

2. The low placement of Henry Fehr's frieze sculptures on the exterior of the Guildhall building affords passers-by an unusually close view of the historical scenes.

3. Portrait of Henry Fehr, the sculptor who designed much of the exterior and interior decoration of the Middlesex Guildhall.

4. The life-size bronze group of *Perseus Rescuing Andromeda* by H.C. Fehr, purchased for the nation in 1894 and now displayed at Tate Britain, Millbank.

## Middlesex Guildhall's Decorative Scheme and Its Creators

It was a chilly Friday morning on 19 December 1913 when a hundred Middlesex Boy Scouts and a hundred Territorial Army soldiers from Middlesex units assembled in front of the newly built Middlesex Guildhall to form the guard of honour at the official opening ceremony. As they and the county dignitaries awaited the arrival of Prince and Princess Arthur of Connaught, and the unfurling of the county flag from the tower, they doubtless had time to study the ornate statues and friezes on the main east façade (fig. 2); and perhaps they conjured up distant or more recent memories of school history lessons to help them interpret the scenes of Norman knights, medieval prelates and Tudor courtiers, or puzzled at the meaning behind the rows of charming medieval ladies looking down from their carved niches.

Some of those present might have read recent press accounts of the building. The rather condescending critic from *The Times*, for example, conceded that 'the new Guildhall … looks as if it had been designed and built with some enjoyment, and as if its absurdities expressed a genuine taste and were not merely sentimental imitations of the absurdities of the past'.[1] *The Sphere*, however, was far more enthusiastic, finding 'the exterior so full of human fancy that one almost describes the building as the most interesting in London'.[2] In any case, both writers might have agreed that the new Guildhall owed a large part of its appeal to its sculptural decoration.

Of the three men chiefly responsible for the building's decorative scheme, only the sculptor, Henry Fehr (1867–1940; fig. 3), received acknowledgement at the opening ceremony. There was no mention of the architect James Gibson's (1861–1951) partner, Frank Peyton Skipwith (1881–1915), who largely devised the scheme of architectural and sculptural ornament, but that is because Middlesex County Council's contract was specifically with Gibson himself. Carlo Domenico Magnoni (1871–*c*. 1950), who carved much of the sculpture, was also unacknowledged, but as a skilled craftsman (and employee of Fehr), he would have expected such anonymity (fig. 1). And since Magnoni was an anarchist refugee under constant surveillance by agents of the Italian state, he would perhaps not have welcomed publicity. (Throughout his forty-one years in England, Italian spies followed his movements and activities.)

Frustratingly little is known about Skipwith,[3] but his education in Germany (at Neuenheim College, Heidelberg) may have introduced him to the exotic vocabulary of Late Gothic and Northern Renaissance art that he exploited to good effect in his designs for the Guildhall. Aged twenty-nine, he had been a partner for only a year when Gibson secured the commission in 1910. His generation had been profoundly influenced by the Arts and Crafts movement, which identified 'Gothic' not in revivalist terms but as an expressive language open to free interpretation.

Many Arts and Crafts architects designed buildings that, while ostensibly Gothic, featured clustered sculpture and naturalistic ornament to enrich the architecture in a wholly original way. These designers found in later medieval art a fertile source of motifs ripe for development. Giles Gilbert Scott's (1880–1960) Liverpool Cathedral (see fig. 36, p. 94), the ornate Lady Chapel of which was consecrated in June 1910, and Robert Lorimer's (1864–1929) Thistle Chapel at St Giles's Cathedral, Edinburgh, which was opened in July 1911, were proof of the continuing vigour of the Gothic tradition.[4]

Skipwith already knew Henry Fehr and his work before their collaboration at the Guildhall, as Gibson had, since the 1890s, regularly chosen Fehr to design the sculptural features of his buildings. Fehr was an eminent sculptor of free-standing statues in bronze and marble, an original member of the Royal Society of British Sculptors and one of the most experienced architectural decorators of the period. Born of Swiss parentage in Forest Hill, south-east London, he had attended the Royal Academy Schools in the 1880s and then assisted Sir Thomas Brock RA. Fehr's early works, such as the bronze group *Perseus Rescuing Andromeda* (1893, Tate Britain), were closely identified with the 'New Sculpture' movement of Alfred Gilbert and his followers (fig. 4). Even in such late works as the Colchester War Memorial (1923), Fehr never abandoned the fluid tendencies of Gilbert's manner.[5]

As well as his work on Gibson's buildings, Fehr produced sculpture for a number of other architects. His terracotta, cast-iron and plaster decorations for Charles Fitzroy Doll's (1850–1929) Hotel Russell (1898; fig. 5), and the terracotta ornament on Doll's shop premises in Torrington Place (1907) – both in Bloomsbury – are in a Renaissance-inspired idiom, whereas his work for Lanchester, Stewart and Rickards at Hull

*Below:* 5. Part of Fehr's elaborate scheme of exterior and interior sculpture (1898) for the Hotel Russell, Bloomsbury, one of several commissions for the architect Charles Fitzroy Doll.

*Below, right:* 6. Henry Fehr (left, wearing cap) with his studio assistants, including the stone-carver Carlo Magnoni (centre, wearing long smock and beret), working on sculptures for Sennowe Park, Norfolk, in 1911.

*Opposite:* 7. Elevation drawing for the east portal of Middlesex Guildhall; the drawing is attributed to Frank Peyton Skipwith and was published in *The Builder* in 1913.

Art School (1904), Deptford Town Hall (1905) and Cardiff City Hall (1906) takes its inspiration from the Baroque. So too does Fehr's most monumental London work, the colossal mermaids on Arthur Blomfield's façade of Victoria station (1909). Before the Guildhall commission, the only architectural works by Fehr that might be characterized as 'Gothic' were the two large *Wars of the Roses* reliefs at Gibson's West Riding County Hall, Wakefield (1898). These are hardly 'archaeological' in their rendering of medieval imagery, but it was probably this very stylistic freedom that appealed to Gibson and was to work equally harmoniously with Skipwith's original Gothic detailing.

Since the mid-1890s Henry Fehr had worked from purpose-built studios at The Avenue, 76 Fulham Road.[6] There he employed a team of assistants who helped with plaster- and clay-modelling and executed stone-carving from his models. Fehr's principal assistant from the early 1900s (and into the 1920s) was Carlo Magnoni, who had

fled his native Italy and then, having been expelled from Switzerland, had settled with his family in London in 1898.

Magnoni's anarchist political attachments did not constrain the exercise of his artistic skills, and his work as stone-carver and sculptor can be found throughout Britain. He was chiefly responsible for carving, from Fehr's models, all the stone figure sculpture outside and inside the Middlesex Guildhall. He remained proud of his work, and in 1934 wrote to his brother of '*l'esecuzione di tutte le sculture del famoso Guildhall, superbo quanto lussuoso edificio pubblico*'.[7]

## Exterior Stone Sculpture

In March 1911, two dashing watercolours by William Walcot (1874–1943) of the design for the new Middlesex Guildhall were published in *The Builder* (see fig. 14, p. 81).[8] They show limited areas of sculptural decoration, but nothing like the extent of carving that would eventually adorn the building. One would expect the County Aldermen of Middlesex to

have taken a close interest in such a conspicuous element of the project, but it appears that the sculptural programme was wholly delegated to the architects and their chosen sculptor.

Indeed, when in October 1913 one of the County Buildings Committee members, Montague Sharpe, called his colleagues' attention to 'the carved frieze now being executed on the East Front of the Guildhall', Gibson replied that '[he] was responsible for the carving and that the designs had not been submitted to the Committee or to anyone'. To which William Regester, the Committee's chairman, added that he 'had specially refrained from taking any responsibility in connection with the designs and that the responsibility for them rested upon the Architect'.[9]

Thus one of the most prominent public buildings in London was lavishly embellished with exterior and interior sculpture without any apparent advisory input from its commissioning clients. This is all the more surprising when one considers that most of the carvings either symbolize the county of Middlesex and its history, or are emblematic of the councillors' and Justices' official duties.

As no archives of Gibson, Skipwith & Gordon have been traced, the precise evolution of the Guildhall's decorative programme is a matter of conjecture. The only known elevation drawing, published in November 1913 but probably drawn in early 1912, shows the 'Entrance Feature' on the east front with two carved friezes indicated but, otherwise, only one figure at the apex of the portal. No sculpture appears over the entrance arch, and the eleven canopied niches are all empty (fig. 7).[10]

Building work began in September 1911, and by April 1912 Gibson was reporting that the 'carvers have started on the East Front on some of the decorative carving' and that 'models for other portions are in hand'.[11] Regester, in his speech at the laying of the foundation stone in May, mentioned two figures (*Justice* and *Prudence*) intended for the east portal, so major parts of the exterior sculpture were obviously in preparation by that date.[12] The carvings over the ground-floor windows were completed in October, when Gibson showed the committee sketches and models for his revised treatment of the tower, which by January 1913 was 'well advanced'. By the autumn almost all the exterior carvings were finished, and the east portal was scheduled for completion in time for the opening in December 1913.

8. Details of sculpture and architecture at the new Middlesex Guildhall, published in *The Sphere* in 1913.

*Opposite, top: 9. Astronomy*, one of the symbolic figures decorating the ground-floor windows.

*Opposite, bottom left and centre:* 10 (a) and (b). Symbolic angel figures form the supporting brackets for the ceremonial balcony on the south wall.

*Opposite, bottom right, and overleaf:* 11 (a) and (b). The underside of the balcony is decorated with carved panels of birds and animals amid foliage.

Writing in September 1913, the critic P.G. Konody was unenthusiastic about the carved figures that were set over the ground-floor windows and 'seem to peer from outside into the rooms'.[13] For the writer in *The Sphere*, however, these and other details were precisely what made the building 'so full of human fancy' (fig. 8).[14] Seemingly growing out of the architectural mouldings, the twenty-five small figures symbolizing arts, science and industry are indeed among the most imaginative features of the building. Beginning on the west side (to the right of the portal) they represent *Dance*, *Communications* and *Astronomy*, and *Mechanics* and *Engineering* (fig. 9). On the south side, flanking the balcony, are *Sculpture* and *Painting*, followed by *Classical Architecture* and *Gothic Architecture*. Along the east front are six pairs of figures, symbolizing *Maritime Industries* – including fishing and shipbuilding – and *Agricultural Industries*, among them fruit-farming and sheep-rearing. The two pairs on the building's north side represent *Learning* (monk and scholar) and *Metalwork* (armourer and goldsmith).

Equally architectonic in character are the six life-size angel figures designed by Fehr as corbels for the Gothic balcony on the south side. Holding emblems of justice, government, law, etc., they are unusual in being positioned as if emerging at right angles from the wall, so that they look directly down on the passer-by. As an 'uncompromising ornamentist',[15] Fehr costumed the figures in the extravagant Renaissance-style gowns and fluted armour favoured by the 'New Sculpture' followers of Alfred Gilbert. There is an interest, typical of the 1900s, in the decorative possibilities of hair, worn either in plaits or as heavy strands framing the angels' feminine faces (figs. 10 (a) and (b)).

Between the corbel figures, the underside of the balcony is ornamented with panels of carved foliage and animals: bats hang amid ivy leaves; a fox wends its way through vines; mice crawl among thistles; and a squirrel feeds on acorns (figs. 11 (a) and (b)). The carvings are typical of the 'real life and invention' that *The Times* critic praised. Fehr used bats again – although more heraldically treated – along with extravagantly whiskered cats' faces, for some of the carvings flanking the windows on the second floor.

The most ambitious component of the Guildhall's sculptural decoration is on the façade facing Parliament Square. In February 1909, when the council still contemplated

12. The east portal, with its rich array of historical and symbolic sculptures by Fehr.

*Opposite, top:* 13. The central frieze, showing King Henry III granting a charter to Westminster Abbey, with, in the centre, the arms of Middlesex surmounting a depiction of Hampton Court's Great Hall.

*Opposite, bottom left:* 14. The left-hand frieze on the east portal, showing King John, surrounded by barons and prelates, granting Magna Carta at Runnymede.

*Opposite, bottom right:* 15. The right-hand frieze, showing Lady Jane Grey accepting the Crown of England.

extending its old building, Gibson had advocated a 'central feature'. What eventually evolved was a tour de force: a gabled portal surmounted by a statue of St George and encrusted with a further fifteen statues (most in canopied niches) surrounding an elaborately carved heraldic centrepiece with narrative frieze, itself flanked on the turret-like side bays by two more friezes in high relief (fig. 12).

Henry Fehr's three friezes depict English historical episodes. On the left, symbolic of the law, are King John and the barons at the signing of Magna Carta. On the right, representing (somewhat obscurely) the county's royal links, is Lady Jane Grey accepting the crown at Syon House, Middlesex. Between them, in reference to the Guildhall's historic location, is King Henry III granting a charter to Westminster Abbey; this subject is divided by a flamboyant carving of the Middlesex coat of arms above a representation of the Great Hall of Hampton Court Palace (also in Middlesex), flanked by a pair of small figures.[16] Placed below the rows of historical characters are the shields of some of the protagonists.

Although the scenes depicted are relatively static, the figures themselves are vigorously modelled, the linear rhythm of their drapery effectively complementing the architecture. Even covered in London grime, as the sculptures were for much of their history, their bravura carving and unusually accessible placing on the building have always made them clearly legible to the passing public (figs. 13–15).

The same crispness distinguishes Fehr's statues of allegorical females that occupy the portal's Gothic niches. Published descriptions are confused, but the figures can be identified by their attributes.[17] The four larger on the outer piers are, on the left, *Architecture* above and *Prudence* below, and, on the right, *Shipping* (wearing a naval crown; fig. 16) above and *Justice* below. Smaller in scale, and in stepped niches following the angle of the gable, the seven statues are (left to right): *Literature, Government, Sculpture* (holding a model of Michelangelo's *Dying Slave*; fig. 17), *Britannia, Music, Truth* and *Education*. On the mullions of the portal's window are two yet smaller figures, representing *Wisdom* and *Law*; even smaller than these are two more *Law* statuettes flanking the Hampton Court relief.

In designing these multiple female figures, Fehr would have been aware of a renowned English prototype, in the form

*Below, left:* 16. The figure symbolizing *Shipping* wears a distinctive naval crown, as used in Royal Navy ships' badges.

*Below, centre:* 17. The allegorical figure of *Sculpture*, depicted holding a model of Michelangelo's famous *Dying Slave*.

*Below, right:* 18. *Queen Eleanor* from the Waltham Cross of 1291–92, by Alexander of Abingdon, was one of the medieval inspirations for Fehr's allegorical figures.

*Opposite:* 19. The west porch, with its figures of *Truth*, *Justice* and *Honesty* and 'plaited' tracery motif.

of the queens depicted on late thirteenth-century Eleanor Crosses. Fehr was far from being a Gothic revivalist, but with their crowned headdresses, graceful poses and columnar gowns, these medieval figures must (even subconsciously) have been an inspirational model for his sculptures (fig. 18). There might indeed be another historical source for the entire east portal conception if, as seems plausible, the architects carried out preparatory research into the decoration of medieval guildhalls. The most obvious example would be the City of London's Guildhall, the early fifteenth-century north porch of which was richly carved with allegorical females. It was known from drawings made before its demolition in the late eighteenth century.[18]

Although the impressive east portal may have been Gibson's idea, the credit for its detailing goes to Skipwith. The published elevation drawing of about 1912 is therefore probably his work. It shows a brilliantly quirky approach to Gothic tracery and cusping, which is here either splayed outwards (rather than inwards as in almost all medieval precedents) or omitted altogether. One finds the same inverted cusping or absence of cusping in the traceried details throughout the building. Their sinuous lines may have suggested to Pevsner and others the 'art nouveau-Gothic' epithet that has become attached to Middlesex Guildhall.

The portal over the west door is a much-reduced variant, carved with just three female statues, of the eastern 'feature': *Truth* stands in a niche above, with little figures of *Justice* and *Honesty* decorating the otherwise plain outer moulding. The niche is inventively linked by 'plaited' tracery forms (without cusping) to two flanking buttresses (fig. 19).

When in October 1912 the council authorized Gibson to raise the height of the tower, a further £750 was allowed for additional carving around its parapet. Fehr's ornamentation consists of shields with the Middlesex arms, crowned portcullises (for Westminster), Tudor roses and heraldic beasts – lions, unicorns and yales (a mythical antelope/goat-like creature with forward- and backward-curving horns).[19]

On each side of the tower, and projecting from brackets immediately beneath this heraldic carving, are eight gargoyle-like figures: the pairs on the north and south faces are angels and those on the east and west faces represent *The Four Winds*. While the angels have conventional Gothic features, the *Winds* are almost Baroque in their twisting poses and naturalistic

Previous pages: 20. Fehr's sculpture on the tower includes a band of heraldic ornament, with gargoyle-like figures beneath of angels and *The Four Winds*.

*Below, left:* 21. Two door-frames in the entrance hall are decorated with miniature lions, reminiscent of those designed by Alfred Stevens in the 1850s for the British Museum.

*Below, centre and right:* 22 (a) and (b). A bear with a shield, and a camel and civic crown, two of the heraldic beasts decorating the north gallery overlooking the former Court 2 (now Courtroom 3).

anatomy (fig. 20). Above the parapet sculpture on the tower's east face stands another of Fehr's allegorical female figures, enshrined within a crocketed Gothic canopy – the tallest feature of the building. She symbolizes *Government* – presumably local government – keeping a watchful eye on the representatives of national politics in the Houses of Parliament directly opposite.

## Interior Sculpture and Carvings in Stone

The original users of the Middlesex Guildhall must surely have been surprised to find such a profusion of sculpture inside. While Gibson and his partners had explicitly responded to the Guildhall's architectural context in their external treatment, there would certainly have been no need to match – let alone surpass – this rich decorative scheme on the inside. Yet it appears that in drawing up their designs, the architects took as many opportunities as possible to create interiors full of symbolic and historical imagery. They did

this in the expectation not only that Fehr would be able to produce many plaster models for carving, but also that his team of craftsmen would be capable of executing them in stone in less than a year. In fact, most of the internal decoration dates from the second half of 1913, and even then was somewhat delayed by a plasterers' strike during the summer.

Apart from such details as the low-relief shields on the entrance-hall columns, there is relatively little purely ornamental work. The majority, whatever its scale, is three-dimensional or in high relief, often with intricate detail. The two door-frame mouldings at the entrance to the former Court 1 (now the Library), for example, are carved with tiny figures (no taller than 12 centimetres/4¾ inches) of seated lions, reminiscent of those modelled in the 1850s by Alfred Stevens (1818–1875) for the iron railings at the British Museum. Stevens had become a much-revered figure among early twentieth-century sculptors, and Fehr's little lions are a discreet tribute to him (fig. 21).[20]

More heraldic animals populate the corbels, label-stops and arch-mouldings of the Council Chamber and courtrooms. Usually set in dense, stylized foliage, they hold shields, repose within crowns or otherwise adopt their distinctive heraldic stances. There is no easily discernible explanation for the particular selection of creatures, but (possibly) each was borne on a shield or was a crest or supporter in a coat of arms associated with the county of Middlesex and its constituent boroughs (figs. 22 (a) and (b)). The arcaded gallery alongside former Court 2 (now Courtroom 3) boasts an especially good set, with lions, a bear, an elephant and a stag. The stag in particular has a number of distinguished forebears from the 1390s – in the form of Richard II's hart emblem – among the carved corbels of nearby Westminster Hall, the Gothic architecture and decoration of which seem a pervasive influence on the Guildhall building.

Half-figures of angels holding symbols of law and government form the corbels supporting the roof-beams.

Wearing veils, or with locks of hair framing their faces, they are typical 'Fehr maidens' of the type already noted in the exterior sculpture. In the carving of these figures, dramatic areas of shadow give prominence to the projecting facial features or symbolic attributes. It is clear that Fehr and Magnoni fully understood the need for bold effects in work that would normally be visible only from floor level. The sculptures' clarity of outline and confluence with the architectural forms also demonstrate the close collaboration of Fehr and his craftsmen with the architects (fig. 23).

In the Council Chamber (now Courtroom 1), the richly carved arches terminate on either side in half-figures of angels beneath Gothic canopies. These angels are younger-looking versions of those in Court 2; like them, their centre-parted hair sweeps down on either side of their faces. They are winsome Edwardian girls angelically garbed, rather than imitations of medieval prototypes (fig. 24).

*Below, left:* 23. One of the symbolic angel corbels supporting the roof-beams of the former Court 2.

*Below, right:* 24. One of Fehr's elegant, Edwardian-looking angels flanking the galleries of the former Council Chamber.

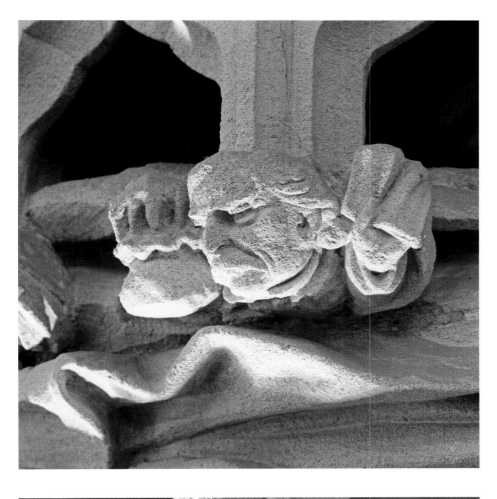

*Opposite:* 25 (a), (b), (c) and (d). In the former Court 1 – now the Library – allegorical crowned figures emerge from beneath Gothic canopies, acting as corbels for the fan-vaulted ceiling.

*Left, below, left, and overleaf:* 26 (a), (b) and (c). The faces of David Lloyd George, sculptor Henry Fehr and carver Carlo Magnoni adorn the corbels of the Library ceiling.

Their somewhat older 'sisters' appear in former Court 1 (now the Library), acting as the corbels for the fan-vaulted ceiling. Here Fehr designed the sculptures not as angels but as allegorical queen-like figures (approximately life-size) symbolizing 'Law', 'Justice', 'Counsel', 'Government' and other concepts appropriate to the room's functions.[21] With their bodies horizontal, they appear to grow out of the wall. Formerly these allegories gazed down on the courtroom, but, with the recent alteration of floor levels, they now scrutinize the users of the new Library (figs. 25 (a)–(d)).

Each monumental figure emerges from under a Gothic canopy, the bosses of which are carved with grotesque faces like the medieval representations of Vices that were often juxtaposed with images of Virtues. Fehr and Magnoni also decided to use these boss-carvings to introduce a topical and personal note: one is a very recognizable portrait of David Lloyd George (Chancellor of the Exchequer, 1908–15) holding a money-bag, while two others feature little demi-figures of Fehr the sculptor and Magnoni the carver, each with their respective artistic implements. There is a delightfully subversive aptness in the image of Magnoni, the Italian anarchist refugee, having his symbolic place in this key part of the judicial system (figs. 26 (a)–(c)).

The official opening of the Guildhall in December 1913 also saw the unveiling of Middlesex's memorial to Edward VII, a marble bust of the late king by the sculptor Percy Bryant Baker (1881–1970). In his speech on that occasion, Prince Arthur of Connaught commented on the excellence of Baker's likeness of his uncle; in fact, the portrait so impressed Queen Alexandra when a version was exhibited at the Royal Academy in 1911 that she commissioned several bronze replicas.[22] The bust was originally placed in the entrance hall, on a stone pedestal designed by the architects and carved (by Fehr's assistants) with the royal arms. Shortly after its installation there were complaints that clients waiting for their court cases were leaning against the bust and its pedestal, necessitating the addition of a protective metal railing. In the redesign of the building, the railing has been discarded and the bust removed to one of the main public areas (fig. 27).

## Woodcarving and Furniture

With its Council Chamber and two courtrooms, as well as anterooms, committee rooms and offices, the new Guildhall required a considerable quantity of furniture, much of it decorative and ceremonial in character. Other woodwork included carved roof-beams, doors and panelling. By a resolution of the county council in June 1912, Gibson and his partners were given responsibility for designing the more elaborate furniture – everything, in fact, but the purely functional office fittings – and were asked to recommend firms to carry out the work.

In his report of April 1912 to the council, Gibson stressed that 'all the fittings should be designed to harmonize with the character of the buildings [*sic*]', estimating the total cost at £13,620. In most cases Austrian oak would be used 'for the panelling, seats, chairs, tables, etc., slightly fumed and treated with a flat unpolished surface'.[23] To give the councillors an idea of what they would get for this substantial expenditure, Gibson arranged a day's visit to Wakefield on 31 January 1913, where he showed the delegation the furnishings he had designed almost a decade earlier for the West Riding County Hall. The visitors were clearly impressed, authorizing an ambitious furnishing programme even though Gibson's office had yet to prepare any designs.

Following the tendering process, the main contracts were allocated in the summer of 1913 to Wylie & Lochhead of Glasgow (Council Chamber), H.H. Martyn & Co. of Cheltenham (Courts 1 and 2) and James Carmichael of Wandsworth (Committee Rooms). Each furniture contract stipulated that all carved work should 'be executed by a Carver to be appointed by the Architect', and that sums of £600 or more should be allowed by each contractor for 'Carving including Modelling'.[24] Although the workforces of both Wylie & Lochhead and H.H. Martyn would certainly have included competent carvers, the significant implication is that the Guildhall carving (other than purely ornamental details) was carried out by a separate team of craftsmen selected by the architects. If so, it seems that the carvers were either employed directly or at least supervised by Henry Fehr, who produced models for all the figural and animal carvings (and much else).

Today, as part of the refurbishment of the building as the UK Supreme Court (UKSC), the original courtroom furniture has been removed to be reused in Crown Courts elsewhere. It was decided, however, that the ornately carved furniture of the former Council Chamber should be retained for the new Courtroom 1. This entailed the careful dismantling, and in some cases repair, of the carved bench-ends and other elements, and their sympathetic adaptation and reconstruction in newly designed furniture units. The chairman's 'throne', with its Gothic canopy and armorial carvings, has been placed in one of the galleries overlooking the court.

Although superficially 'Late Gothic' in overall style, with resonances of Pugin's furnishings for the Palace of Westminster, the Guildhall's decorative woodwork and carved furniture exhibit the same stylistic freedom and

eclecticism as its external features. Without copying historical prototypes, the designers took inspiration not only from Gothic but also from a range of Northern Renaissance sources, the kind of early sixteenth-century Flemish and northern French woodwork that can be seen in a number of English churches, colleges and houses.[25]

One characteristic motif, derived ultimately from Classical cameos, is known as 'Romayne' work: profile heads, carved in low relief, used for bench-ends and to embellish panelling and furniture. Fehr designed carvings reminiscent of this type for the outer faces of the former Council Chamber benches. They portray an array of English kings and queens – presumably chosen because of their particular Middlesex connections – including Stephen, Edward III (wearing fancifully anachronistic armour), Henry VIII, Mary Tudor and Elizabeth I (figs. 28 (a) and (b)).

Additional bench-ends are carved either in relief with heraldic beasts (lions, a stag and an ox, and the mythical unicorn, griffin, yale and enfield – the last a fox-wolf-eagle hybrid), or with simpler panels of foliage and stylized Italianate shields. With their volute-like top mouldings, the bench-ends themselves are quite un-Gothic in style. In fact, much of the woodwork seems to celebrate, playfully and without a trace of antiquarian pedantry, the gradual stylistic transition out of Gothic that one associates with the Tudor era.

Among the Council Chamber carvings reused in the furnishings for Courtroom 1, the most impressive are the three-dimensional creatures that serve as finials on some of the bench-ends, or as armrests for benches. The finial beasts are miniature masterpieces of wood sculpture, skilfully translating the taut energy of Fehr's original plaster or clay models into grained oak. Avoiding excessively projecting or fragile shapes, Fehr designed his lions, bears and wolves as compact, crouching forms whose contours seem – as so many medieval carvings do – to invite human touch as well as close inspection. No doubt they often proved a pleasing distraction during more humdrum council meetings (figs. 29 (a)–(e)).

Equally vigorous in design and carving are the armrests, carved either with demi-figures of animals (including a hare and a boar) or with complete figures of lions and other predators, their stylized bodies beautifully arched from back

to front of the seats (fig. 30). The refurbishment of these animal carvings to fit the new seating, carried out by David Podmore in his Yorkshire workshop, is one of the most successful conservation projects within the conversion of the Guildhall to the UKSC.

High above the carved benches is the pseudo-hammer-beam roof with its angel supporters, which is surely a distant descendant, albeit much abbreviated and with no structural function, of the great timber roof (1393–1400) of Westminster Hall on the other side of Parliament Square.[26] Indeed, Fehr's angel figures, although not strictly medieval in style, do display a rather more Gothic/hieratic quality than the carved furniture below. The galleries allow a good view of the roof carvings, especially the angels at the corners, which, unlike their more symmetrical companions, are cleverly placed to face into the room.

At the entrances to the anteroom outside the former Council Chamber (now Courtroom 1), the two glazed doors are crowned on each side by a canopy containing carved kneeling figures. One pair might represent the Old Testament characters Ruth and Naomi. Although they are

very finely carved, their dark colouring and placing over the doors make them relatively inconspicuous – an example of the abundance of artistic detail within the building that might be missed by a casual visitor (fig. 31).

## Stained Glass and Other Glazing

The extensive scheme of ornamental glazing throughout the Middlesex Guildhall was, like much else, supplied by a firm specifically approved by the architects. They selected Abbott & Co. of St John's Studios, Lancaster, which had previously manufactured glazing for a number of Gibson's buildings, including Walsall Town Hall (1905) and St James's Infirmary, Wandsworth (1909). Founded at the end of the nineteenth century, the firm mainly produced leaded-light glazing for churches, chapels and public and commercial buildings in the North of England. There were occasional London commissions, such as windows for the Hotel Russell in Bloomsbury, but it appears from the surviving archives that Middlesex Guildhall was its largest and most prestigious work in the capital.[27]

Abbott & Co. employed about fifteen craftsmen, and, as well as purely decorative glazing, carried out more elaborate stained-glass windows either from its own designs or from those of architects or independent artists. The style of the Guildhall work and the absence of any relevant designs in the firm's archives make it likely that Gibson's office was responsible for the glazing patterns. No doubt Abbott first produced sample panels to show the varied types of materials to be used. If Skipwith can be credited with most of the non-sculptural detailing for the building, this may also include the decidedly 'Arts and Crafts' glazing.

The majority of the leaded glazing is in fact internal, but the ingenious arrangement of light-wells enables all the major windows to be naturally lit. This includes the armorial stained-glass windows, some incorporating figures, which feature in the main staircase, courtrooms and Council Chamber. Tinted, textured glasses, with coloured inserts in leaded borders, are used in windows elsewhere (for example, in the ground-floor corridors), while clear 'patent polished plate' glass with intricate leading patterns is featured in doors and screens. In 1915 *The Builder* commented that the glazing was 'in absolute harmony with the design of the building', and praised especially the 'fine richness of tone' in the

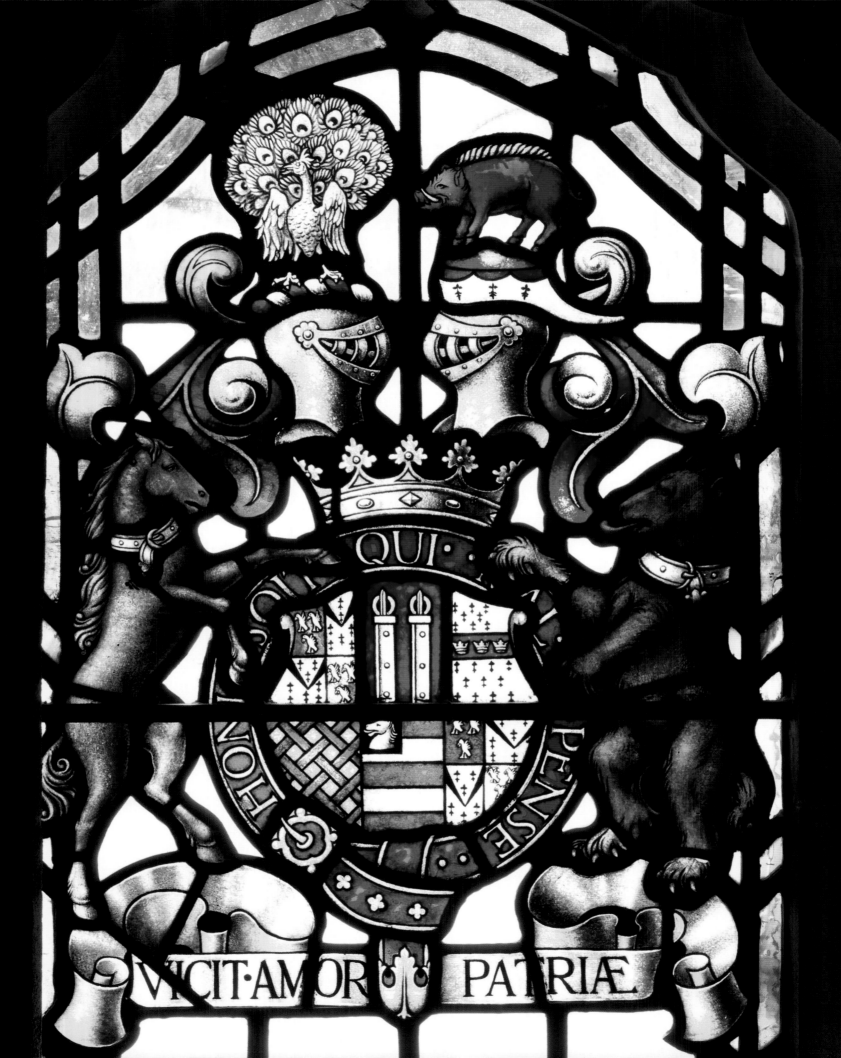

QUI

HON... PENSE

VICIT·AMOR·PATRIÆ

stained-glass figures of the Council Chamber (Courtroom 1) windows.[28] These six representations of *Virtues* were designed by Fehr (for which he was paid £5 by Abbott & Co.), and may well be his only work in the medium.[29] Each is 'surrounded by rich haphazard spots of ornament in colour' in the tracery lights. Like the main lights below, which are of tinted quarries with armorial inserts, the *Virtues* are glazed in 'rich Norman slabs' with very broad leads (figs. 32, 33 and 34 (a) and (b)).

Used extensively throughout the Guildhall windows, 'slab' glass was a relatively new material, the manufacture of which had been devised by the architect E.S. Prior (1857–1932) in the late 1880s. It became closely associated with the designers and architects of the Arts and Crafts movement, who valued its particular qualities of brilliant luminosity and irregular colouring. Clearly, these effects were appreciated by the Guildhall's architects, as the specifications were altered during the course of the work so that additional windows could be glazed with Norman slabs instead of the cheaper 'Ambetty' textured glass.

The conspicuously 'hand-made' character of 'slab' glass and the necessity for heavy, almost coarse, leading engendered a style characterized by one artist as glazing 'with careless care'.[30] *The Builder*'s critic admired this treatment in the armorial windows of what was then Court 1, where 'to break the monotony the arms have been, as it were, dropped in casually, a very happy result being obtained'.[31]

Similarly characterful, although more delicate, are the windows in the Justices' sitting-room, where the geometric

35. James Gibson and his partners designed elaborate patterned leading for the glazed screens and doors throughout the building.

*Opposite:* 36. Abbott & Co.'s decorative glazing in the Justices' sitting-room includes vignettes of stylized landscapes.

glazing is interspersed with scenes of windmills, bridges and castles, painted in simple linework with touches of yellow stain 'on Crown sheet haphazard' (as described on the Abbott & Co. job sheet) – a stylishly modern interpretation of seventeenth-century domestic glazing (fig. 36).[32]

The clustered concentration of motifs found in the exterior architecture is echoed in the glazed wooden doors and screens, the lead-lines forming structured patterns of verticals interrupted by chevrons, roundels and other devices, somewhat like the reticulation of Perpendicular Gothic tracery. The effective integration of the leaded glazing within the design of the panelled woodwork, and its formal links to much of the architectural detail, further suggest Skipwith's hand (fig. 35).

## Plasterwork and Tiling

The ornamental plasterwork, entrusted by the architects to Gilbert Seale & Son of 22 George Street, Camberwell, is of two types. The first, as used for the fan-vaulted ceiling of the former Court 1 (now the Library), on the main staircase and as a wall-covering in the entrance hall and elsewhere, is an artificial stone material referred to in the contract documents as 'Stuc'. The second, used for decorative cornices and for the ceilings of the principal anterooms, is another patent material known as 'Sirapite', a hydrated gypsum compound particularly suited to moulded decoration.

Gilbert Seale & Son had previously worked with both Gibson and Fehr, notably at Walsall Town Hall, and the company's experienced workforce would have been familiar with all the necessary collaborative procedures involving architects, sculptor and builder. Following the architects' detailed drawings, Seale's own craftsmen made the moulds for the ornately modelled fan-vaulting in the former Court 1, incorporating such elements as the central royal arms, which were probably modelled by Fehr. Installation of the plasterwork then entailed the delicate task of fixing the moulded sections to the structure put in place by the main contractor's craftsmen. It is said that tea was used to stain the finished plaster to the right stone-like tint. Pointing was then applied to heighten the effect of masonry joints. The results are convincing, although a real stone vault across this span is not structurally possible (fig. 37).

Where surfaces were not designed to replicate stone, the decorative treatment in white plaster was broadly inspired by

Opposite: 37. The impressive fan-vaulted ceiling (in plaster) of the Supreme Court's Library, which was formerly Court 1.

*Below:* 38. Modelled plasterwork by Gilbert Seale & Son in the anteroom of the Council Chamber (now Courtroom 1).

*Below, right:* 39. The tiled dado in green and dark blue is one of many Arts and Crafts elements designed by Gibson and his partners.

the sixteenth- and seventeenth-century traditions of English plasterwork favoured by George Bankart and other Arts and Crafts designers.[33] Plain areas are contrasted either with wreath-like features of high-relief foliate or heraldic decoration, as in former Court 2 (now Courtroom 3), or with framing borders and cornices moulded with low-relief floral or foliate patterns, as in the first- and second-floor anterooms. The latter are especially impressive: sinuous stems of flowers and fruits trail along the ceiling beams and cornices, while the corner spandrels are adorned with delicately modelled sprigs of symbolic national flowers and plants (fig. 38).

A striking feature of corridors throughout the building is the green tiling, which extends from the skirting to dado level. Unevenly glazed in a rich grass-green interspersed with narrow bands of dark blue, the wall-tiles – which appear to have been substituted by the architects for the mosaic dados originally specified – add to the distinctly Arts and Crafts character of the interiors, providing colour and interest in areas that might otherwise lack them (fig. 39).

## Light-Fittings and Metalwork

On 15 April 1913, H.H. Martyn & Co. was instructed to proceed with the manufacture of the electroliers, from the architects' designs, at a cost of £1960. Specific designs for the bronze and wrought-iron light-fittings, many of which are still in use, were provided for different parts of the building.

One recurring motif is an embossed shield, either plain or adorned with the Middlesex arms, linked by sections of repoussé scrollwork or stylized foliage. The largest pendant lamps, as in the former Council Chamber, have a central framework of slender, interlinked Gothic shafts fixed to the central corona of shield-shapes; from these the lights hang within a ring of embossed metal roses. Elegant but simpler light-fittings are used in the corridors. Shield and rose motifs appear on the lamps fixed at intervals on the main staircase, but there they are surmounted by bronze statuettes of lions, probably cast from a model by Fehr (figs. 40 (a) and (b)).

Few elements better illustrate the architects' commitment to an integrated decorative ensemble than the metal door fittings, with their exquisite Gothic tracery

EXAMPLES OF SOME OF THE WORK SUPPLIED
TO THE MIDDLESEX GUILDHALL

patterns. Along with the locks and ironwork, they were manufactured (from Skipwith's designs, perhaps) by James Gibbons of St John's Works, Wolverhampton. In style they resemble Late Medieval French lock-plates, examples of which could have been studied by the designer at the Victoria and Albert Museum (fig. 41).[34]

Gibbons's firm also made the ceremonial key used for the opening of the Guildhall (fig. 42), as well as the staircase ironwork and, on the exterior, the rainwater hoppers moulded with a floral ornament and the date 'AD 1913'. In July of that year the council decided not to reuse (as originally planned) the old cast-iron railings from the Guildhall of 1893, and an additional £650 was allowed for new wrought-iron railings – emblazoned with the repeated letter 'M' for Middlesex – which were designed by the architects and made by Gibbons.

**Middlesex Guildhall Collection**

The historic county of Middlesex acquired by gift or other means a significant collection of works of art, primarily

*Opposite, top, left and right:* 40 (a) and (b). Bronze light-fittings, made by H.H. Martyn & Co. of Cheltenham, on the main staircase.

*Opposite, bottom left:* 41. James Gibbons of Wolverhampton manufactured the Gothic-style door-handles designed by F.P. Skipwith.

*Opposite, bottom right:* 42. An advertisement for Gibbons's firm, showing door-fittings for Middlesex Guildhall, and the key used for the ceremonial opening. The advertisement was published in the *Modern Building Record*, 5 (1914), 169.

*Above:* 43. Tapestry with the Royal Arms of King George III, made for the Middlesex Sessions House at Clerkenwell in the 1780s.

portraits of Lord Lieutenants and other dignitaries, which will continue to be displayed in the new Supreme Court. These include works by the two great English portraitists of the eighteenth century. In one of the main courtrooms is Sir Joshua Reynolds's (1723–1792) *Earl of Northumberland* (later the 1st Duke; the frame is by Thomas Chippendale, see fig. 6, p. 202); and Thomas Gainsborough's (1727–1788) *Hugh Percy, 1st Duke of Northumberland* (exhibited at the Royal Academy in 1783; see fig. 6, p. 15), now graces the new Library.

The earliest portrait, attributed to the Flemish artist Paul van Somer (*c.* 1576–1621), depicts Sir Baptist Hicks (1st Viscount Campden; 1551–1629), magistrate, philanthropist and courtier in the reigns of James I and Charles I, and builder of Hicks' Hall, the first purpose-built sessions house of the Middlesex Justices (see fig. 5, p. 15). Among later paintings depicting chairmen of Middlesex County Council are two by distinguished Late Victorian artists: *Ralph Littler* by Sir Hubert von Herkomer (1849–1914) and *William*

*Regester* (chairman when the Middlesex Guildhall was built) by the Hon. John Collier (1850–1934). Ethel Mortlock's *2nd Duke of Wellington* (the Lord Lieutenant of Middlesex from 1868 to 1884) clearly shows the sitter's resemblance to his famous father, the victor of Waterloo.

The large tapestry of the royal arms (fig. 43), a relic of the eighteenth-century Middlesex Sessions House (at Clerkenwell), dates from the early years of George III's reign (1760–1820). The arms, with their distinctive quartering (in the lower right-hand of the shield) with its Elector's crown, are those borne by the Hanoverian kings. Although the tapestry is now somewhat faded, its symbols of government and law – and, perhaps surprisingly, the exuberantly rococo design – are well suited to its current setting.

### War Memorials

From 1924 the Middlesex Guildhall was associated, through the placing of various war-memorial sculptures and plaques, with those county residents who served and died in the

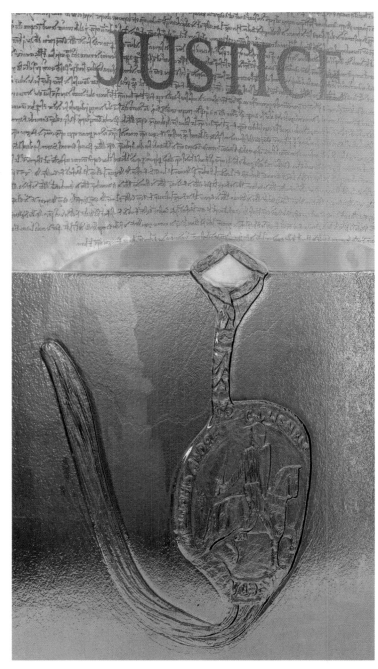

*Above:* 44. The Middlesex Memorial to the dead of the First World War, by Richard Goulden, with its bronze figure of Private Robert Ryder, VC.

*Above, right:* 45. Bettina Furnée's glass doors for the Library of the Supreme Court, featuring the text and seal of Magna Carta.

*Opposite:* 46. The glass-and-carved-walnut Library balustrade, with the 'river of text' by Richard Kindersley.

armed forces during the two world wars. The principal memorial, commemorating Middlesex men and women of the 1914–18 war, is now sited on the south wall of the main entrance (fig. 44) and is the work of the sculptor Richard Goulden (1877–1932), best known for his Margaret Macdonald memorial in Lincoln's Inn Fields.[35] The other First World War memorial, by an unknown but accomplished maker, is in an Arts and Crafts style with embossed lettering and inset enamel plaques.

### Newly Commissioned Furnishings

Symbolic images and texts are the dominant theme of the new furnishings and decoration of the Supreme Court, as explained in the chapters by Lady Hale and Hugh Feilden in this book. As a constitutional innovation, the court

required a new emblem that would express its national identity and jurisdiction. It was recognized that heraldry can do this far more effectively than more transitory media. Yvonne Holton, artist at the Court of the Lord Lyon, King of Arms (the Scottish heraldic authority), has combined the English rose, Scottish thistle, Welsh leek and Northern Irish flax in a device the stylish simplicity of which makes it ideally versatile for a variety of applications.

The visitor sees the UKSC emblem on the left-hand side of the east portal of the building and also, on entering, engraved – with text from the judicial oath – on the glass screen by Bettina Furnée. Furnée has contributed several text pieces to the courts. The entrance screen inventively uses the flowers of the UKSC symbol as decorative flourishes in the lettering. Just beyond the screen are the doors to the Library,

which Furnée has sandblasted with a facsimile of Magna Carta, complete with King John's seal. Two key phrases from the charter are superimposed on the overall design (fig. 45).

On entering the entirely new Courtroom 2, one sees a curved glass screen, engraved with words written by Eleanor Roosevelt (the only woman quoted in the many texts adorning the building), forming a lobby partition while also allowing a view of the room beyond. Furnée has placed the band of upper-case lettering on clear glass between two wider bands of sandblasted basket-weave pattern, denser at the base and lighter at the top (see fig. 32, pp. 90–91). Beyond the screen, the UKSC emblem appears in colour above the west wall, its symbolic plant forms providing, in a simplified form, the motif for Sir Peter Blake's Wilton carpet design, a modern version of the kind of heraldic ornament

used by Pugin in the Palace of Westminster. Blake's carpet, with differing backgrounds of green, blue or crimson, is used throughout the building, sometimes (as in the Library) with a large central roundel against a field of small repeating devices.

Relieving the predominantly white space of Courtroom 2 are hand-printed textile hangings by the Timorous Beasties design partnership, founded in Glasgow by Alistair McAuley and Paul Simmons. These fabrics also incorporate the rose, thistle, leek and flax, but in a more naturalistic form, the stems of which extend upwards, parallel with the two tiers of tall windows on either side.

In his designs for the glass-and-carved-walnut balustrade of the Library, Richard Kindersley has made the words of philosophers, reformers and activists into a flowing river of text that surrounds the central staircase (fig. 46). The

47. The sleek, functional lines of Tomoko Azumi's courtroom desks in oak and black walnut.

*Opposite:* 48. The bronze portrait relief of HM Queen Elizabeth II by sculptor Ian Rank-Broadley, commemorating the opening of the Supreme Court in October 2009.

calligraphy is of an italic form, suggesting the humanistic intellectual tradition of the Renaissance and its Classical inspiration. This lettering heritage, freely interpreted, can also be discerned in Kindersley's carved inscription – featuring the poem written by Andrew Motion, then Poet Laureate, to mark the creation of the Supreme Court – on the curved stone bench facing the main entrance.

With a visually austere but skilfully utilitarian approach, Tomoko Azumi (working in collaboration with Luke Hughes) has met the challenge of designing new 'working' furniture for an elaborately decorated historic building. In her desks and chairs for courtrooms and Justices' rooms, an important consideration was to integrate, with some flexibility, the necessary ICT facilities. These have been accommodated in portable trolleys designed for use in the different courts. European oak and American black walnut were chosen to harmonize with the existing woodwork and reused original furniture (fig. 47).

To commemorate the opening of the Supreme Court by Her Majesty The Queen, the sculptor Ian Rank-Broadley created a bronze portrait relief for the main entrance. The half-length portrait (fig. 48) depicts Her Majesty in profile, crowned with a tiara, and wearing the Sovereign's robes of the Order of the Garter. Her hand is outstretched in a gesture intended by the artist to suggest the Crown as the ultimate source of justice in the realm. There is an impressive play of contrasts between the three main elements of the sculpture: the dignified and sympathetic realism of the portrait, the formal elegance of the inscription and the Titianesque drama of the voluminous robes. Since 1998, Rank-Broadley's image of Queen Elizabeth II has been used on UK and Commonwealth coinage, contributing to a distinguished series of numismatic portraiture throughout her reign. The new relief marks the continuing royal connection with the building since its opening by HRH Prince Arthur of Connaught in 1913.

# THE DESIGN OF THE SUPREME COURT OF THE UNITED KINGDOM

HUGH FEILDEN

*The special interest of the historic Guildhall has been preserved, and the building uplifted and given a new use that is far more significant than the original.*

## Choosing the Site

As an architect, the opportunity to be engaged in a project to create the United Kingdom Supreme Court (UKSC) in the Middlesex Guildhall on Parliament Square was unique. I knew from my experience of working with other courts in historic buildings that there would be a demanding brief that was bound to provide opportunity and challenge, and so it proved. The key design criteria agreed between the Department of Constitutional Affairs (DCA) and the Law Lords were a strong public presence, good accessibility for all, openness and a design appropriate for an institution at the apex of the United Kingdom's legal system. In 2004 Feilden+Mawson was asked by the DCA to review two listed buildings, which at that stage were part of a longlist of possible locations for the proposed UKSC. These were the New Wing of Somerset House and the Middlesex Guildhall (fig. 2).

The DCA provided an outline schedule of requirements that had been developed in close co-operation with the Law Lords. This defined the spaces that the Law Lords considered essential for the successful operation of this new and independent institution, and thus supplied us with criteria with which to test potential sites. The core requirement was for three courtrooms, each laid out in a manner similar to the committee rooms then being used by the appellate committee in the House of Lords (see figs. 7 and 8, p. 41). This layout supported the 'collegiate' approach (as opposed to an 'adversarial' one) that the Law Lords adopt in their work. The new courts had, however, to be larger, allowing more Justices to sit, and were also to provide more room for the advocates, legal teams and the general public. In order to underpin the independence of the institution, the building had to be self-contained and self-sufficient, providing all the administration and support services required by the Supreme Court. It would also house the Judicial Committee of the Privy Council (JCPC; then at 9 Downing Street) and that committee's administration and support services (fig. 3). The Supreme Court could not, however, share a building with any part of the Court Service for England and Wales, and ideally would not share one with any other organization. There would be rooms for each of the twelve Justices of the Supreme Court and for two visiting Justices. An important requirement was a full law library, and also significant space to store and manage case papers. This was a very challenging brief for any site to fulfil. Fortunately, the field had been narrowed by the time I was appointed in January 2004.

The DCA had considered a longlist of around forty-two sites, which, based on the initial requirements, was rapidly reduced to a shortlist. The sites had to be the right size, available and near to either the Palace of Westminster or the Royal Courts of Justice. Although a preference had been expressed (among the project-management team, and later by some Law Lords) for a clear site to allow the design of a new building, only one such site appeared on the shortlist, in Victoria Street, and that would have been completely dwarfed by surrounding buildings and would therefore have had a poor public presence. Two existing historic listed buildings were on the final shortlist: the New Wing of Somerset House and the Middlesex Guildhall. I prepared conservation statements for both these sites, and initial option studies for all the final three shortlisted sites. Feilden+Mawson also consulted the planning authority, Westminster City Council, and English Heritage, the

9ᵗ 2006

Stephen Wiltshire.

Secretary of State's adviser on the historic environment, because we wished to build a close working relationship with them. This relationship, sustained throughout the programme, ensured that we were able to present imaginative designs and proposals that had the support of the local planning authority and met the desires and aspirations of the Law Lords. After all this initial work, there was clear consensus that the Middlesex Guildhall was most suitable for the new Supreme Court.

The old Middlesex Guildhall had three main advantages. First was its location on the west side of Parliament Square, which was widely accepted as being symbolically appropriate, standing close to the legislature (the Palace of Westminster), government (as represented in Brydon's Government Buildings, which now house HM Treasury), and the established Church with its link to the monarchy (Westminster Abbey). Second, it was the right size. At about 6000 square metres (64,583 square feet) gross internal area, it was comfortably big enough to satisfy the brief (initially around 5000 square metres/53,819 square feet gross and finally 5700 square metres/61,354 square feet gross). The New Wing at Somerset House, another front-runner on the shortlist, was much bigger and would have been difficult to adapt as a separate entity. Third, the Guildhall, already owned by the DCA and therefore readily available once the workloads of the existing Crown Courts had been moved to new locations, had a limited long-term future as a Crown Court. The Guildhall building itself was also more amenable to alteration than the New Wing of Somerset House, in particular because of the requirement for the courtrooms to be double-height. There were no double-height spaces of sufficient floor area in the Grade I-listed former government offices facing Waterloo Bridge. The Law Lords themselves had also formed the view that Somerset House would not be suitable. The rooms potentially large enough to be used as courtrooms were at ground level and very near the street, which presented serious security problems. With this in mind, the DCA project-management team sought a letter from English Heritage confirming its acceptance in principle of either of the proposals. This was in advance of any detailed design, so our initial proposals for both sites involved relatively few alterations to the sensitive areas of the historic fabric. After some discussion, English Heritage expressed a preference for Middlesex Guildhall as being more likely to be able to accommodate the brief for the UKSC without unacceptable loss of its historic worth or harm to its architectural interest.

In a statement to Parliament in December 2004, the Lord Chancellor announced that the Middlesex Guildhall was the preferred location for the UKSC. This was subject to proposals that satisfied the Law Lords, who still had to approve the detailed design and who also questioned the initial, conservative approach to alterations to the fabric, which Westminster City Council and English Heritage had advised. This condition was subsequently enshrined in the Constitutional Reform Act 2005.

**Developing the Design**

Once the preferred site had been announced, the DCA appointed a full design team. All the architectural practices on the Court Service 'framework agreement' (an approved list of professional firms from which the Court Service

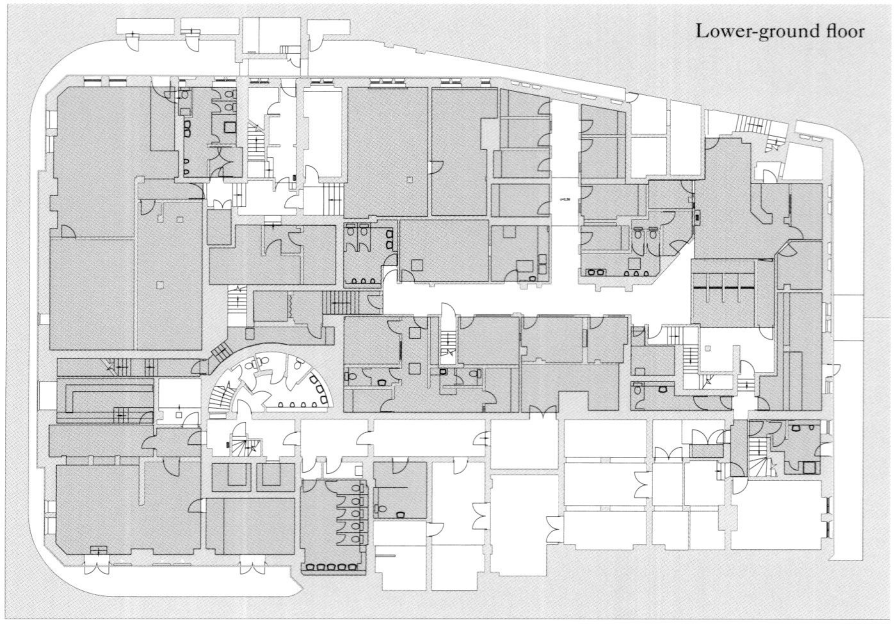


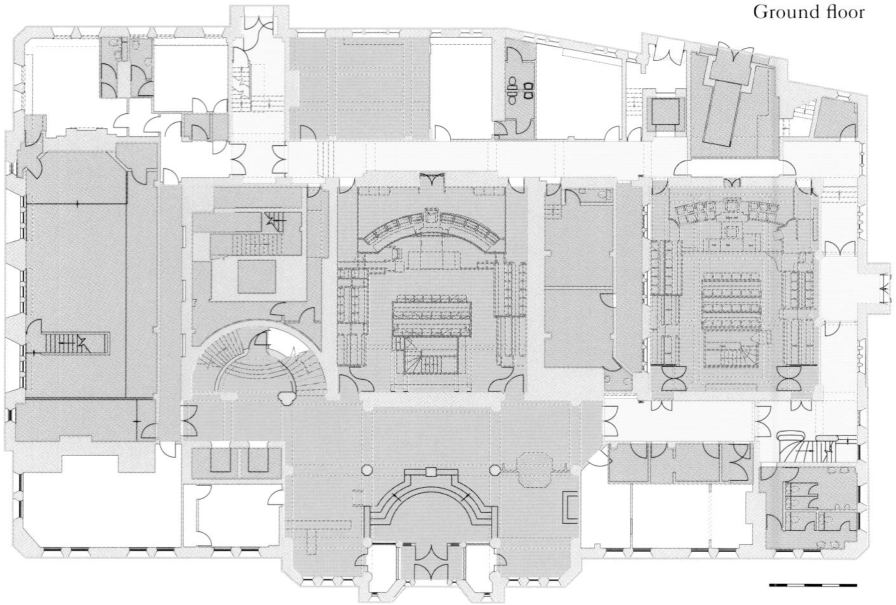


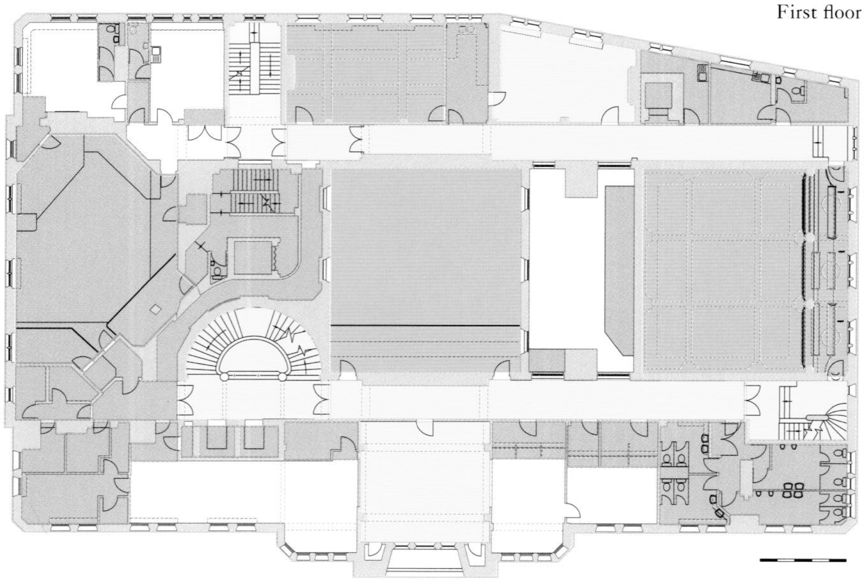


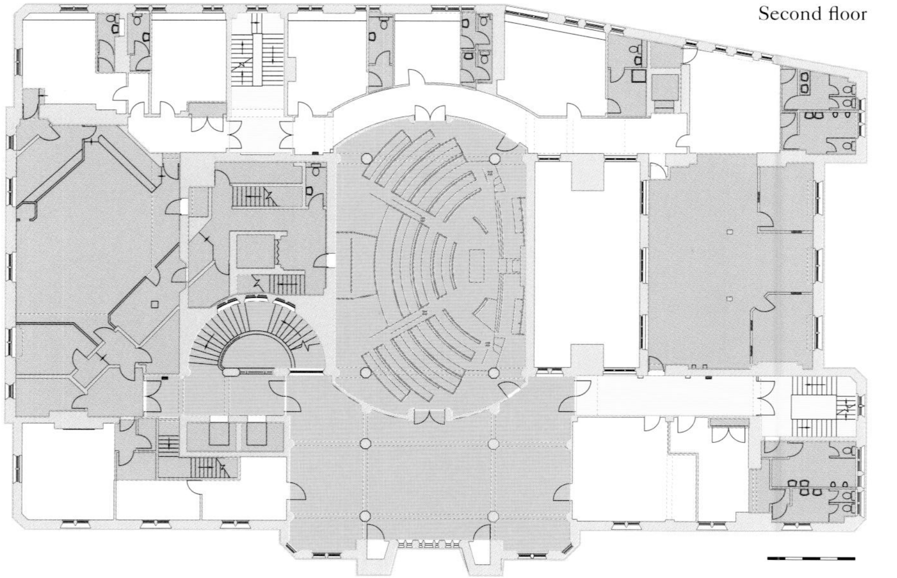


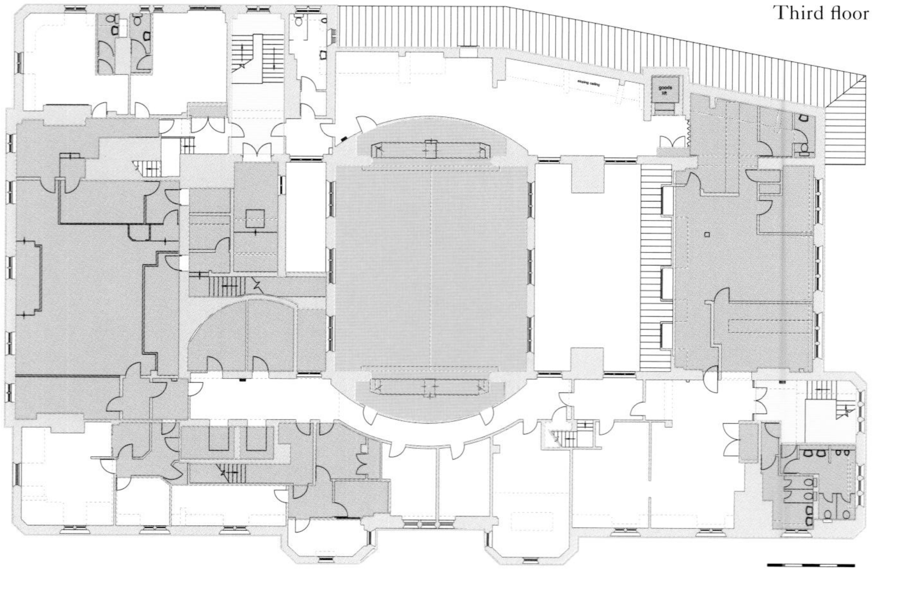


Most sensitive

Potentially sensitive

Not sensitive

Recent intervention

4–8. Drawings showing the sensitivity analysis of the lower-ground floor, the ground floor, and the first, second and third floors of the building. This assessment identifies the relative significance of different parts of the existing historic fabric, and is used to inform proposals for change. The general intention was to concentrate changes in areas of lower sensitivity and to avoid change to fabric of high sensitivity.

*Right:* 9. North–south section. The original courts are shown shaded in purple. The light-wells are open to basement level.

*Right, centre:* 10. North–south section, 1986. The building was converted to Crown Courts use in 1972 and then altered extensively in 1985 to create a total of seven Crown Courts. This was achieved by completely filling the southern light-well and partially filling the northern light-well, dramatically reducing the amount of natural daylight within the building.

*Right, bottom:* 11. The feasibility study assumed that the new courts would be in the three historic Crown Courts, and showed that the space requirements for the UKSC would fit comfortably within the existing building. At this stage, as the architects awaited detailed discussion of the brief's requirements, significant demolition within the light-wells was not proposed.

chooses for a particular project) were invited to present proposals and fee bids. Part of the tender process required the competing practices to demonstrate how they would integrate their work with the developing 'World Squares for All' proposals for Parliament Square and its surroundings. Foster+Partners was involved in this ambitious masterplan, and because we had worked with that company on the first phase of World Squares for All at Trafalgar Square, and also on the renovation of Government Offices Great George Street, it seemed sensible for my practice to team up with Foster again. Despite strong competition, the Feilden+Mawson/Foster+Partners team was appointed to act as technical advisers (see Credits, p. 214, for a list of the project team).

Our first tasks were to develop the design and technical brief, then to expand the conservation statement into a full conservation plan assessing the significance of the building and the relative sensitivity of the spaces and fabric, and finally to investigate the building itself in further detail (figs. 4–8). The sketch scheme that had been prepared to test the feasibility of adapting the Middlesex Guildhall for the Supreme Court was used as the basis for initial discussions with the end users, the Law Lords (figs. 9, 10 and 11). This scheme showed the existing historic courts and the former Council Chamber reused as the three courtrooms; the Library on the ground floor, as we were mindful of the high floor loads from book storage; administrative offices and support staff on the upper floors; and the Justices' rooms on the top floors. The northern light-well would be cleared down to the ground floor and the southern light-well partially opened up. The existing entrances would all be reused, and the general public would use the main entrance off Parliament Square. Secure access for staff and Justices would be at the rear. The exterior of the building would change very little, apart from the creation of a pedestrian-friendly space outside the main entrance, achieved by closing the southern end of Little George Street to vehicular traffic.

The Law Lords, who as part of their engagement with the project programme had formed a subcommittee to monitor and review the progress of the design, felt strongly that this approach was still too conservative with regard to the courtrooms. A design workshop was held with them and

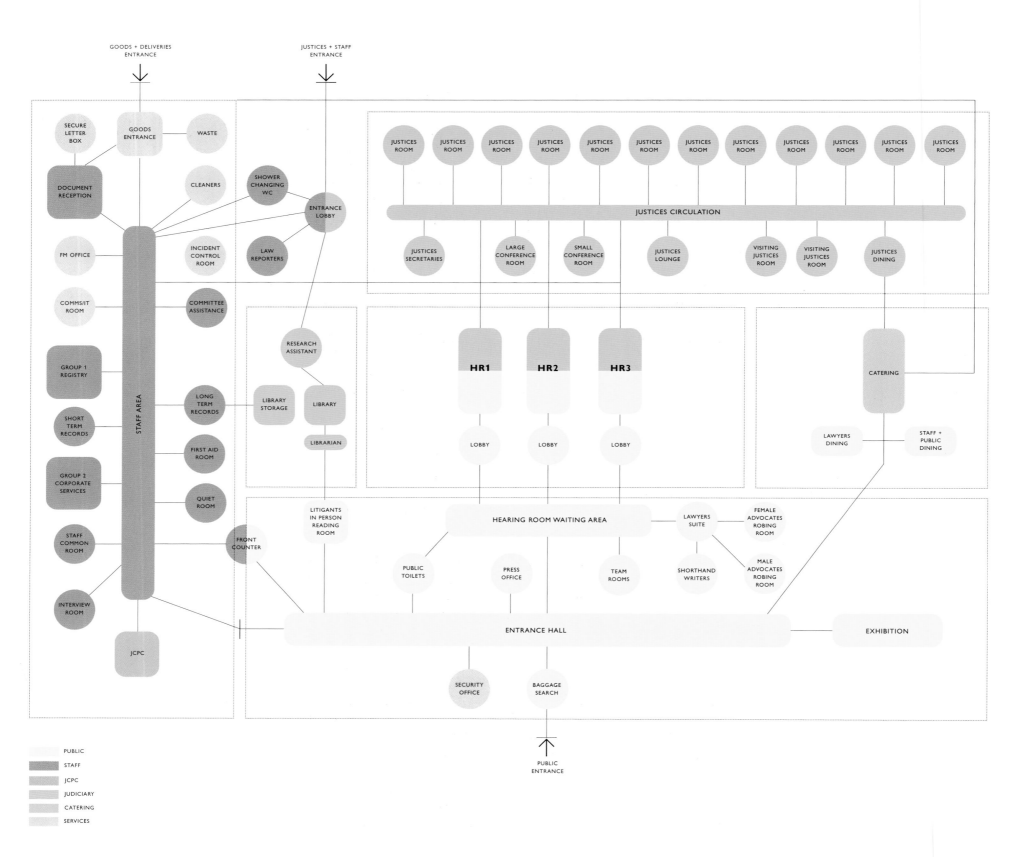

GOODS + DELIVERIES ENTRANCE

JUSTICES + STAFF ENTRANCE

SECURE LETTER BOX

GOODS ENTRANCE

WASTE

DOCUMENT RECEPTION

CLEANERS

SHOWER CHANGING WC

ENTRANCE LOBBY

JUSTICES ROOM

JUSTICES ROOM

JUSTICES ROOM

JUSTICES ROOM

JUSTICES ROOM

JUSTICES ROOM

JUSTICES ROOM

JUSTICES ROOM

JUSTICES ROOM

JUSTICES ROOM

JUSTICES ROOM

JUSTICES ROOM

JUSTICES CIRCULATION

FM OFFICE

INCIDENT CONTROL ROOM

LAW REPORTERS

JUSTICES SECRETARIES

LARGE CONFERENCE ROOM

SMALL CONFERENCE ROOM

JUSTICES LOUNGE

VISITING JUSTICES ROOM

VISITING JUSTICES ROOM

JUSTICES DINING

COMMS/IT ROOM

COMMITTEE ASSISTANCE

STAFF AREA

RESEARCH ASSISTANT

GROUP 1 REGISTRY

LONG TERM RECORDS

LIBRARY STORAGE

LIBRARY

HR1

HR2

HR3

CATERING

SHORT TERM RECORDS

FIRST AID ROOM

LIBRARIAN

GROUP 2 CORPORATE SERVICES

QUIET ROOM

LOBBY

LOBBY

LOBBY

LAWYERS DINING

STAFF + PUBLIC DINING

STAFF COMMON ROOM

FRONT COUNTER

LITIGANTS IN PERSON READING ROOM

HEARING ROOM WAITING AREA

LAWYERS SUITE

FEMALE ADVOCATES ROBING ROOM

INTERVIEW ROOM

PUBLIC TOILETS

PRESS OFFICE

TEAM ROOMS

SHORTHAND WRITERS

MALE ADVOCATES ROBING ROOM

JCPC

ENTRANCE HALL

EXHIBITION

SECURITY OFFICE

BAGGAGE SEARCH

PUBLIC ENTRANCE

PUBLIC

STAFF

JCPC

JUDICIARY

CATERING

SERVICES

with representatives of the staff and the legal professions from all parts of the United Kingdom. This reached the clear conclusion that the manner in which the Supreme Court operated could not be accommodated by using the existing historic court furniture layout, which was arranged in a way that reflected an adversarial form of justice and therefore did not suit the way the new court would work. It was clear that the requirements of the Supreme Court would in certain areas test the desire to preserve the historic fabric. The argument was made that the cultural significance of the new Supreme Court outweighed the significance of the historic courtroom furniture, and that the need to accommodate the business process of the Court would justify the alteration of historic fabric that we would normally seek to preserve. So we moved away from our first design ideas, and developed a more interventionist approach. This building was, after all, an important new expression of the law, in an ideal location, and was capable of being changed without losing its integrity or interest. An option to keep one historic court untouched was rejected. Lord Bingham, the Senior Law Lord, made it clear that the new Supreme Court should not be expected to sit 'in the attic of a museum'. The Law Lords were trying to achieve an atmosphere that was conducive to the style of learned debate and discussion that characterizes their proceedings. The central historic court on the ground floor (Court 1), in particular, was thought to be too dark and oppressive to achieve this. The obvious alternative to using it as a courtroom was to designate it as the Law Library.

Design is always an iterative process, so we took a step back and decided to look again at the processing of a typical case as it passed through the Supreme Court, and the considerable paperwork involved at each stage, from initial delivery of papers to the court to lodging of decisions in the Law Library. This assessment confirmed the balance required between open shelving and long-term storage, and demonstrated the need to allocate more administrative space near the main entrance at ground-floor level. We also visited the House of Lords, the judges' chambers in the Royal Courts of Justice, the JCPC in Downing Street and other 'benchmark' sites, such as the new High Court Library in Edinburgh, and, later, the new courts in Glasgow. Concurrently, the Law Lords were visiting other Supreme

Courts around the world, and feeding back their impressions. Although none was an exact equivalent in either size or function, the Supreme Court in Israel was a favourite, particularly for its use of natural light. This reinforced a desire to have at least one modern courtroom in the Supreme Court. Meanwhile, other elements of the brief, such as security requirements, the IT strategy, the internal environment of the building, business processes and staffing were being developed in detail, all captured in a continually expanding design brief (fig. 12).

Externally, the World Squares for All project in Parliament Square and its surroundings was still live (as discussed earlier by Chris Miele), and it was thought that the design of external spaces in front of the new court would follow from that scheme. This was no small matter. The Middlesex Guildhall is built on an island site that has no land associated with it: there is no more than street and pavement on all sides. It faces Little George Street, which is separated from the west side of Parliament Square by the raised area of grass known as Canning Green, but was then largely screened by two big trees in front of the building. At that time Foster+Partners was working on the masterplan for Phase Two of World Squares for All. The main feature of that scheme was the closure of the south side of Parliament Square to vehicular traffic, linking the central grassed area to St Margaret's Church. Concurrently, an area-wide security review was in progress, which could also have had a considerable effect on traffic and pedestrian movement in the locality. Our work had to be developed despite the uncertainty surrounding these proposals – which, as things turned out, have not been implemented. We were determined to make the new Court a significant presence on Parliament Square. The symbolism of its location proved to be very effective in explaining its function, and, as Jeremy Musson discusses in his chapter, the original architect of the Guildhall had conceived of the tower as a counterpoint to that of St Margaret's Church. The current layout of Parliament Square is much as George Grey Wornum (1888–1957) had proposed it after the Second World War, and English Heritage was keen that the Supreme Court proposals should reinforce his design (fig. 13).

At sketch design (RIBA stage C) the scheme had still not coalesced and was an awkward imbalance between preservation of the historic fabric and emerging ideas of what the Supreme

12. Functional relationships diagram. This diagram is an extract from the design brief, and was used to test the feasibility study and to develop early sketch schemes.

13. George Grey Wornum's drawing of Parliament Square. The central square should be the main viewing point for the whole of Parliament Square, but current traffic management makes it difficult for pedestrians to reach it. The World Squares for All masterplan proposed reconnecting the central square with St Margaret's churchyard, but – as discussed in Chris Miele's chapter – that plan is not being implemented.

Court should be (fig. 14). To avoid altering the main building fabric, the light-wells, being low-sensitivity spaces, were still being used for vertical transportation of lifts and services. The Library was at this stage located in the former Court 1 on the ground floor, but still used a large area of the basement for storage. The new court was also on the ground floor on the south side, but this did not leave enough room for a reception desk for the administrative areas close to the main entrance. The approach to be taken to bomb-blast mitigation – which in turn would dictate whether or not the building could be wholly or partially naturally ventilated – had not been decided. This was a particularly important decision if we were to achieve our target of a Building Research Establishment Environmental Assessment Method rating of 'Excellent' (BREEAM is a methodology developed by the BRE to assess the energy performance and sustainability of a project). A further series of workshops was held from which there emerged some key ideas.

**Key Ideas**
Unlike a trial court and many other Supreme Courts around the world, the United Kingdom Supreme Court does not have a defendant in the dock or witnesses who give live

evidence from a witness box. Its purpose is to decide important points of law, sometimes clarifying and sometimes developing the law. This means that the Supreme Court does not need docks, witness stands, jury boxes and the like, features typical of a criminal court. As already mentioned, the atmosphere has been likened to a learned seminar, and the initial model and layout tested were those used in the House of Lords committee rooms. Here there was a U-shaped bench arrangement and a central lectern at which advocates would stand to address the Law Lords (fig. 15).

As the Law Lords thought through the way in which they would work, and considered the opportunities for change and improvement, a different model emerged, based on a shallower, crescent-shaped bench for the Justices, and a similar bench for the advocates, who would stand to speak from where they sat, rather than moving to a lectern (fig. 16). This would speed up the flow of presentation, which could otherwise be interrupted by advocates moving about with volumes of papers in tow. It was important, however, that the Justices would be seated at the same level as the advocates, and not, as Lord Bingham described it, 'half-way up the wall' as they are in the most traditional courtrooms. This meant that the existing historic furniture layout, both in the original

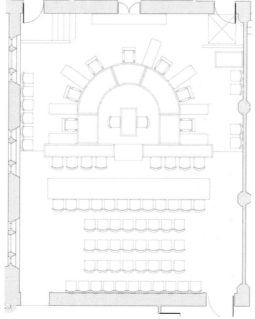

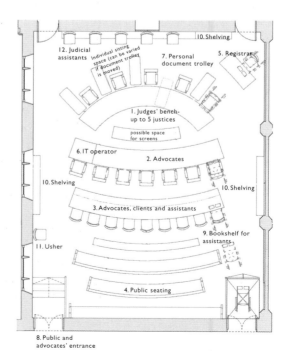

courtrooms and in the former Council Chamber, could not be reused, nor could this furniture be easily adapted, because in all three courts we had to raise the floor level to provide proper sight lines.

There was also a very clear desire to have a different feel in each court, and to include one modern courtroom. The original schedule of requirements called for two large courtrooms and one small, but this was clarified as one court capable of sitting five Justices, another to sit up to seven, and a third capable of accommodating nine. To provide an appropriate setting for the proceedings of the court it was felt that it was critical to create a sense of space. All the courtrooms were therefore expected to be double-height, which was why they had been placed in existing historic courts in the sketch proposals. Creating a modern courtroom for the Supreme Court would therefore require either the total stripping-out and reconfiguration of one of the historic courts (which would be very controversial), or the creation of a new double-height space within the building (which was going to be more acceptable to the Law Lords, the planning authority and English Heritage).

The former Council Chamber was suitable in principle for the nine-seat Courtroom 1, provided its main axis was rotated through 90 degrees (fig. 17). The northern historic court on the ground floor was deemed to be suitable for five Justices and therefore tentatively designated as being the principal courtroom for the JCPC.

**Equal Access for All**
Although the cases heard by the Law Lords in the House of Lords were in principle open to the public, making the building accessible to people was not a straightforward matter. Once in the building it was not easy to find the correct committee room, and services available to visitors and users alike were extremely limited. Even when people found the right room, there might not be a place to sit, particularly if there were more than two parties with their legal teams. Cases that created strong public interest in the House of Lords sometimes had to be moved to a larger room to accommodate the public. Greater transparency has always been at the heart of the creation of the Supreme Court. Easy public access was therefore a key requirement, so that people could see for themselves how important points of law that

affect or interest them were decided. Situated on the west side of Parliament Square, with its own front door, the Supreme Court is a much more accessible and less daunting prospect for the first-time visitor than was the case at the House of Lords.

The requirement for easy access extended not only to visiting members of the public, but also to that hardy band known as litigants in person, people who for whatever reason eschew professional legal representation and bring their case forward themselves. This is rare, but the facilities for such people must be provided. A specific room for litigants in person was added to the brief, close to the Library, so that, through the librarian, they could use its

17. The arrangement of the former Crown Court (no. 3), as photographed in 2006. This was the original Council Chamber. Feilden+Mawson undertook studies to see whether this furniture could be adapted, but concluded that there was no satisfactory solution.

18. The addition of the bust of King Edward VII to the front entrance in 1913 blocked the original clarity of the area. This, combined with security equipment and pressure on the space within the Crown Court complex, made the entrance cluttered and confused. For the Supreme Court, much greater clarity was required.

*Opposite, top:* 19. This architect's section from 1911 shows the original design intent before construction started. A number of vertical ducts were added during construction, beginning the process of closing up the light-wells.

*Opposite, bottom:* 20. The ground-floor plan from the contract set of 1911. It shows the two original courts and an uncluttered front entrance hall. Two garages for motor cars, an innovative feature for the time, are shown top right.

facilities to research and prepare their case. It was also important that the front desk to the court's administrative offices should be near the front door, to speed the process of such litigants' submissions.

## A Front Door

While the Guildhall has a perfectly good front door, the approach to it, the signage around it and the space immediately inside were far from ideal for the new use. The approach had to be both more generous and more accessible to people on foot (of all different abilities). At least one tree needed to be removed to give a clear view of the building. The memorial plaques on either side of the door and the heraldry above it had to be either covered or removed, and the space inside the front door completely redesigned. In particular, the bust of King Edward VII, which had been added at a late stage in the original construction of the Guildhall, restricted and confused the circulation (fig. 18). This fine bust (discussed by Peter Cormack in the previous chapter) was after much discussion relocated to the cafe at the base of the northern light-well. Externally, the main entrance had also to provide an attractive and distinctive backdrop for television and newspaper coverage, as is the case with 10 Downing Street and the Royal Courts of Justice. It is hoped that the front door of the Supreme Court might, in time, achieve the same kind of instant public recognition.

## Security

All courts in the United Kingdom have a public side and a restricted, secure side (similar to landside and airside at an airport), with security checks on entry to the building. The Supreme Court follows this pattern. There is a requirement for baggage search before entry to the public side of the building. This same stringent checking procedure applies to public visitors and to the legal teams using the building (despite some eloquent pleas for a separate entrance and fast-tracking facilities). And so the main entrance had to be large enough for teams to queue at peak times, while accommodating visitors. Paperwork being delivered to the building also has to be checked in securely.

The Justices and staff enter the restricted side of the building directly, at the rear. The separation into public and

restricted areas, enforced internally by the door-lock system, gives a vertical division to the layout of the interior of the building – public side to the front, restricted side to the rear – with the two sides meeting in the courtrooms, where they are separated by the notional bar in front of the Justices' bench.

In its use as a Crown Court, the Middlesex Guildhall not only had a clear separation between public and restricted areas, but also contained custody areas with separate circulation, and jury and witness areas, although not with dedicated circulation. Since it was originally designed as council offices with only two courts attached, and later altered to become a seven-court centre, the interior layout we found when we started work was extremely confused in its circulation and did not meet modern best practice; some aspects, such as the van dock, were incapable of being brought up to the required standard.

In addition to the vertical internal separation into public and restricted sides, there was a growing feeling that the building should also separate into horizontal layers, floor by floor, with the most private areas – the Justices' rooms and the space for their secretaries and legal assistants – at the top of the building, public areas at the lower levels, and the courtrooms and facilities for the legal teams and their clients in the middle.

## Restoring the Clarity of the Original Building

The contract drawings for the construction of the Guildhall in 1911 show the light-wells clear and unencumbered (figs. 19 and 20). When the building first opened, a number of vertical risers and service runs were added, but not enough to prevent daylight reaching the heart of the building.

The conversion to seven Crown Courts in the 1980s continued this incursion by filling the southern light-well entirely with a custody core (transporting prisoners from the cells in the basement to the docks in each courtroom), and the northern light-well partially with jury retiring-rooms and mechanical and electrical service runs and risers. The quality of natural light within the building, already compromised by filling the light-wells, was made worse by net curtains and film on the windows, placed there to mitigate the effects of bomb blast. From our experience at the Treasury near by, we knew what a dramatic improvement could be achieved by

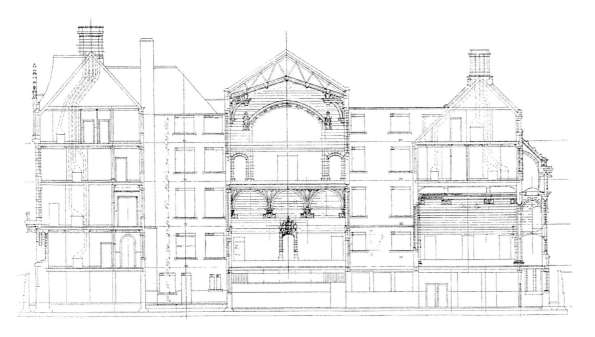

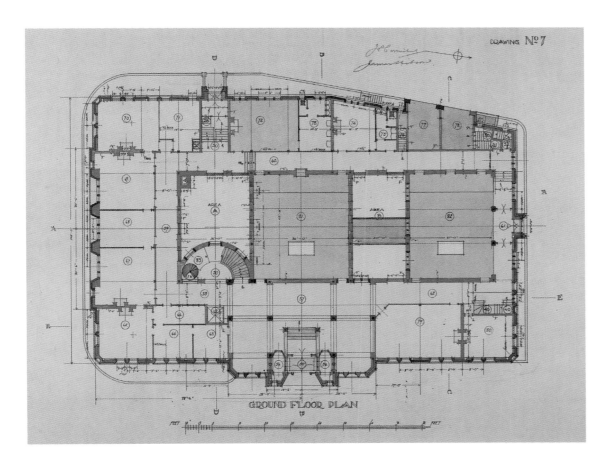

GROUND FLOOR PLAN

DRAWING No 7

removing such alterations and restoring the clarity of the original building, clearing the light-wells and replacing the net curtains with a modern bomb-blast solution. With clarity of plan form and natural daylight restored, finding one's way about is much easier, as we had anticipated it would be. Likewise, this return to something like the original plan and circulation makes all the rooms, not just the principal ones, more attractive.

### Vertical Transportation

Our initial approach had been to use the light-wells for lifts and some vertical risers, continuing the previous pattern of changes to the building. This had been done successfully at the west end of the Treasury renovation. The light-wells in the Guildhall are smaller, however, and a decision was made to place new lifts inside the building and to leave the light-wells clear. Also, all new vertical risers had to be cut through the existing floor plates. This meant greater intervention in the historic fabric. The containment of these risers proved to be more difficult than was expected.

### Explaining the Law and Interpreting the Building

Given that our aim was to encourage the public into the building, some explanation of what the Supreme Court was for and what it did – beyond the simple necessity of stating which cases were being held where – was an integral part of making the process of justice more accessible to a wider public. This was fundamental to the brief from the very beginning of our involvement. It has been achieved by creating a public exhibition space, part of which explains the role of the court and part of which relays hearings. The exhibition space has the capacity for changing or travelling exhibitions as well as for permanent static displays, together with the flexibility to evolve to meet changing educational needs, and to be large enough to take parties of schoolchildren. To mitigate the increased level of intervention in the historic fabric, part of the exhibition is an interpretation and explanation of the building and the history of the site.

### Integrating IT and Broadcasting

The ability to broadcast the court's proceedings was a core requirement enabled in the Constitutional Reform Act 2005. This created a range of additional design challenges, from the

location of equipment to the position of cameras and their interface with the historic fabric. Integrating IT facilities into the Justices' and advocates' benches was also important, even though a paperless courtroom was felt to be far distant. WiFi and other services are also provided within the building.

## The Library as a Body of Knowledge

The schedule of requirements for the Library called for a large shelf run, which could not be fitted into any single room within the building. There were early discussions about whether the library should be digital, but the technology was not felt to be sufficiently robust to do away with books yet, nor were the users prepared to do so. The Library itself contains the body of knowledge that *is* the law, being expanded incrementally by every decision made in the Supreme Court. It would be used by the Justices and their researchers, and its content could generally be divided into a core collection used regularly and a larger section of books and references that would be used less frequently. This allowed much of the book storage to be in dense rolling racks or double shelving, but emphasized the need for the working section of the Library to be easily accessible and to provide a good working environment.

There was a symbolic resonance in placing the Library at the heart of the Supreme Court, and with the original furniture removed, there was an opportunity to enhance the drama of the space. Early ideas revolved around the balance between open shelving and compact rolling-shelf book storage in the basement, and the possibility of reusing the existing dock-stairs aperture to move from one level to another. This resulted in sketches of a central drum stack containing a staircase (fig. 21). As the use of the lower-ground level was opened up from plant and storage to public use, there was less storage space available, and more shelving was needed in the main Library. The earlier ideas were then inverted, by forming a larger floor opening to create a triple-height space surrounded by open shelving, which is double depth in places to provide the required shelf run. Around the perimeter of the new opening the double-depth shelving was kept low in order to form a continuous reading shelf, important for users who tend to browse the shelves looking for references (fig. 22).

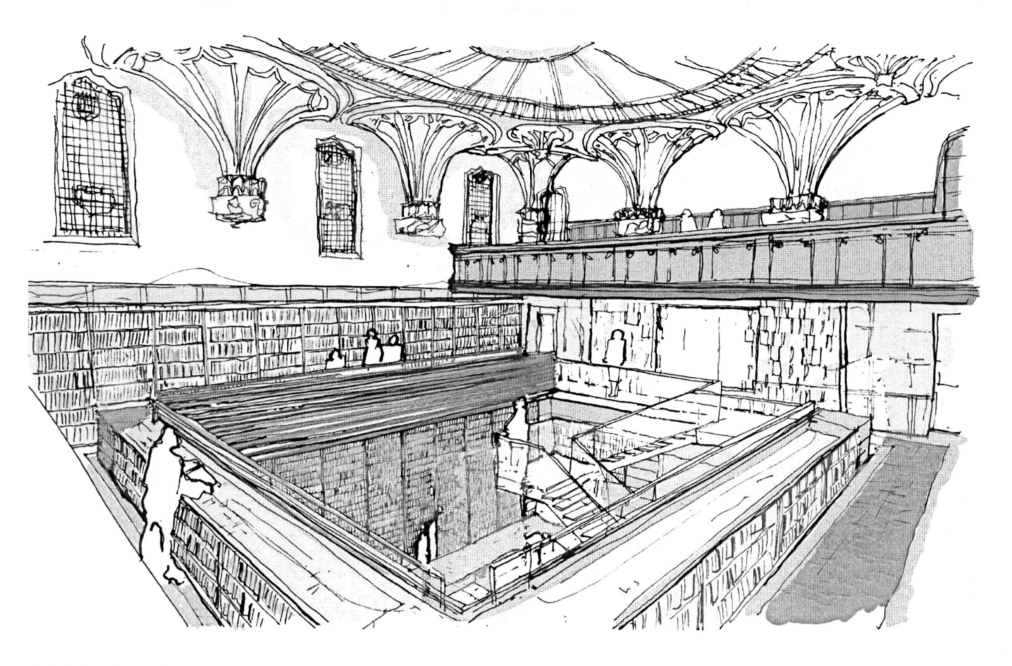

## A Collegiate Atmosphere

The schedule of requirements called for fourteen Justices' rooms, one for each of the Justices and two for visiting or supporting judges. The original intent was to fit them all on to one floor, in order to create a collegiate atmosphere in this most private area of the building, but that could not be done. The Justices, with their secretaries and legal researchers, could be fitted over two floors, the researchers sharing space with the law reporters who prepare the official reports of the court's judgments. The Justices would also have a sitting-room and a dining-room, so that they could entertain guests to formal lunches or dinners, although the catering on site would be limited to a cafe, open to staff and the public.

## Facilities for the Legal Teams

The workshops held to discuss the evolving scheme soon identified that the provision in the original space schedule for the legal teams presenting to the court needed to be

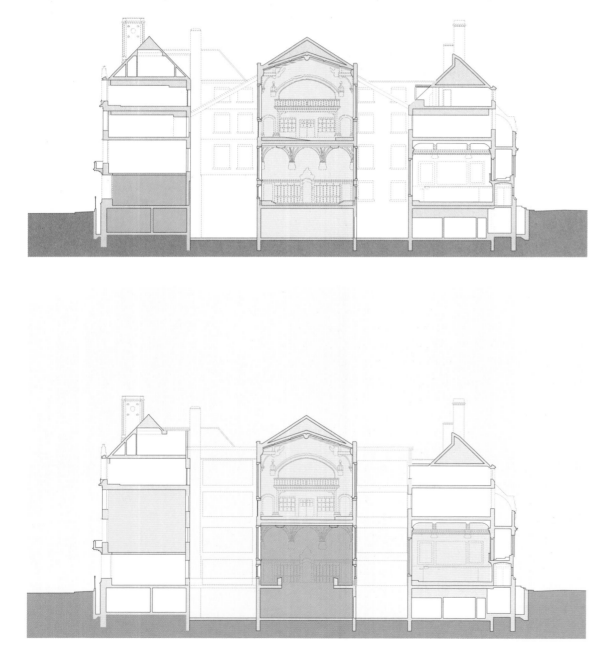

increased significantly to be effective. A much larger general lawyers' room was provided, with Internet access so that lawyers attending the court, usually senior in the profession, could keep in touch with their offices. Associated with this space were robing-rooms, and conference rooms that could provide a secure and private base for the teams and clients attending a hearing. This was felt to be particularly important for lawyers coming from Scotland, Northern Ireland and other parts of the world for cases heard in the JCPC. The lawyers' room also had to house the Scottish advocates' library, which was not part of the main legal library, but was provided by the Scottish legal profession for their members' use.

**Integrated Art and Crafts to Match the Original**
The existing Guildhall has extravagant, inventive Gothic detailing, displaying high levels of craftsmanship. The works of renovation and alteration to the Guildhall to create the new Supreme Court had to match the quality of the original, but using modern art and craftsmanship. The Middlesex Guildhall Collection (owned by the Middlesex Guildhall Collection Trust), which generally predates the building, would be retained, restored during the renovation and rehung. This decision left little room for new paintings, so new artwork was integrated into the design of the interiors.

**A New Approach to the Historic Building**
The above concepts were developed and refined in step with the brief, and as this happened it became clear to me that the conservative approach to the reuse of the building that had guided our initial ideas would have to be challenged. An early, and very bold, idea from Foster+Partners was to put the main public entrance underground, replacing Canning Green to create a long ramp down to the level of the Guildhall. This would have allowed as much room as was necessary for security facilities, which could have been placed outside the existing building, and would also have allowed for a separate fast-track entrance for legal teams through the existing front door. This concept also led to the idea of stacking the three courts in the centre of the building, starting on the lower-ground floor and ending with the former Council Chamber on the second and third floors (fig. 24). Unfortunately, this approach was very costly, and, perhaps

more to the point, would have introduced too much uncertainty into the project programme. More time would have been needed to acquire the land and relocate the statues of either Abraham Lincoln or George Canning or both, assuming that a new location for these listed sculptures could even be agreed – no small task given that the City Council has identified this and the wider area as a 'Public Sculpture Saturation Zone' in its local plan (with a consequent presumption against any new monuments around Parliament Square). At this point, in light of the emerging new requirements, the overall project timetable was extended by one year to 2009. This effectively removed management pressure to preserve as much of the building as possible to reduce construction time.

The thinking behind the ramp idea did, however, lead to a different approach to the use of the basement, now renamed the lower-ground floor, which was previously allocated to plant and support facilities. The new concept diagram also changed our approach to the use of the two light-wells, and I saw the advantages of opening them right down to lower-ground-floor level, as had originally been intended. This led us to place the cafe at lower-ground level in the northern light-well, and an enlarged exhibition space alongside. We also decided to remove the proposed lifts from the light-wells and to reuse the existing shafts plus one new lift near the restricted entrance for staff, although this eventually led to a less elegant solution for integrating the vertical risers.

More fundamental was the decision to locate the Library in the ground-floor Court 1, and move the new 'modern' courtroom to the south side of the building. This part of the building had been completely rebuilt internally in the 1980s, and offered most scope for the significant alteration that would be required to create a new double-height courtroom. We also considered other, more radical, interventions, including widening the front entrance space, reinforcing the main entrance axis from the front doors to what was now to be the Library by creating a window opposite the front doors, enlarging the existing dock stairwell in the Library to improve connection to the lower-ground floor below, and replacing corridor windows and walls alongside the light-wells with floor-to-ceiling glass (fig. 25).

Simultaneously, we were receiving more detailed survey information on the state of the existing building, and discussing this more radical approach with English Heritage

and the planning department of Westminster City Council. These creative discussions defined a conceptual envelope of what might be possible, having regard to all circumstances, and enabled us to identify which aspects of the proposals would be controversial. The most difficult issue emerging was how to justify radical intervention, in particular the need to remove the historic court layout and furniture to create the courtrooms required for the Supreme Court and the new Library. This indeed turned out to be the most contentious part of the works, ultimately leading the Victorian Society and SAVE Britain's Heritage to mount a legal challenge in the High Court against Westminster City Council's decision to issue the necessary listed building consent.

**Refining the Design**

By early 2006 the design was rapidly coming together, pushed forward by rigorous analysis of the primary concept. At the suggestion of Lord Mance and Lady Hale, who were concerned about the noise and distraction of traffic passing very close to the ground-floor windows on the southern side, what became the new Courtroom 2 was moved up from the ground floor to the first floor, behind the existing balcony. This shielded the room most effectively from traffic noise and provided visual privacy. The reinforced-concrete structure – dating from the 1980s – in the southern wing was capable of losing a floor to create, through the judicious insertion of structural steelwork, a double-height space. This new structure also increased the carrying capacity of the attic floor, allowing more and heavier plant to be placed there, and consequently freeing up space on the lower-ground floor.

The initial approach to the Library, of forming a central bookstack around an enlarged existing aperture, was turned inside out, so as to create a large central floor void surrounded by a reading gallery with open bookshelves at both ground- and lower-ground-floor levels (fig. 26). This has opened up the former courtroom as a triple-height space and allows a much better view of its ornate decorative ceiling. The size of the proposed window from the front entrance to the Library expanded and contracted as its benefits and limitations were ironed out, but eventually this opening became a glass door inscribed with a facsimile of Magna Carta. The solution was arrived at in response to a new element of the brief, which was the need for an occasional ceremonial route into the building

24. North–south section sketch scheme, with underground ramp. This early scheme proposed bringing the public into the building via a ramp under Canning Green, and stacking the three courts vertically in the centre of the building. But the basement court would have had too low a ceiling, and there was no effective use for Court 2 on the north side of the ground floor.

25. The north–south section scheme at planning stage. The courts are all double-height, on three different floor levels, with the 'modern' court inserted into the area that was rebuilt in the 1980s. The light-wells are open down to the basement and glazed over at roof level. To improve daylight and clarity within the building, new windows are shown inserted into the west walls of the light-wells. The Library is central and triple-height.

from the front door, through the glass screen dividing the
entrance hall, and into the Library. This idea influenced
the layout of the redesigned front entrance, and later the
treatment of the area outside the front door to the building.

Once we had decided to move the new courtroom up a
floor, there was now room to put the administrative offices and
their front desks on the ground floor of the south side. This in
turn allowed for the whole of the front of the building at first-
floor level to be redesigned as an extended suite of rooms for
the legal teams, with conference rooms on the corners, robing-
rooms and lavatories in the interval, and a large common room
in the centre of the building.

The rooms for the Justices and their support staff were
spread over the second and third floors, with plant above them
in an enlarged roof space. The light-wells were enclosed by
glazing them over with blast-resistant glass, avoiding the need
to protect or encapsulate the stained-glass windows in the
Library, the new Courtroom 1 and the associated waiting-
areas. The plant platform on top of the main semicircular
staircase was removed, leaving room for a private terrace at a
high level for the Justices to use as an informal meeting-space.

The bases of the light-wells, being protected from the
weather, could be used as the public cafe on the north side
and as a Justices' reading and research gallery and librarian's
office on the south side.

Externally, little had to be done to the building apart
from cleaning and repairing the stonework and adding security
cameras. The approach to the main entrance off Parliament
Square was to be improved by closing Little George Street
to vehicular traffic and raising the former road surface to
pavement level in order to create a much larger pedestrian
space at the front of the building. The potential removal of the
tree blocking the view to Parliament Square and of external
lighting was left until World Squares for All proposals were
completed. Likewise, the provision of external physical
security measures was left until the central Whitehall security
area upgrade was resolved.

### Planning Approval and Listed Building Consent

The UK has a comprehensive system regulating physical
changes to buildings and to their uses. Running in parallel to
this normal planning regime is another that deals specifically
with changes to nationally protected or 'listed' historic
buildings, of which the Middlesex Guildhall is one, identified
at Grade II* in the national list, a designation applying only
to the top 5 or 6 per cent of all officially protected historic
buildings. The extensive discussion we had with both
Westminster City Council and English Heritage over a two-
year period to explore and refine design proposals is fairly
typical when dealing with listed buildings that are undergoing
significant changes. And so the submission of applications
for planning, conservation area and listed building consents
to Westminster City Council in June 2006 was a significant
milestone for the project. Prior to the applications being
lodged, a public exhibition was held over three days in the
Royal Institution of Chartered Surveyors building next door.
The response from those who attended was generally positive,
but we knew that we had vociferous opponents who believed
that we were seeking to change too much, in particular the
original courtroom furniture we were proposing to remove.
Nonetheless, removal of the historic court furniture was
fundamental to the successful operation of the Court.

Of course, we met the objectors to explain the scheme
and our rationale. Our argument was, simply, that the
international cultural significance of the creation of the UKSC
outweighed the national cultural significance of the historic
fabric that would be altered, displaced or lost. A lot of
misinformation was circulating, in particular that Middlesex

Guildhall had a long-term future as a Crown Court Centre. This was demonstrably untrue, because of insuperable limitations it presented for the handling and transfer of prisoners – conditions found in no other London Crown Court. These problems were especially pertinent for a building located in an area with such sensitive security issues. Despite our lengthy discussions, the objection to the removal of the original layout and furniture in the ground-floor courts and in the former Council Chamber remained. The general solution adopted in consultation with English Heritage was to move the furniture from the original courts to another London Crown Court. We agreed, however, to adapt the furniture in the former Council Chamber for reuse in Courtroom 1, keeping as much of it as possible, not only on site but also in the room where it had originally been (fig. 27).

After much discussion and refinement of detail, and a packed Planning Committee meeting with last-minute submissions from the objectors, planning permission, conservation area consent and listed building consent were granted unanimously by Westminster City Council, subject to a long list of conditions and a legal agreement or planning obligation – often called a section 106 agreement after its statutory provision. This contractual agreement is between an applicant for planning permission – as it was then, the DCA – and the relevant planning authority. One of the conditions required the provision of a published record of the building, and this book was conceived in part to discharge this particular stipulation.

Otherwise the planning conditions were standard. The key elements of the section 106 agreement associated with the planning consent that needed addressing by the design team were the requirements for the conservation and rehanging of the Middlesex Guildhall Collection and the provision of public art. The DCA also agreed to contribute to the cost of public works proposed by Westminster City Council at the junction of Broad Sanctuary and Little George Street.

While the section 106 obligations were financially significant, the listed building consent conditions had a potentially more serious effect on the programme, in that a number of them were so-called 'precedent' conditions, which would have to be cleared *before* any of the approved development could be started. This is not unusual in listed building consents, but in this case we sensed that the particular stringency and extent of the conditions reflected the sensitivity and controversy surrounding the proposals, and so we continued to develop the design and detailing to satisfy the conditions before construction started. The critical areas were the detailed design of the Library, the front entrance, the final design of the new windows to the light-wells, and the agreement of precise proposals for the future use of the historic furniture from the old courts and Council Chamber.

Detailed study of the furniture and original contract documents for the building showed that the court furniture had been designed and supplied by H.H. Martyn & Co. of Cheltenham, and, although ornate, was not exceptional for the period. The Council Chamber furniture supplied by Wylie & Lochhead of Glasgow incorporated sculpture and reliefs by Henry Fehr (1867–1940), who had designed all the other sculpture inside and outside the building, and was of greater significance. (Peter Cormack discusses the decorative arts of the building in the previous chapter.) The solution agreed with English Heritage and Westminster City Council was to relocate the original court furniture to another London Crown Court (eventually agreed to be the Snaresbrook Crown Court Centre) and to retain as much as possible of the remaining Council Chamber furniture, even where that meant adapting it, as demonstrated in the reuse of the carved bench-ends retained within what would become the principal courtroom. Furniture

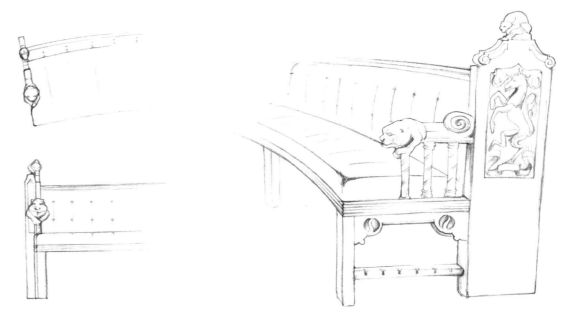

*Below:* 28. A computer-generated image of the front entrance, exploring the integration of artwork into the security screen.

*Below, right:* 29. Following discussions about ceremonial occasions, what was to have been a window into the Library became a pair of glass doors that are etched with a facsimile of Magna Carta.

*Opposite, top:* 30. The emblem of the United Kingdom Supreme Court is used in a number of ways around the building, especially on glass screens, windows and window blinds.

*Opposite, bottom:* 31. The new carpet, designed by Peter Blake. Three background colours were chosen for use, variously, in public areas, the courts, and the areas restricted to the Justices. The colours were chosen to complement existing shades in the building, such as the green wall tiles.

designer Luke Hughes was brought in to advise on the practicality of this approach, and the proposals were agreed.

Still, we had determined opponents, and at the end of the three-month period within which a planning consent may be challenged, SAVE (together with the Victorian Society) applied for a judicial review of the planning and listed building consents on the grounds that Westminster City Council had not properly considered the advice contained in national planning policy guidance on the historic environment (PPG15). This was, frankly, a traumatic time for us all. We saw it as a test of the arguments we had put forward in preparing the applications, in particular that the cultural significance of the Supreme Court could outweigh the impact on the historic fabric of the building that was to house the court, although in fact the challenge was made on a technical procedural point. The hearing was held in the High Court on 26 March 2007, and judgment delivered shortly afterwards, rejecting the arguments put forward by SAVE and the Victorian Society, and in the process clarifying aspects of the law as it applies to historic buildings and associated guidance. Although the Judicial Review was

primarily concerned with whether the correct process had been followed, there was a certain satisfaction to be gained from the fact that the decision to grant listed building consent for the Supreme Court had been considered at the highest level and had in itself led to a clarification of the law. Thus the Supreme Court achieved one of its objectives before it was even built.

### Interiors and Integrated Artwork

For some time prior to the planning applications a team from Feilden+Mawson had been developing an art strategy and an interior-design package, working with an Art Panel chaired by Lady Hale. The panel's strategy was accepted by Westminster City Council and incorporated into the section 106 agreement. Following the agreed strategy, the panel decided how new artwork could be incorporated into the fabric of the building. Their vision was for a ceremonial route from outside, through the front doors, across the entrance hall and into the Library through the new central doorway. There had to be a glass screen across the entrance hall (fig. 28), to separate those who had gone

through the security scanner from those who had not. There were to be glass doors into the Library (fig. 29), and another glass screen isolating the entrance to Courtroom 2 on the southern side. All these were to be treated as works of art. The Library itself presented another opportunity to enhance the stairway down to the lower-ground floor and the balustrade surrounding the newly opened-up space on the ground floor. Bettina Furnée was commissioned to design the decorations for the glass screens and doors, and Richard Kindersley to decorate the Library.

An additional requirement of the Constitutional Reform Act 2005 was the design of an official emblem (fig. 30). It was felt that this might also be used as the Court's heraldic badge. Yvonne Holton, the Scottish herald painter, was commissioned to design this. She devised a lively composition of plants representing each of the four nations within the United Kingdom, encased in the sign for Libra, the scales, which also happens to be the letter Omega, the final letter in the Greek alphabet, symbolizing the final court of appeal. This emblem and elements of it have been used in numerous manifestations throughout the building. The four plants also appear in stylized form in the vibrant new carpets that Sir Peter Blake was commissioned to design for the building (fig. 31).

By using art to enhance the fabric of the building, it was possible to fulfil the section 106 agreement. The panel suffered one disappointment, however. It had hoped to improve the appearance of the outside of the building by installing four standing stones to represent the four nations within the jurisdiction of the Supreme Court. It became clear to us that such a radical idea in such a sensitive spot would not have the support of either Westminster City Council or English Heritage. Our other ideas, based on landscaped benches, had a better reception and were approved.

## Procurement and Delivery

At the beginning of the project the procurement route for the construction was undecided. The route chosen is known in the construction industry as PDS, which stands for Private Developer Scheme and is sometimes described as 'lease and lease back'. The purpose of such an arrangement is to pass the design risk to the contractor, who takes on all design responsibility and associated risk after planning approvals, working with a new design team. The Ministry

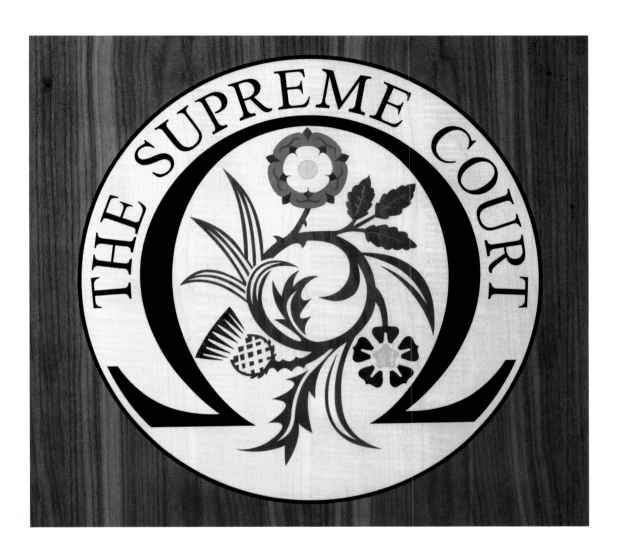

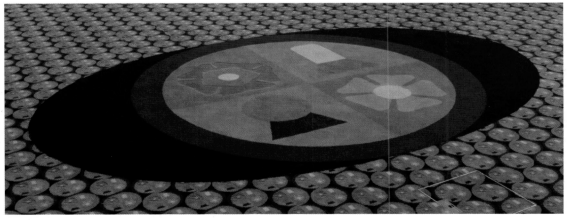

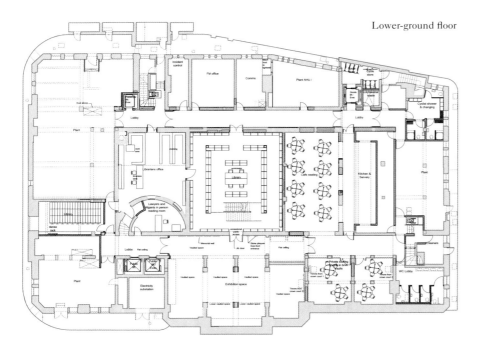

Lower-ground floor

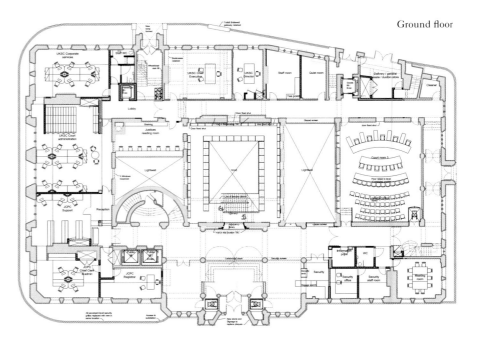

Ground floor

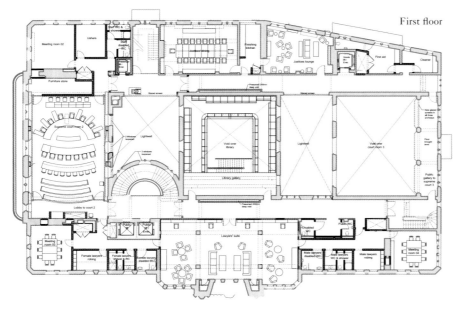

First floor

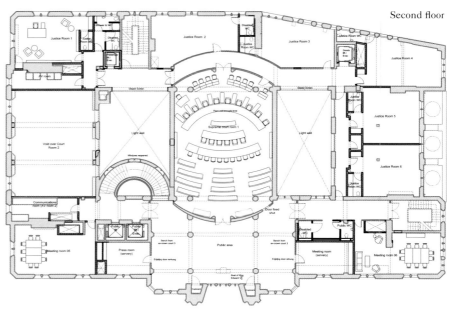

Second floor

32 (a)–(e) Plans of the scheme, as approved by Westminster City Council.

*Opposite:* 33. Her Majesty Queen Elizabeth II unveiling the bronze portrait relief of her at the opening ceremony for the Supreme Court of the United Kingdom on 16 October 2009.

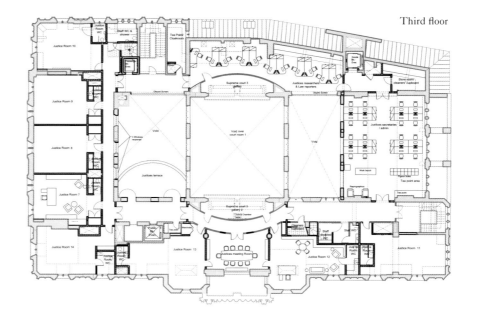

Third floor

of Justice (formerly the DCA) programme team retained Feilden+Mawson, the original design team, to ensure the quality of the end result (figs. 32 (a)–(e)). The plans approved by Westminster City Council formed the basis for the contract with the developer.

The project had to be advertised through the Official Journal of the European Union (OJEU). The process resulted in a shortlist of developers and then a preferred bidder, which was Kier, with Wallis as its contractors and Gilmore Hankey Kirke as its architects. This team was appointed, and work started on site in June 2007. My practice remained as technical advisers to the Ministry of Justice, continuing design work on the interiors, furniture and art packages, reviewing the developer's team's proposals and helping to discharge the outstanding planning and listed building consent conditions. Direct works (such as signage), the work for the Middlesex Guildhall Collection, and the IT systems were managed outside the building contract, and a selection process for the designers of the exhibition space led to the appointment of Easy Tiger Creative.

The developer's team took responsibility for the delivery of the construction project from start on site to the handover of a usable building, including discharge of many of the planning and listed building conditions still outstanding. This could be time-consuming, as each submission, unless agreed by Westminster City Council to be capable of being dealt with by exchange of letter, went through the full planning and listed building determination process, taking a minimum of eight weeks even when decisions were handled by officers with delegated authority. There was added pressure because failure to comply with the terms of a listed building consent is potentially a strict criminal liability, and there is no such thing as retrospective listed building consent. No one wanted the new court to be accused of being guilty of a criminal offence.

There were the usual unexpected discoveries as the building works progressed, such as the extent to which the roof steelwork had rusted at eaves level and at the top of the tower where the original design had been changed, probably during construction, and steels inserted across the corners to carry the turrets. This led to additional work, but the team managed to accommodate it within the timetable.

And so it was, amid a flurry of paperwork concluding the planning and listed building conditions consents, that the former Guildhall building was handed back to the Ministry of Justice on 18 March 2009, on programme to the day.

There then followed a period of commissioning and running-in of the building systems, and dealing with minor defects, while the Middlesex Guildhall Collection, art from the JCPC and other furniture were brought to the building, and the new furniture installed. In May 2009 the Law Lords confirmed their contentment with what had been delivered. The building was formally handed over to the court in July, allowing the new organization three months to set up and prepare for the start of the new legal year, which from time immemorial has begun on 1 October. The formal opening by Her Majesty The Queen took place on 16 October 2009 (fig. 33).

34. The curved stone seating integrates security provision and creates a generous space in front of the court's main entrance.

*Opposite:* 35. The main entrance is now much more visible. Its newly cleaned façade reveals the lively quality of Henry Fehr's carvings.

## External Security

At the planning stage the security risk to the Supreme Court building was assessed as being similar to the risk to the Royal Courts of Justice, and so no additional security measures outside the building were thought necessary. While the general severity of the threat did not change during the construction period, its perceived nature, however, did. This led to a requirement for an external perimeter of vehicle-blocking bollards, which were being installed around other government buildings in the area. Given the lack of room around the Guildhall, there was space only for a line of bollards at the edge of the pavement. But at the front of the building there was room to do something more creative. Outside the main entrance, security has been achieved by building a semicircle of stone-clad benches facing the front doors. I designed these to match the detailing designed by Wornum elsewhere in Parliament Square (fig. 34). The poem specially written for the Supreme Court by the then Poet Laureate, Andrew Motion, is carved into the seat backs. This creates a positive and welcoming space in front of the main entrance, and has also allowed a complete re-laying of the pavements on a simple pattern – elaborate paving designs having been rejected. Another important benefit was the removal of the superfluous plane tree, opening up the view of the front of the building. Newly cleaned, this façade now presents itself clearly towards Parliament Square, balancing St Margaret's Church, as was originally intended (fig. 35).

## Assessing the Results

At the time of writing, it is still not possible to say exactly whether the hours spent designing and discussing the proposals will really deliver as I hoped they would. In truth, only time will tell how well the building works for the people it is intended to serve – principally the court users, the staff and the Supreme Court Justices, but also the general public who are interested in how the Supreme Court decides points of law that are of importance to the people. But some of the key architectural ideas can already be judged.

The reintroduction of natural light to the interior of the building has worked very well. Clearance of the light-wells and removal of net curtains have restored the quality of daylight evident in early photographs, and this has made it much easier to find one's way about. The full-height glazing of the corridors to the light-wells on the west side has had a dramatic effect, particularly at attic level (fig. 36). A deep clean of the building's fabric, together with coherent signage, also helps.

The entrance hall has lost its clutter and confusion, and now feels bright and spacious (fig. 37). Moving the bust of King Edward VII was the right thing to do, and its new location in the northern light-well displays it to advantage. The relocation of the Middlesex Regiment War Memorial to the south side of the entrance has also worked well.

The ground-floor administrative areas have been combined into one suite of office space, improving openness and flexibility. The legal teams' suite on the first floor is among the most impressive of the newly created rooms in the building and should live up to expectations (fig. 38).

The Justices' rooms have suffered more than most from the need to provide air-handling equipment throughout the building, with lower ceilings inserted to carry the ductwork and equipment rather than relying on natural ventilation; this has led to some awkward angles and corners in a few rooms. But each of the rooms has its own individual character, with plenty of space for books and enough extra room for small meetings, so it is hoped that the Justices will soon feel at home (fig. 39). When working with an old building, however, there will always be such compromises. The compensation comes from breathing new life into the building, and ensuring that it will be handed on to the next generation.

A key space is the new Library. Opening up the former court by one floor has enhanced the observer's appreciation of the elaborate ceiling, which is now seen to even greater advantage, with all the intended drama. Through its simplicity, the shelving enhances the original detailing of the courtroom, which can now be appreciated, including the sculpted portraits of those who contributed to the original building. The space has also been considerably enhanced by the removal of the suspended light-fittings of the 1980s and the repositioning of all artificial light on to furniture and out of the principal volume (fig. 41).

The progression of inscribed glass screens, which starts in the front entrance and continues into the Library with texts chosen by the Law Lords and becoming pithier as the observer moves farther into the building, has worked well. The law is expressed in words, and the use of words within the integrated artwork is apposite. The final panel of illuminated glass on the Library balcony is most effective (fig. 40).

40. The Library well, viewed from the basement. The inscriptions on the balcony are intended as gentle reminders to Library users.

*Opposite:* 41. In the Library, the original ceiling has been cleaned and relit, to great dramatic effect.

*Opposite:* 42. Courtroom 3, showing the view towards the Justices' bench.

43. Courtroom 2. This view from the public entrance shows the contrasting feel of the modern court.

A striking feature of the original building was the green-and-blue ceramic tiling that lines the corridors and staircases. These tiles did not show to their best advantage when teamed with dull institutional carpets and paint on the walls above them. Now they are matched by Sir Peter Blake's striking carpet design, which brings out the best in the tiles. The two together make the corridors and staircases bright and welcoming.

The three courtrooms have achieved the individuality required. Courtroom 3, on the ground floor, was probably best observed originally from the bench. Bringing the floor up to that level uniformly has improved the sense of the space for all other users (fig. 42). Otherwise, it is the least

altered of the major historic rooms, retaining original light-fittings and the fine Reynolds portrait of Hugh Percy (when still Earl of Northumberland) in its original position. Courtroom 2, on the first floor, created by the removal of one floor, is unmistakably modern, with clean, uncluttered lines and strong natural light; it is surprisingly quiet given its location next to Broad Sanctuary. The illuminated stylized emblem of the Supreme Court, which hangs above the Justices' bench, gives direction and containment to the space without being overbearing (fig. 43). Courtroom 1, on the second floor in the old Council Chamber, has benefited most from the opening up of the light-wells to restore daylight. This, together with internal cleaning, has transformed a dark

44. Courtroom 1, designed to seat
up to nine Justices in the area below
the balcony.

space into an open and uncluttered one (fig. 44). The reused
furniture looks very fine and shows that modern craftsmen
can match the standards and quality of earlier generations.
Relamping the historic light-fittings in Courtrooms 1 and 3
has also helped, and all three courtrooms benefit from the
new carpets.

I feel that the loss of historic fabric through renovation
and reconfiguration to the new use is more than offset by the
long-term beneficial use that the building now has, and I am
confident that the strategic conservation goals have been
achieved. The cheerful spirit created by Henry Fehr's work,
having been dulled down by the alterations of the 1980s,
is now evident again, in both the old and the new work.
Overall, the most successful aspect of the scheme is the
generous level of natural light, as the architect James Gibson
(1861–1951) originally intended. It improves the clarity of
the building and makes it easier to use. This enhanced
lighting, taken together with the new decorative art, is true
to the exuberant spirit of Fehr's original carvings. Looked at
as a whole, then, I believe the special interest of the historic
Guildhall has been preserved, and the building uplifted and
given a new use that is far more significant than the original.

# SUPREME AND HIGH COURT ARCHITECTURE IN THE COMMON-LAW TRADITION: AN INTERNATIONAL PERSPECTIVE

G. A. BREMNER

'It seems to be a thoroughly British sentiment that our Courts of Justice shall always surpass all other structures in durability, ... firm set on their foundations and built four-square to all the winds that blow ...'

Sir Frederick Lugard, Governor of Hong Kong (1912)

*Previous page:* 1. The United States Supreme Court, Washington, DC (1929–35). A marble temple designed by Cass Gilbert.

2. Final design of the Hong Kong Supreme Court (*c.* 1900) by Aston Webb and E. Ingress Bell.

3. Plan of the Hong Kong Supreme Court, showing the simple, geometrically proportioned layout based on a series of intersecting rectangular spaces that culminate in the central or 'large' court space situated beneath the dome.

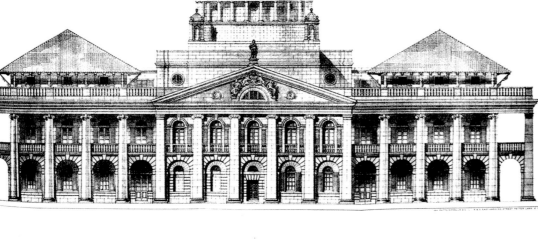

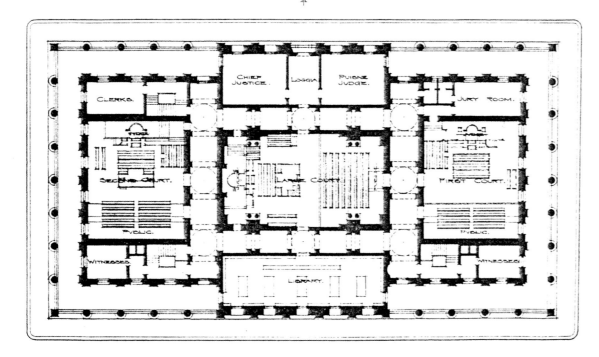

As we commemorate the creation of the UK Supreme Court (UKSC), it is worth reflecting on how the common-law system (of which this court now represents the apogee) was exported and given monumental form in Supreme and High Court buildings abroad. It is surprising perhaps that in this process many of Britain's former colonies managed to establish higher courts before the United Kingdom.

Architecture has played a distinguished role over the years in symbolizing ideas of law and justice. A 'good' or 'bad' court building can make all the difference to the way the law is perceived and respected in any given context. This is the lesson one might take from looking at how the notion of justice has been fabricated in court architecture through the ages. If a court of law could not administer justice practically, then it at least had to look as though it could in theory. In this respect, there has not always been a happy correspondence between the image conveyed by court buildings and the decisions taken within them.

This chapter will consider a selection of High and Supreme Court buildings from around the world. These buildings have been chosen primarily for the way in which they capture and represent ideas relating to common-law practice over the past two centuries, and how this practice has been transformed or adapted in the face of social and political change. I will look at the broad shift in the symbolism of court architecture from age-old concepts of order and authority, through such notions as identity and independence, to ideas of transparency, openness and accountability. In creating a new Supreme Court for the United Kingdom, the project team had to find a way to express these several concepts within the constraints of a historic building, alterations to which were carefully regulated and themselves subject to administrative and legal processes.

### 'Temples of Justice': Classical Architecture and the Majesty of the Law

If there is one style or 'language' of architecture that has a particularly close relationship with the law it is classicism. The classical language of architecture, at least since the Renaissance, has come to symbolize order, stability and tradition. Even in ancient times, through its association with important public and religious institutions, classicism was seen to embody the gravitas and decorum essential to the expression of civic virtue. Despite the myriad transformations and permutations that the classical language of architecture has undergone since, it has never entirely lost this ability to stand for and communicate authority.

With the rise of the British Empire came an equivalent enlargement in the sphere of common-law practice and its variants. Like the ancient Romans before them, the British were keen to carry and reproduce their social, cultural and political institutions wherever their empire took them. One building that epitomizes the relationship between classical architecture and the extension of the common-law tradition abroad is the Hong Kong Supreme Court, designed by

Sir Aston Webb (1849–1930) and E. Ingress Bell (1837–1914) in about 1900 (fig. 2). Located in one of Britain's most geographically isolated and politically tenuous colonies of the nineteenth century, this building was imagined from the very beginning as an unflinching statement of British colonial rule. Despite the frequent injustices under British law in Hong Kong, the new court was understood to signify something noble in the minds of the colony's governing elite, capturing in the self-assured mass of its form the rule of law as the principal cornerstone of British imperial government.[1]

But the Hong Kong Supreme Court was no ordinary work of classical architecture. It was an intelligent and knowing amalgam of many late seventeenth- and early eighteenth-century English sources, ranging from the architecture of Sir Christopher Wren, John Webb and Nicholas Hawksmoor, and after them Sir John Vanbrugh, Colen Campbell and William Kent. Indeed, as Webb and Bell themselves made clear, the building's dome was to echo that of Wren's great masterpiece in London, St Paul's Cathedral.

Webb and Bell's decision to adopt a specifically English, as opposed to French or Italian, style of classicism was significant. It was a style (later referred to as 'Edwardian Baroque') that was seen to have distinct national and imperial connotations.[2] Owing to its late seventeenth-century origins, architects saw this style as corresponding with the rise 'of that Greater Britain which has come to be such a factor in the civilization of the world'. According to this logic, the buildings of Wren and others suddenly became 'the national style, – the vernacular of the country … a living, working, architectural reality, as much a part of England as its literature or its great school of painting.'[3] Thus, in designing their building in this particular style, the architects of the Hong Kong Supreme Court were seeking to assert imperial authority and the rule of law in a culturally specific and identifiable way (fig. 3). In this sense, British architects of the period, such as J.M. Brydon (1840–1901, author of the passages above and architect of the Government Buildings near to the Guildhall, on one side of Parliament Square), sought to draw direct parallels between late seventeenth- and late nineteenth-century British history. The age of Wren, it was believed, was a period of unity, prosperity and unfettered expansion much like their own.

Webb and Bell were not the only architects who considered a modern version of English Baroque classicism appropriate for court buildings. Edward Mountford (1855–1908) also adopted it in his design for the Central Criminal Court (Old Bailey) in London (1900–06; fig. 4), and flashes of it appear in buildings as late as the Supreme Court in Singapore (1936–39; fig. 5), designed by Frank Dorrington Ward. At the Old Bailey, however, Mountford drew inspiration not from St Paul's Cathedral but from that other masterwork by Wren, the Royal Naval Hospital at Greenwich.

Themes of identity and empire were also a factor in the selection of the site for the Hong Kong Supreme Court. The land was reclaimed from Victoria Harbour as part of the Praya Reclamation Scheme in 1895. Owned by the Hongkong and Shanghai Banking Corporation (HSBC), the immediate area was envisaged as a public garden and referred to as Royal Square (later Statue Square) after a memorial to Queen Victoria's Golden Jubilee was unveiled there in 1896 (fig. 6). Directly to the east of this site were the grounds of the Hong Kong Cricket Club, and to the south City Hall and the original HSBC headquarters building (1886). In time, other socially eminent institutions, such as the Hongkong Club, relocated to this site.

*Below, left:* 4. The Edwardian Baroque splendour of Edward Mountford's Central Criminal Court (Old Bailey), London (1900–1906).

*Below:* 5. The Supreme Court, Singapore (1936–39), by Frank Dorrington Ward.

At the unveiling of the queen's statue in May 1896, a prominent local resident and businessman, Catchick P. Chater (1846–1926), observed that, even after the colony's most familiar names had vanished and been forgotten, the statue would 'remain to impress upon those who follow us the rights and privileges which, under British laws, they will ever enjoy'.[4] Here Chater drew on the eternal appeal of self-determination afforded under British law. In so doing, he was attempting to invest the site, indeed, the whole city, with a distinct aura of British liberal and constitutional idealism. In this sense, when the new Supreme Court took its place among the other distinguished piles on the site, it was entering a space that had already been characterized by a particularly 'British' idea of justice.

A more explicit association linking the law, identity and architecture was made at the ceremony for the laying of the Supreme Court's foundation stone in 1903. The then governor of Hong Kong, Sir Henry Arthur Blake, sought to remind those present of the authority by which British colonial rule had been built and maintained. Making direct reference to the architectural character of the building, Blake emphasized its symbolic power by observing how, 'with its lofty dome', the new court would be 'a fitting and proper temple for the pure, impartial and incorruptible administration' of British law.[5] These sentiments were reiterated nine years later upon the building's completion. At the opening ceremony in 1912, Sir Frederick Lugard (1858–1945), who had succeeded Blake

as the colony's governor, noted that, although it had taken long to build and had cost a great deal of money, the new court 'in [its] massive granite walls and pillars … stand[s] unrivalled in the Far East'. 'It seems to be a thoroughly British sentiment that our Courts of Justice shall always surpass all other structures in durability,' he added, 'firm set on their foundations and built four-square to all the winds that blow, as an outward symbol perhaps of the Justice which shall stand firm though the skies fall, and which we take pride in associating with the British flag. … It is a grand conception – it is the conception on which the British Empire has been built.'[6]

Thus architecture is transformed into a universal truth: the classic and enduring monumentality of the new Supreme Court building was a corollary to the indissoluble tenets of British law and liberty. In the context of empire, this was clearly understood to have wider historic significance. The language of architecture from which the building was composed and the legal system that was administered within its walls were both influenced in various ways by the empire of ancient Rome. With the capacity for architecture to bear meaning across time and space in this way, the Hong Kong Supreme Court would remain as testimony, it was believed, to the achievement and righteousness of British and, indeed, European civilization in Asia.

One of the earliest and finest evocations of this self-conscious, Neoclassical tradition in court architecture, and one from which Webb and Bell no doubt drew inspiration, is the Four Courts building in Dublin (1786–1802; fig. 7). This structure, designed by James Gandon (1743–1823), was originally the seat of the Lord Chancellor and Lord Chief Justice of Ireland under British rule, and today houses the Supreme and High Courts of the Republic of Ireland. Like the Hong Kong Supreme Court, Gandon's Four Courts is distinguished by a grand and stoic demeanour. Its prime riverfront position on the Liffey, just along from that other great masterwork by Gandon, the Dublin Customs House, amplifies the commanding presence of the architecture and, with it, the political power of the colonial authority.

It had long been the ambition of the civic authorities in Dublin to furnish the city with a more stately and commodious form of administrative architecture. By the 1750s the time was right to reclaim the buildings in and around the Inns Quay from 'prostitutes and thieves', and to erect in their place an

government based in Dublin Castle.[8] High-minded officials viewed architecture and urban 'improvement' as one of the most effective means of expressing the benefits of imperial union, both economically and artistically. The rule of law, and the security of a constitution, were central to this ideology of supposed benign domination. Thus, the Four Courts, with its sentinel-like dome peering across the Dublin skyline, reflected not only ideas of prosperity, civilization and the dignity of state brought by union, but also, and more specifically, the political authority of Westminster.

As a work of monumental public architecture, Gandon's Four Courts had its reverberations abroad too. One was the Supreme Court building in Melbourne (1873–84; fig. 8). With the discovery of gold in the colony of Victoria in 1851 came considerable wealth and, in turn, a substantial increase in the magnificence of Melbourne's architecture. For many years, however, the effects of this prosperity eluded the colony's principal legal institution. It was not until the early 1870s that the decision was finally taken by the government to consider a new, purpose-built facility to house the Supreme Court. Amid much controversy over a corrupt competition process, the commission was finally awarded to Alfred Louis Smith (c. 1830–1907; with A.E. Johnson) for a classically inspired, 'modern Italian' structure containing eight courtrooms over two storeys, capped with an imposing colonnaded dome. In form at least, this dome is modelled on Gandon's exemplar in Dublin. Such a reference would

*Above:* 7. The Four Courts, Dublin (1786–1802), by James Gandon.

*Right:* 8. The Supreme Court, Melbourne, Australia (1873–84), by Alfred Louis Smith (with A.E. Johnson). The building's dome is modelled on Gandon's Four Courts in Dublin (above).

imposing 'Suit [*sic*] of Buildings' for public convenience.[7] Although originally planned as public offices, by the 1780s this project came to include what was described at the time as a 'Hall of Justice' – the building that would eventually become Gandon's Four Courts. Again, as with the Hong Kong Supreme Court, the scale and magnificence of this building must be understood in the wider context of British colonial policy in Dublin and its relationship to the idea of civic improvement.

Landmark buildings in Dublin, such as the Royal Exchange, the Customs House and the Four Courts, were public projects commissioned against the backdrop of local politics and as such intended as symbols of Unionist sentiment. They were paid for by the government in Westminster through the agency of an administrative

probably have seemed odd in the public architecture of a British colony at this time were it not for the fact that many of the prominent figures in the Melbourne legal establishment were immigrants from Dublin and thus influenced the design.[9]

From the beginning the Supreme Court in Victoria enjoyed exceptionally wide powers. The Act of Establishment of 1852 defined its jurisdiction at common law as equivalent to the three principal courts in London.[10] Not coincidentally, the site for the new court was located at the western end of Melbourne, one of the highest points in the city and where most lawyers had their chambers. When completed in 1884, the building, with its prominent dome, was the tallest and most visible architectural landmark in Melbourne – a fitting accomplishment, perhaps, for an institution that was the embodiment of the rights and freedoms of a fledgling society soon to achieve its independence.

In the United States of America we see something different. There the classical tradition in architecture had accrued its own set of associations after that nation's independence from Britain in the late eighteenth century. Rather than representing ideas of order, regularity, power and

empire, classicism in America came to signify such notions as freedom, rationality, modernity and the equal rights of man. It was in no way to be associated with the tyranny and authoritarian rule of imperial Rome, but instead with the virtue of republican Rome and the liberty of ancient Greece, then imagined to be the birthplace of representative democracy.[11] In this sense, the new American nation imagined itself as youthful, idealistic and hopeful, unencumbered by the prejudices of the Old World. It was to be the beacon and future of humanity, and its state architecture was to reflect this, including buildings constructed to administer the law.

We see this idealism first emerge through the towering figure of Thomas Jefferson (1743–1826) and his design for the Capitol building in Richmond, Virginia (1785; fig. 9). Ironically, Jefferson modelled this building on the Maison Carrée at Nîmes, which he described as 'the most beautiful and precious morsel of architecture left to us by antiquity'. The fact that it was a prime example of Roman imperial architecture did not seem to matter, for Jefferson understood it as a work of republican genius.[12] Notwithstanding this inherent contradiction, in using such a model as the basis for the first civic building of the new United States of America, Jefferson was attempting, in his own words, to 'improve the taste of my countrymen, to increase their reputation, [and] to reconcile to them the respect of the world'. In so doing, Jefferson gave what might otherwise have been a generic idiom a specifically national expression.[13]

It was from this tradition that the design for the first permanent US Supreme Court drew inspiration. Although the commission was initially given to Henry Bacon, architect of the Lincoln Memorial (1922), it eventually fell to Cass Gilbert (1859–1934), an architect who had made his name designing such dignified public buildings as the Minnesota State Capitol in St Paul (1895–1905) and the United States Custom House in New York City (1899–1907). Gilbert's design was nothing if not grand, and it is hardly surprising, given the building's magnitude and significance, that he described it as the 'most important and notable' work of his career.

At first glance the US Supreme Court appears like the Parthenon with wings (fig. 10). Its main entrance portico, comprising sixteen fluted Corinthian columns of glistening white Vermont marble, is on such a scale that upon passing through it for the first time Chief Justice Harlan Stone wryly

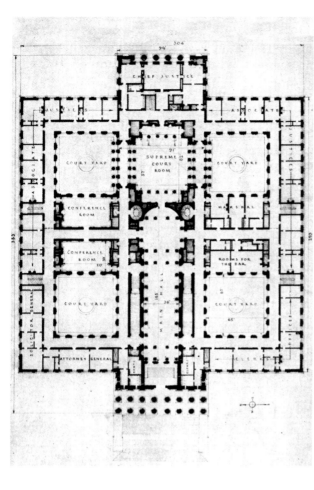

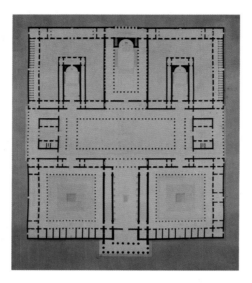

*Left:* 11. Plan of the US Supreme Court.

*Below:* 12. Henri Labrouste's Prix de Rome plan for the Cour de Cassation, Paris (1824).

*Bottom:* 13. The stark and monumental interior of the Entrance Hall at the US Supreme Court.

remarked that he felt like 'a beetle entering the Temple of Karnak'.[14] As with the Lincoln Memorial, the use of white marble was intended to reflect the Supreme Court's purity and clarity of purpose as the third and co-equal branch of government, at the same time symbolizing the irreproachable ideals of the Union.[15]

Indeed, one cannot help identifying the grand, projecting temple front of the US Supreme Court with that of Jefferson's original Capitol building in Virginia, the initial home of the administration of that Union (see p. 180). Such an exemplar must have been on Gilbert's mind when considering how he might capture the primacy of the American judicial system in built form – it had, after all, housed what was known as the General Court Room of the Commonwealth of Virginia for more than fifty years. In plan the new Supreme Court was no less grandiose (fig. 11). Gilbert's layout was based in part on the famous Beaux Arts architect Henri Labrouste's (1801–1875) Prix de Rome project for the Cour de Cassation of 1824 (fig. 12). As in Labrouste's design, Gilbert's plan comprises a large square block with a projecting temple front and a major hallway connecting the entrance lobby to the main courtroom.[16] Like the exterior of the building, the lobby or 'hall', as it is known, shimmers with polished marble surfaces in a monumental neo-Greek idiom, as though it were the *cella* or *sanctum sanctorum* of a grand pagan temple (fig. 13).

Such a space has special significance in the context of the US Constitution. The lobbies of American courthouses were supposed to play a similar role to that of the Hall of the People in the US Capitol. They were intended as gathering-places – grand waiting-rooms – where attorneys could meet informally with their clients, or where the 'citizenry' could access the machinery of justice through the symbolic gesture of openness and inclusion that such spaces conveyed.[17]

But at the US Supreme Court this idea is taken to an extreme. Its severe grandeur tends to leave an unnerving rather than agreeable impression upon the minds of those who visit. In trying to express the central role of the law in the federal constitution of the United States, the building borders on the imperious. This is something the Chief Justices themselves sensed when it was finally completed in October 1935. Justice Stone observed that it was 'bombastically pretentious' and therefore 'wholly inappropriate for a quiet group of old boys'. Another Justice sardonically remarked: 'What are we supposed

14. The Royal Courts of Justice, the Strand, London (1866–82), by George Edmund Street.

15. Medieval sections of the Palais de Justice, Paris (the old Royal Palace).

to do, ride in on nine elephants?'[18] It was not all irony, however. In later years certain amenities were added for the well-being and amusement of the staff, including a basketball court on the top floor – a facility affectionately referred to as 'the highest court in the land'.

Despite initial misgivings over the architectural magnificence of the US Supreme Court, the building has now taken its place among the other, equally imposing monuments that comprise the government sector of Washington, DC. Indeed, the building's grandiloquence was in a way a fitting reflection of the political status that the once modest republic had achieved by the early twentieth century. In this sense, the US Supreme Court is not so far removed from the Hong Kong Supreme Court in expressing notions of power and authority over and above its primary function as a court of law. Its position in a wider symbolic landscape was likewise inseparable from the idea of the District as a 'new Rome' at the centre of a burgeoning economic (and territorial) empire.[19]

## A Gothic Interlude: Cultural Identity and the Search for Authenticity

The classical tradition in court architecture did not go unchallenged. By the mid-nineteenth century new stylistic trends were beginning to emerge in the world of architecture, especially in Britain. This was the time of the Gothic Revival, a movement championed by such luminaries as A.W.N. Pugin and John Ruskin, who sought to give modern British architecture a moral dimension on the basis that Gothic was a truthful style, expressing honestly its methods and materials of construction. It was also the time of the 'Battle of the Styles', a debate that pitted the proponents of classical and of Gothic architecture against one another in an effort to identify an appropriate style for modern society.[20]

Perhaps the most distinguished building erected in this style is a short distance from Parliament Square, the Royal Courts of Justice by G.E. Street (1824–1881; fig. 14). Completed in 1882, sixteen years in the making, and looking like some great, sprawling medieval palace, this impressive structure provided London with an equivalent to the Palais de Justice in Paris – the latter being a genuine medieval precinct in the heart of the city, and one that to this day houses the Cour de Cassation, the highest court in France (fig. 15).

Although the influence of the Gothic Revival was beginning to wane by the time the Royal Courts of Justice were completed, the project presented a creditable case that court architecture could be in a style other than classical.

One factor leading to the rise of the Gothic Revival in secular architecture was its supposed national credentials. Gothic architecture was generally considered among younger members of the architectural profession in Britain at the time to be an indigenous and therefore a more authentic style of architecture. It was a style that, despite its Continental origins, was understood to reflect the characteristics of a particular place, and a style that could be traced back to the origins of English culture with its tradition of individual liberty protected by the common law. There was, to be sure, a certain romance to reviving Gothic architecture. Nevertheless, these associations seemed to fit naturally with the image of the law as a historical product that had evolved over centuries.[21] And so, once established as a legitimate national style, it was not long before the Gothic Revival began influencing the design of court buildings outside the United Kingdom, particularly in its colonial dominions.

The earliest examples of this type in the former empire are in New Zealand and Canada. The old Supreme Court in Auckland (1865–68) by Edward Rumsey (1824–1909) is a good if modest exemplar of the idiom (fig. 16). A pupil of the prolific Sir George Gilbert Scott (1811–1878), Rumsey emigrated to New Zealand via Melbourne in the early 1860s. Not surprisingly, his design for the Supreme Court bears more than a passing resemblance to aspects of Scott's original (but unexecuted) design for the new Government Offices in Whitehall (1857), a design that was seen by many as heralding a new age of secular Gothic in Britain.[22]

It was a similar story in Ottawa, where the Supreme Court building (1874; demolished) designed by Frederick J. Alexander (1849–1930) was nestled among what is perhaps the grandest and most visionary array of civic Gothic buildings on one site anywhere in the world (fig. 17). Although a rather modest affair like Rumsey's (it was originally a construction-site workshop), Alexander's building was still very much part of that wider conception for Parliament Hill later described by the Canadian poet and historian William Campbell (1861–1918) as revealing 'to us [the French and British peoples of Canada] not only universal beauty and inspiration', but also symbolizing 'our common ideal, … our common ancestry, and our common Christianity' (fig. 18).[23]

This new taste for the Gothic style in court architecture also made its way to India. High Court buildings in Calcutta, Bombay, Madras, Hyderabad and Lahore (now Pakistan) all adopted this style in one form or another (figs. 19 and 20). Indeed, the Gothic, with its pointed-arch construction, had a natural affinity with the Mughal architecture of India, and offered the opportunity to create a uniquely synthetic style (the 'Indo-Saracenic') by blending aspects of European rational planning and medieval architecture with elements from local traditions. The results of this cross-fertilization were often spectacular, achieving a degree of splendour – to the point of ostentation – considered essential by some British officials in commanding the majesty and authority of the law.[24]

This search for national-origin myths, represented by the Gothic Revival, survived into the twentieth century. The current Supreme Court of Canada is a curious case in point (fig. 21). Designed by Ernest Cormier (1885–1980) in 1938, this building appears at first glance to be a severe take on the 'Château-Baronial' manner that had become popular in Canada

by the late nineteenth century. This style of architecture came to be associated with the identity of Canada's first colonial settlers and administrators (the French and Scots). The Château-Baronial style was an offshoot or variant of the Gothic Revival in its romantic and culturally inspired imagery, and by the early twentieth century, with the completion of the Confederation Building in Ottawa in 1927, had received a national seal of approval from the federal government.[25] In adopting a heavy, abstract version of this style, the Supreme Court of Canada, perched high above the Ottawa River like a medieval citadel, was not only making a statement about the authority and independence of the judiciary, but also reinforcing the idea of architecture as a vehicle for the expression of cultural identity.

## Modernism and Transparency: Court Architecture in the Late Twentieth Century

With the rejection of historical styles in the twentieth century, the language and meaning of court architecture changed significantly. This transformation was accompanied by the dismantling of Britain's global empire and the independence of its former colonies. By the mid-twentieth century, court architecture had begun to abandon images associated with authority, permanence and grandeur for those suggesting openness, access and transparency. These characteristics and associations had previously been present, sometimes explicitly, sometimes not, in the imagery of earlier court buildings, especially in post-independence America. But by the 1950s the tables had turned decidedly in favour of openness and transparency, and these values continue to inform ideas of representation in court architecture to this day.

Among the earliest and best-known examples of this Modernist trend in court architecture are the High Court of Punjab and Haryana, Chandigarh, India, designed in 1951 by Le Corbusier (1887–1965), and the High Court of Australia, Canberra (1975–80), by Colin Madigan (born 1921) of the firm Edwards Madigan Torzillo & Briggs.

At Chandigarh, Le Corbusier was given free rein to plan and develop a new capitol precinct for the government and administration of the Indian Punjab. A new city was necessary after British withdrawal from India and Partition in 1947, which left Lahore – the old administrative centre of the Punjab – on the Pakistan side of the border. Apart from an Assembly (Parliament), a Secretariat and a Governor's Palace, the only other piece of administrative machinery required for this new city was a High Court. Le Corbusier's arrangement of buildings reflects to some extent their constitutional role, with the Governor's Palace (not built) at its head, followed by the Assembly and the High Court buildings facing each other across the main public space, and the Secretariat off to one side (fig. 22).

Although the layout of greater Chandigarh was based on the Congrès International de l'Architecture Moderne (CIAM) Athens Charter of 1933 (in which planned cities were to be divided into separate zones for work, dwelling, administration and recreation), the monumental scale and composition of the new precinct that Le Corbusier designed look more towards the heroic scale of Sir Edwin Lutyens's (1869–1944) designs for New Delhi, particularly his magisterial Viceroy's House (1912–31).[26] At the same time, the High Court at Chandigarh is a calculated response to the prevailing climate and the architectural traditions of the region, especially the masterworks of the great Mughal emperors to be found in Delhi, Agra and Fatehpur Sikri, although these earlier sources may not be evident at first glance.

As built between 1951 and 1958, the High Court of Punjab and Haryana is essentially a concrete box with open sides (fig. 23). Its dominant feature is the vaulted roof, which hangs over the building like a giant upturned parasol. This element was intended, among other things, to convey the 'shelter, majesty and power of the law'. It also alludes to modern technology in the form of an aeroplane wing, and harks back to Le Corbusier's earlier ruminations on such ancient Roman structures as the Basilica Constantine. But its most immediate parallel is to be found in the classic Diwan-I-Am, or public audience hall, that formed part of the ancient Mughal palaces at Delhi and Agra.[27] Le Corbusier's skilled synthesis of these images and associations in the architecture of the High Court gave the building the necessary cultural and technological connotations that reflected Jawaharlal Nehru's (1889–1964) vision for Chandigarh as 'the first large expression of our creative genius, founded on our newly earned freedom'. Here the architecture of the law becomes a generalized symbol of a new nation, not of the law in particular.

Nehru's notion of 'freedom' (democracy) was articulated by Le Corbusier through the idea of transparency. The expression of this idea begins with the building's plan, in

*Below, left:* 22. Plan of the capitol precinct, Chandigarh, India (1956), showing the relationship of key civic institutions.

*Below:* 23. The High Court of Punjab and Haryana, Chandigarh, India (1951–58), by Le Corbusier.

*Opposite, top:* 24. Plan of the High Court of Punjab and Haryana, showing the internal relationship of the courtrooms.

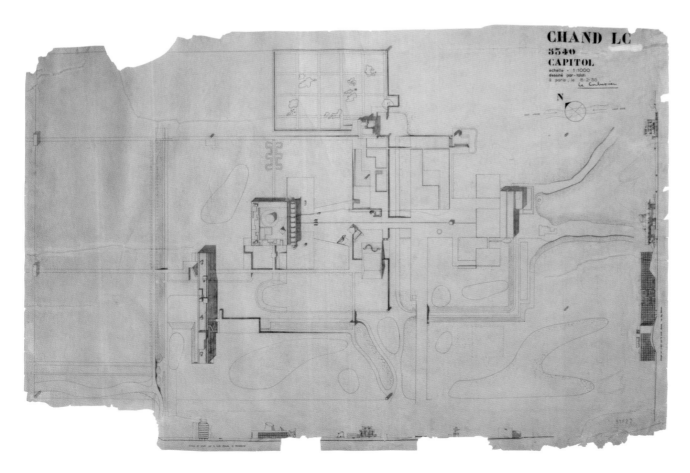

which the main internal spaces are arranged in a clear and rational way (fig. 24). Immediately to the left of the main-entrance concourse is the largest of the courtrooms, the Supreme Court itself; to the right are the eight minor courtrooms, positioned one after another in phalanx-like succession. The genius of this design is the way in which the internal arrangement of spaces is so clearly reflected on the exterior of the building. As one approaches the court, the most prominent feature is the entrance – unmistakable in its gaping yawn and teeth-like columns in primary colours. The location, scale and number of courtrooms within then emerge through a subtle interplay of visual cues evident in the main structural components of the building, and through a technique of spatial layering that gives order to these elements.

The architectural device that affects this layering is the *brise-soleil* screen, draped across the front of the building like a great perforated curtain (fig. 25). This screen is not only permeable (spatially and visually) but also divided by a series of vertical and horizontal elements that correspond with the basic dimensions of the principal spaces inside. The formal arrangement is repeated farther back by the main structural columns that rise up through the building, terminating with the dramatically sculpted arches of the parasol, each of which runs the full width of the building and corresponds to the main spaces.

What one ends up with in the architecture of the High Court at Chandigarh is not so much literal transparency,

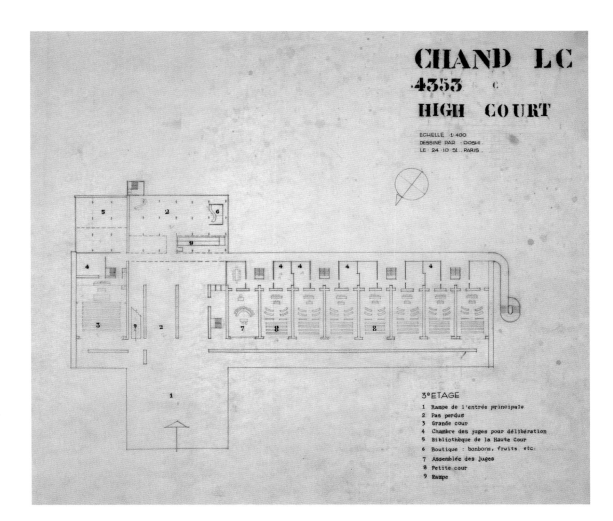

CHAND LC
·4353     c
HIGH COURT

ECHELLE  1:400
DESSINE PAR · DOSHI
LE  24·10·51 . PARIS .

3°ETAGE

1  Rampe de l'entrée principale
2  Pas perdus
3  Grande cour
4  Chambre des juges pour délibération
5  Bibliothèque de la Haute Cour
6  Boutique : bonbons, fruits. etc.
7  Assemblée des juges
8  Petite cour
9  Rampe

although there is obviously some element of that, but an
architecture that reveals itself completely through the clear
expression of the building's internal spaces on the exterior.
This has been likened to a Cubist montage of overlapping
planes and surfaces, which enables certain components of
the architecture to come forward or recede according to one's
perspective or proximity.[28] The resulting tension between
inside and out – the surfaces and their attendant spaces
appear to abut, intersect and slide past one another under
the intense Punjabi sun – was appropriate for the emerging
modern state of India.

The High Court of Australia is also a building conceived
for a planned urban context, and like its counterpart in
Chandigarh, its architecture makes little sense divorced from
its position in the wider masterplan for Canberra. Designed
by Walter Burley Griffin (1876–1937) in 1912, the plan for
Australia's capital city is an unusual combination of informal
Garden City principles and formal, Baroque axial vistas. As a
consequence, the urban scale of Canberra is vast, with grand
avenues and wide open spaces separating many of the city's
major buildings over kilometres (fig. 26). The result is a low-
lying, dispersed and heavily vegetated city – described by
some as a 'city in the bush'. In such an environment the
form and texture of a building are easily lost as they compete
with the stark chiaroscuro effects of the Australian sunlight
playing off the manmade lake and expanses of native flora.
Here, mass and colour are crucial, hence the massive,
clean-cut external modelling of the High Court in off-white
concrete (fig. 27).[29]

The court itself was established under the Australian
Constitution (section 71), which was drafted in preparation
for independence and the formation of the Commonwealth
of Australia in 1901. The appointment of the first bench,
however, had to await passage of the Judiciary Act in 1903.
The High Court of Australia is the final court of appeal for
both federal and state cases.

Despite the extent of its jurisdiction, the High Court did
not require a building with a particularly large or complex
programme. Apart from an ample public concourse, the
building houses only three courtrooms, chambers for seven
Justices, a main registry, a library and corporate services
facilities. It is nonetheless an important building symbolically,
for prior to its inauguration the bench of the High Court had to

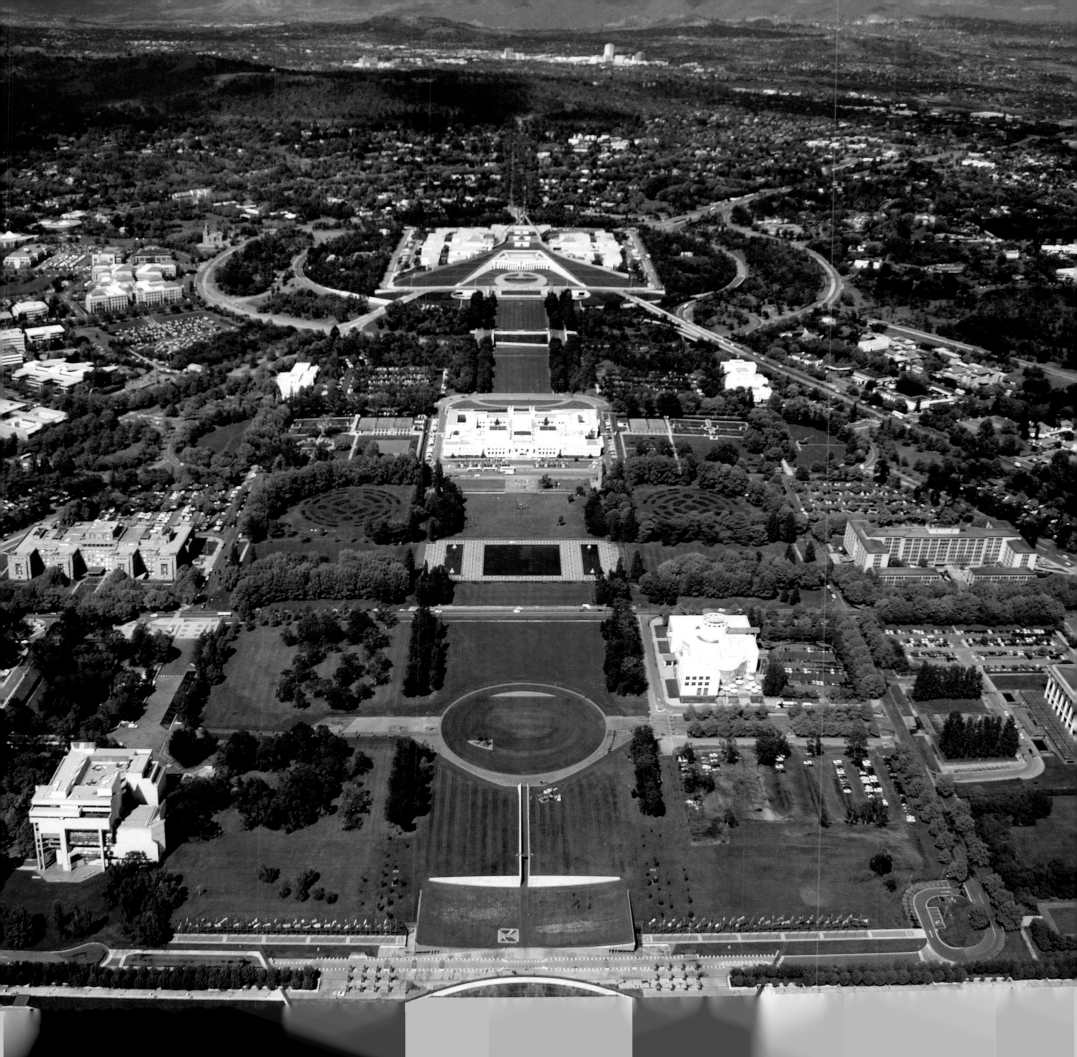

27. The High Court of Australia, Canberra (1975–80), by Colin Madigan of Edwards Madigan Torzillo & Briggs.

*Opposite, left:* 28. The steel-trussed glass wall on the ceremonial front of the High Court of Australia allows light to penetrate deep inside the building.

*Opposite, right:* 29. The light and open space of the main entrance foyer in the High Court of Australia.

travel on circuit to individual states. With the completion of the new building in 1980, the High Court finally found a permanent home in the heart of the nation's capital, within the so-called 'Parliamentary Triangle'. In this respect, the location of the High Court in relation to corresponding institutions of Australian government, such as Parliament House, is similar to that of other planned cities, including Washington, DC, Chandigarh and even Brasília.[30]

Although the architecture of the High Court of Australia appears somewhat overbearing from the outside, it is fundamentally a building of light and space. Its vigorous external massing is essentially a response to the brief, which insisted that it impart 'a sense of strength and security'. The main entrance, facing away from Lake Burley Griffin, comprises a giant glass wall that enables those approaching to see deep inside the building (fig. 28). The main public hall is expansive, rising some 24 metres (79 feet) to a deeply coffered ceiling supported by two slender concrete columns. This is an exhilarating space. It creates a sense of openness and continuity that, in conjunction with the main stair and *promenade architecturale* linking the first four levels, visually connects the main components of the building, including the three courtrooms (fig. 29). The daylight that penetrates emphasizes the clean, crisp lines of the architecture, conveying a sense of clinical efficiency. All is illuminated and nothing hidden from view.

Although the High Court of Australia makes use of large, unframed glazing, allowing for high levels of visibility and light, more recent court buildings have taken the idea of transparency and its associations even further. A case in point is the new Commonwealth Law Courts complex in Melbourne (1995–99), designed by Paul Katsieris of Hassell Architects (fig. 30). Located a stone's throw from the classically inspired Supreme Court (mentioned above), this building incorporates courtroom facilities and office space for the High Court Registry, the Australian Federal Court and the Family Court. It is a seventeen-storey, L-shaped building, divided in two by a generous atrium space rising nine storeys and extending the length of an entire city block (figs. 31 (a) and (b)). The atrium represents one of the main design initiatives of the court, intended, as its architect noted, to capture not only a sense of reciprocal visibility (outside–in and *vice versa*), but also the grandeur and poise associated with the expanse of the Australian interior.[31]

Indeed, ideas of 'light' and 'accessibility' abound in this building. Chief Justice Michael E.J. Black has observed that the original stakeholders of the project wished to have a building that would, through its physical presence, reflect 'the place of law in a free society'. It was hoped that the building would make the law open to the scrutiny of all citizens – both functionally and figuratively – and in this way ensure the justice system is accountable to the people it serves.[32] The material qualities of the building are intended to communicate the condition and responsibilities of the law in a free, democratic state. This association between freedom and the law is expressed tangibly in the etching of words from chapter 3 of the Constitution on parts of the building's glass façade. These words cast shadows across the bodies of people entering the court, reminding them of their legal rights.

Similar ideas form the inspiration for the new Supreme Court of New Zealand, Wellington (2006), by the firm Warren and Mahoney (fig. 32). This building, currently under construction, is particularly interesting for the way it incorporates the existing fabric of the old Supreme Court, a classical building erected in 1881 but vacated and closed in 1993. The new complex thus palpably represents continuity and change, a dialectic that is an essential attribute of any common-law system. The principal element of the design is the orb-shaped central courtroom, encased in what is

essentially a glass box protected by a monumental bronze screen depicting in abstract form the branches and leaves of native New Zealand trees. In an attempt to 'encourage an atmosphere of inclusiveness', the activities of the court will be visible from outside.

This idea is one that originated in what is perhaps the most impressive of new court buildings in recent years, the Constitutional Court of South Africa in Johannesburg (2001–2004; fig. 33). Designed by the firms OMM Design Workshop and Urban Solutions, this building is no less remarkable for the dramatic transformation in South African society that led to its creation than for the unique and emotive symbolism of its architecture.

In a response to the changed political circumstances under which South Africa's new Constitution was formed, one of the main objectives of the court was to capture the idea of 'unity in diversity' underpinning the new South Africa. The ideas that were most salient in the conception and realization of this building, however, were those of equality and human rights. At the court's official opening on 21 March 2004 – South African Human Rights Day – the then President of South Africa, Thabo Mbeki, observed that the building would be, above all, 'a shining beacon of hope for the protection of human rights and the advancement of human liberty and dignity'. On entering it, the visitor can see inscribed on the lintel above the main door the words

*Opposite, left:* 30. The Commonwealth Law Courts, Melbourne, Australia (1995–99), by Paul Katsieris of Hassell Architects.

*Opposite, right, top and bottom:* 31 (a) and (b). The main atrium of the Commonwealth Law Courts, Melbourne.

32. Design for the new Supreme Court of New Zealand, Wellington (2006), by Warren and Mahoney.

33. The Constitutional Court of South Africa, Johannesburg (2001–2004), by OMM Design Workshop and Urban Solutions.

'human dignity, freedom, equality' in the hand of each of the Justices who were incumbent during the time that the court was being built.

The social and political upheavals that led to the creation of the Constitutional Court of South Africa called for a particularly complex iconographic programme. The question for those involved in the building's design was not only *who* and *what* should be represented but also *how*. This presented a difficult challenge. Acknowledging the altered political condition of South Africa after 1994 was one thing; trying to come up with an equally radical and suitable form of architecture to match was another. Anything too traditional or monumental ran the risk of being interpreted as perpetuating the past. Something modish ran the risk of trivializing the Constitution itself. On this point, Justice Albie Sachs observed that it was important that the new building be 'gentle rather than imposing; inviting rather than forbidding; entrancing rather than monumental; human rather than austere'. As a result, it is full of symbolism expressing the past, present and future of South Africa and its politics. The angled piers in the foyer signify trees under which indigenous Africans traditionally administered justice (fig. 34). The main doors are carved with the twenty-seven human rights enshrined in the Constitution in the official languages of South Africa, including Braille and sign language (fig. 35).

The starting point for the brief was the all-important idea of reconciliation and the corollary of that, the notion of redemptive justice. This idea was given full and powerful expression by erecting the court on the site of the old Johannesburg Fort, a complex of buildings that housed the infamous Number Four 'native' prison in which numerous political detainees and leading anti-apartheid activists were incarcerated during the apartheid era. The new court building incorporates elements of these prison buildings, including 150,000 bricks from those sections that were demolished. This gesture was a reminder of the iniquities of the past, and expressed the metaphor of rebuilding that had enabled a new beginning for South Africa after the Truth and Reconciliation Commission.

Those parts of the building that incorporate these fragments include the 'Great African Steps' leading up to the court, and the dry-packed brick wall directly behind the judges' podium. Similar to what will appear in the Supreme Court of New Zealand when complete, a ribbon window was cut into this wall at ground level, revealing the feet and legs of the public as they walk past outside (fig. 36). This device not only enables the public to see proceedings, but also reminds the judges of the presence of the people whose liberty they are bound to respect through the rule of law, thus representing, in the words of Justice Sachs, 'a non-racial, non-sexist universe – from thigh to ankle at any rate'.[33]

In its own way the new UK Supreme Court is a building that straddles these different approaches to court architecture. Like the New Zealand Supreme Court, it incorporates the fabric of an existing historic building; like those precedents in the Gothic Revival style of the mid- to late nineteenth century (of which it is a late example), it suggests something about the history and traditions of Britain; and like so many new court buildings of the late twentieth and twenty-first centuries, it attempts to express notions of openness, transparency and accountability. It even conveys in the solidity of its exterior an air of that stability and grandeur normally associated with classicism. In these ways it is no less a fitting symbol of the process of constitutional reform in Britain, and the law's place within it, than other new court buildings.

# EPILOGUE: MEMORIES OF THE MIDDLESEX GUILDHALL AS A CRIMINAL COURT, 1968–2007

FABYAN EVANS

*When it was proposed in 2003 that the Guildhall should cease to be used as a Criminal Court in order to provide premises for the United Kingdom Supreme Court, this was met with some incredulity …*

I first passed through the front door of Middlesex Guildhall with my pupil master, Neil Denison, in 1968. In common with many who have done so, I was surprised to learn that there was a criminal court located in Parliament Square. The charm of this part of Westminster is enhanced by the retention of institutions, including schools and churches, that have local rather than national functions, and Middlesex Guildhall made a valuable contribution to them (fig. 2).

At that time the criminal jurisdiction of Greater London had been divided into five sessions areas, and the Guildhall housed the Middlesex Quarter Sessions, which covered north-west London, an area that roughly corresponded to the old county of Middlesex. The process of 'gaol delivery' had formerly required the court to hold a session once a quarter in order to ensure that all who were awaiting trial for offences triable by a jury were brought to justice within a reasonable time. These sessions had previously very often been completed in a matter of days, but this had long since ceased to be possible. By 1968 the jurisdiction of the court included the rapidly developing Heathrow Airport, and the lists were never cleared by the end of the quarter, even though many

crimes that would be tried at Crown Court level today, such as wounding with intent, had to be committed to the permanent assizes at the Central Criminal Court.

The building still retained all the trappings of a county guildhall. The two courtrooms on the ground floor remained as they were when first built, and the former Council Chamber, still with electronic voting panels that resembled the sort of equipment seen in Edwardian servants' quarters, was used as a permanent third court on the second floor (figs. 3 and 5 (a) and (b)). Two committee rooms, with splendid views over Parliament Square and towards the west door of Westminster Abbey, were also pressed into service as courtrooms when the need arose (fig. 4). Prisoners, many of whom had to be handcuffed to a prison officer, were escorted around the carpeted corridors, and were bemused to find that the dock consisted of a ladder-back chair in front of a polished mahogany table with a direct view of the Palace of Westminster and the clock tower containing Big Ben. Many defendants sitting in the dock of Court 2 were totally unaware that the portrait of Hugh Percy, painted while he was the Earl of Northumberland, which was hanging behind them and

*Above, left:* 3. The chairman's throne in the old Council Chamber. The throne has since been relocated to one of the galleries overlooking the principal courtroom of the Supreme Court, Courtroom 1.

*Above, centre:* 4. One of the two committee rooms that were used as courtrooms, showing the room laid out for that purpose, prior to the building's recent conversion.

*Above, right, top and bottom:* 5 (a) and (b). The voting panel and individual electric buttons in the old Council Chamber used by the Middlesex County Councillors.

remains in the same place today, was by Sir Joshua Reynolds (1723–1792) and worth a fortune (fig. 6). Up to the closure of the court, judges had the privilege of lunching in the Judges' Mess in the presence of another magnificent portrait of Percy – who had by then become a duke – by Thomas Gainsborough (1727–1788; see fig. 6, p. 15). This painting can now be seen hanging in the new Library. The building is probably unique in housing two portraits of the same man by these two great artists.

The chairman and permanent deputy chairmen of the sessions had similar status to County Court judges. They dressed in wigs and black court dress and were addressed as 'My Lord' as opposed to 'Sir', the title that was normally used to address judges in the rest of the country who would sit unrobed at Quarter Sessions. This was an anomaly that had arisen many years before, when a chairman of London Sessions had also been a peer of the realm.

In 1968 the chairman of Middlesex Sessions was Ewen Montagu QC (1901–1985; fig. 7), who had achieved national fame when he recorded in his book *The Man Who Never Was* (1953) the wartime operation involving a cadaver faked to resemble an officer in the Royal Marines carrying plans for an Allied attack on Greece and Sardinia, which was washed up in the Mediterranean Sea. Montagu was not the most popular of judges. He was impatient and appeared to regard the trial process as an unwelcome preliminary step to the imposition of the sentence. When it came to sentence, however, he was generally regarded as sound and humane, often displaying an accurate instinct for the prisoner who was prepared to try and mend his ways. He had frequent clashes with experienced junior counsel during the course of jury trials. Sir Harold Cassel (1916–2001) was a fearless opponent. On one occasion, after a particularly acrimonious exchange, Cassel drew attention to the panelling behind the judge's chair, listing all the names of the chairmen of Middlesex Sessions – commencing with Judge Jeffries and ending with Montagu – and commented that in between them there had been some very good judges. They had included Henry Fielding and his brother, John Fielding, 'The Blind Justice' (1721–1780), whose portrait also hung in Court 2 and now hangs in the principal courtroom (the old Council Chamber; fig. 8).

In common with other Quarter Sessions, Middlesex had its own Bar Mess. Members were entitled to use a luncheon room at the rear of the building, overlooking a bomb site

*Opposite:* 6. Portrait of Hugh Percy when Earl of Northumberland (1762), by Sir Joshua Reynolds.

*Above:* 7. Ewen Montagu, QC, 1954, later chairman of Middlesex Sessions.

*Right:* 8. Portrait of Sir John Fielding, Middlesex Justice, by Nathaniel Hone.

where one could park a car for five shillings a day and upon which now stands the Queen Elizabeth II Conference Centre. Members of the Mess were encouraged to lunch there, and those who did not do so missed a valuable experience. There was always someone on hand who could give timely advice. It was a convivial gathering. James Crespi, a member of the Bar who was later lucky to survive the IRA bomb in the Old Bailey, could be heard quoting James Boswell's *Life of Johnson* at a large round table in the corner. The activities of the Mess extended beyond the provision of food. Young members of the Bar could join what was known as 'the Soup List' and thereby acquire briefs to prosecute for the Metropolitan Police. The Mess was sufficiently small to provide a valuable and discreet means of self-regulation and education before the introduction of formal advocacy training; careers were saved by a timely word in the ear; self-confidence, so essential in moderation for effective advocacy, was enhanced by the odd word of praise for a good cross-examination or speech to the jury; in the best traditions of the Bar that continue today, a strong work ethic and fearless representation of the client's interests, while adhering to rigorous standards of integrity, were taken to be the norm.

With the introduction of the Courts Act in 1971, Alan Trapnell, the chairman, assumed the title of Resident Judge, and the full-time deputy chairmen became circuit judges. Little else changed except for the amount of work. This grew in quantity on account of the increasing number of cases that qualified for legal aid. Now that young members of the criminal Bar were no longer dependent upon dock briefs – a practice that had involved prisoners engaging counsel to represent them, for a modest but instantly payable fee, from barristers sitting in court – the size of barristers' chambers that specialized in criminal work, and the calibre of those who became members of them, rapidly increased. As can happen in an institution with such a pleasant environment, there was no shortage of very experienced staff employed by the court and other support agencies who relished the opportunity to continue working there. Walter Ball, who was the Senior Clerk from the Solicitor's Department of the Metropolitan Police, undoubtedly knew far more about criminal practice and procedure than any counsel he briefed. Many a prosecutor who was experiencing difficulties would be rescued by some whispered advice from

the bench behind him about a precedent that instantly provided the answer to an unmeritorious submission from his opponent. A respectful but happy rapport developed between bench and Bar. At one Bar Mess dinner for the judges, the Junior, who was describing in jocular vein cases that had been tried by each judge, announced that Judge Bill Hughes, who was a popular member of the Garrick Club, had had a case but drunk it. Luke Hughes, his son, is the furniture-maker who has designed the bookshelves for the new Supreme Court Library.

By 1982 the volume of work had increased to such an extent that satellite courts were opened in the old County Court at Willesden and at Wellington Barracks, where proceedings had to stop at 11 am every day to allow the passing noise of the band of the Brigade of Guards to abate. The decision was taken to refurbish the Guildhall, and it was expected that the judges and staff would move to the newly opened Crown Court at Southwark for two years so that the

9. The board listing the chairmen of Sessions and Resident Judges who sat in the Guildhall until it ceased to be a Criminal Court in 2007.

*Opposite:* 10. The old Council Chamber as a Crown Court.

*Page 206:* 11. Court 1, facing the bench.

*Page 207:* 12. Court 1, looking towards the jury box.

work could be carried out. Those who expected to return to work at the Guildhall, permanently or as visiting lawyers, were therefore dismayed to find that no work seemed to be in progress. When Lord Hailsham was in his last term as Lord Chancellor, however, he reputedly provided an impetus for visible work to commence, and in 1988 the doors finally reopened for business after a period of six years, with seven fully operational and secure courtrooms, three of which had been faithfully restored to their former glory. Suzanne Norwood became the Resident Judge. She was joined by Derek Clarkson QC, the only judge to return to the Guildhall who had previously sat there for any significant length of time. There was soon a queue of others, myself included, who became interested in joining their ranks. In 1995 I was delighted to be appointed as Resident Judge, a post I then held for ten years. Roger Chapple, who was appointed to that role for the last two years of the court's existence, was the last to have his name inscribed on the panelling behind the judge's chair in Court 1 (fig. 9). In 2007 Ian Cheeseman, who had been employed as Security Manager since before the temporary closure in 1982, still remained in post.

Much of the work that had previously been committed to the Guildhall had been diverted during its closure to Isleworth and Kingston Crown Courts. The court was entrusted with a local jurisdiction over cases committed from Marlborough Street and Marylebone Magistrates' Courts. These came from a catchment area that provided some high-profile allegations of misconduct in nightclubs and restaurants by well-known sporting personalities – allegations that were rarely proved to the satisfaction of a jury. The court performed a useful role in absorbing cases from other venues in order to relieve listing problems or to avoid them being tried in a particular locality because of their notoriety. The caseload began to require judges who were sufficiently experienced to try certain classes of offender, such as those accused of serious fraud. In the 1980s circuit judges around the country had found themselves trying offences that had previously been within the exclusive province of High Court judges. In London these had been tried at the Central Criminal Court, but by the 1990s cases of rape and child abuse were regularly transferred or committed for trial at the Guildhall. They were followed by cases of murder for judges who were authorized to preside over them.

When it was proposed in 2003 that the Guildhall should cease to be used as a Criminal Court in order to provide premises for the United Kingdom Supreme Court, this was met with some incredulity, not only by those who were currently working there, but also by the vast majority who had visited the building in the past. It had been thoughtfully modernized and restored some twenty years earlier in a way that preserved its fine architectural features, and it had continued to perform an important role in the administration of criminal justice in London on or near a site that had been used for that purpose for more than two hundred years (figs. 10–12). The architectural correspondent of *The Times*, Marcus Binney, who took a leading role in a campaign organized by SAVE Britain's Heritage to retain the court in its present state, commented to me that he had not realized, until he visited the premises, quite how the court 'hummed'. Furthermore, the configuration of the building, with its courtrooms that were custom-built for jury trials and contained fine carved furniture, was clearly unsuitable for the cerebral work of the new court. Although much of the fine carving from the Council Chamber has been retained, the extensive changes that have taken place to the interior of the building as a whole have surely proved this to be so.

I made no secret of my opposition to the project and was disappointed when the building was finally chosen for its new role. Many members of the judiciary felt the same. However, it is some comfort to know that the Guildhall has not been converted into a faceless block of administrative offices, as some believed might have become its fate in 1984. In spite of a general regret that it has ceased to be a court where people accused of crime are tried by their peers, it is only fitting that it has gone on to become the highest court in the land.

ENDNOTES,
SELECTED SOURCES,
CONTRIBUTORS'
BIOGRAPHIES AND CREDITS

## From County Hall to Supreme Court

Acknowledgements: I am most grateful to Elizabeth Prochaska, my legal assistant, for help with the research; to my colleagues Lord Hope and Lord Carswell, for advice on Scotland and Northern Ireland; and to Chris Miele and to Merrell, for their helpful suggestions.

1 The history of Middlesex and the administration of justice on this site is largely taken from C.W. Radcliffe, *Middlesex: The Jubilee of the County Council 1889–1939* (London: Evans Brothers, 1939).

2 *Westminster and London improved* (1766), cited in P. Hunting, *Royal Westminster* (London: RICS, 1981).

3 For example, W. Besant, *Westminster* (London: Chatto & Windus, 1897), p. 10; C. Thomas, R. Cowie and J. Sidell, in *The royal palace, abbey and town of Westminster on Thorney Island*, MoLAS: Archaeological Excavations (1991–98) for the London Underground Limited Jubilee Line Extension Project, 22 (London: Museum of London, 2006), p. 35, comment that this 'provides a persuasive route for a road but without any archaeological evidence it must remain speculation'.

4 This history is largely taken from Emma Mason, *Westminster Abbey and Its People, c. 1050–c. 1216* (Woodbridge: Boydell Press, 1996); see also Emma Mason, 'Introduction', in *Westminster Abbey Charters, 1066–c. 1214*, London Record Society, 25 (1988).

5 Walter Thornbury, 'The City of Westminster: Introduction', in *Old and New London*, 6 vols (London: Cassell, Petter & Galpin, 1873–78), IV (1878).

6 P. Temple, ed., *Survey of London: 46, South and East Clerkenwell* (New Haven, Conn., and London: Yale University Press for English Heritage, 2008), pp. 96–104.

7 Radcliffe, *Middlesex*, pp. 39–40.

8 See S. Jones, *The History of the Crown Court at the Middlesex Guildhall* (2008, unpublished, available from the Supreme Court Library).

9 This means that they cannot be removed from office except on an address to the monarch from both Houses of Parliament in cases of inability or misbehaviour.

10 HL Deb. (series 5) vol. 614, cols 419–20 (22 June 2000).

11 *R (Jackson)* v. *Attorney-General* [2005] UKHL 56, [2006] 1 AC 262; *R (Countryside Alliance)* v. *Attorney-General* and *R (Derwin)* v. *Attorney-General* [2007] UKHL 52, [2008] 1 AC 719.

12 The Gregorian calendar was adopted for all Great Britain in 1751.

13 *Greenshields* v. *Magistrates of Edinburgh* (1709), 1 Rob 12, 1 ER 356.

14 *Mackintosh* v. *Lord Advocate* (1876–77) LR 2 App Cas 41.

15 The Welsh Assembly government and the Scottish and Northern Irish Executives; the Welsh and Northern Irish Assemblies and the Scottish Parliament.

16 The sad story of Soane's battles with Frederick Robinson, Chancellor of the Exchequer, and Charles Greville, Clerk to the Privy Council, is told by Ptolemy Dean in *Sir John Soane and London* (Aldershot, and Burlington, Vt.: Lund Humphries, 2006).

17 The last of the 'old' Commonwealth countries to leave was New Zealand, which set up its own Supreme Court in 2004.

18 Most cases come from Trinidad and Tobago and Jamaica, which plan in due course to transfer them to the Caribbean Court of Justice; many others come from the Bahamas, which does not.

19 For example, the British Virgin Islands and the Cayman Islands.

20 For example, appeals from the General Medical Council and the General Dental Council, now transferred to the High Court. Appeals from the Disciplinary Committee of the Royal College of Veterinary Surgeons remain for the time being.

21 For example, $4000 (roughly £2500) from the Bahamas; $1500 (roughly £151) from Trinidad and Tobago.

22 *MacLeod* v. *MacLeod* [2008] UKPC 64, [2009] 3 WLR 437.

23 *Sanatan Sharma Maha Sabha* v. *Attorney-General of Trinidad and Tobago* [2009] UKPC 17.

24 *Mitchell* v. *City of Glasgow Council* [2009] UKHL 11, [2009] 1 AC 874.

25 *White* v. *White* [2001] 1 AC 596; *Miller* v. *Miller* and *McFarlane* v. *MacFarlane* [2006] UKHL 24, [2006] 2 AC 618.

26 *R (Ahmad)* v. *Newham London Borough Council* [2009] UKHL 14, [2009] 3 All ER 755.

27 *R (Corner House Research)* v. *Director of the Serious Fraud Office* [2008] UKHL 60, [2009] 1 AC 756.

28 *R (SB)* v. *Governors of Denbigh High School* [2006] UKHL 15, [2007] 1 AC 100; *Savage* v. *South Essex NHS Foundation Trust* [2008] UKHL 74, [2009] 1 AC 681.

29 *R (Williamson)* v. *Secretary of State for Education and Employment* [2005] UKHL 15, [2005] 2 AC 246; *R (Wright)* v. *Secretary of State for Health* [2009] UKHL 3, [2009] 1 AC 739.

30 supremecourt.gov.uk.

## Law Lords and Justices

1 In much of this chapter I have relied heavily on the detailed and pioneering work of Professor Robert Stevens, former Master of Pembroke College, Oxford: in particular, 'The Final Appeal: Reform of the House of Lords and Privy Council 1867–1876', *Law Quarterly Review* (hereafter '*LQR*'), 80 (1964), 343, and *Law and Politics: The House of Lords as a Judicial Body, 1800–1976* (London: Weidenfeld & Nicolson, 1979). Most further references to the latter work are given at the relevant places in the text.

2 A.S. Turberville, 'The House of Lords as a Court of Law, 1784–1837', *LQR*, 52 (1936), 189 (p. 205); Louis Blom-Cooper and Gavin Drewry, *Final Appeal: A Study of the House of Lords in Its Judicial Capacity* (Oxford: Oxford University Press, 1972), p. 32; Stevens, *Law and Politics*, p. 8.

3 Sir William Holdsworth, *A History of English Law*, 7th edn, rev. 1956, ed. A.L. Goodhart and H.G. Hanbury, with introductory essay and additions by S.B. Chrimes, 17 vols (London: Methuen: Sweet & Maxwell, 1956), I, 442.

4 During the nineteen years of his Lord Chancellorship, Lord Hardwicke was the only peer qualified to hear appeals: Nicholas Underhill, *The Lord Chancellor* (Lavenham: T. Dalton, 1978), p. 168.

5 [1898] *Appeal Cases* (hereafter 'AC') 1.

6 Turberville, 'The House of Lords as a Court of Law', pp. 203–204.

7 *Ibid.*, pp. 208–209; Stevens, *Law and Politics*, pp. 21–23.

8 See, for example, the view strongly expressed by Lord Holland: Stevens, *Law and Politics*, p. 23.

9 Blom-Cooper and Drewry, *Final Appeal*, pp. 24–25; Stevens, *Law and Politics*, pp. 18, 43.

10 Blom-Cooper and Drewry, *Final Appeal*, p. 25; Stevens, *Law and Politics*, pp. 28, 31.

11 Blom-Cooper and Drewry, *Final Appeal*, p. 25; Stevens, *Law and Politics*, p. 40.

12 R.E. Megarry, 'Lay Peers in Appeals to the House of Lords', *LQR*, 65 (1949), 22; Stevens, *Law and Politics*, p. 32.

13 Stevens, 'The Final Appeal', p. 349.

14 Megarry, 'Lay Peers in Appeals', p. 23.

15 Stevens, *Law and Politics*, p. 108; Appellate Jurisdiction Act 1887.

16 [1901] AC 427, which led to trade-union protection in the Trade Disputes Act 1906.

17 [1925] AC 578, condemning a council's policy of equal pay for women workers.

18 See T. Bingham, 'The Old Order Changeth', *LQR*, 122 (2006), 211 (p. 218), citing Hailsham of St Marylebone, *A Sparrow's Flight* (London: Collins, 1990), p. 378; Hailsham, 'The Duties of a Lord Chancellor', published by the Holdsworth Club, p. 22 (address given on 12 June 1936).

19 Bingham, 'The Old Order Changeth', p. 217.

20 *Ibid.*, p. 219, citing HL Deb., cols 468–71 (22 May 1969).

21 See Lord Hope of Craighead, 'Voices from the Past – the Law Lords' Contribution to the Legislative Process', *LQR*, 123 (2007), 547–70.

22 See Bingham, 'The Old Order Changeth', pp. 218–19.

23 HL Deb. (series 5) vol. 614, cols 418–20 (22 June 2000).

24 *London Street Tramways Co Ltd* v. *London County Council* [1898] AC 375.

25 *The Spirit of the Laws*, trans. and ed. A. Cohler, B. Miller and H. Stone (Cambridge: Cambridge University Press, 1989), Part 2, II, chapter 6, p. 157.

26 *The Federalist*, no. 81 (1788).

27 Ithaca, NY: Cornell Paperbacks, Cornell University Press, 1966, p. 140.

28 Cited in Bingham, 'The Old Order Changeth', p. 213.

29 Underhill, *The Lord Chancellor*, pp. 177–78, 185.

30 Holdsworth, *History of English Law*, XVI (1966), pp. 30–31; Parl. Debs. (series 3) vol. 34, cols 440–74.

31 Parl. Debs. (series 3) vol. 34, col. 442; see also cols 444, 453.

32 *Report*, Cmd 9230, chapter X, p. 74, para. 42.

33 R.F.V. Heuston, *Lives of the Lord Chancellors 1885–1940* (Oxford: Oxford University Press, 1964), p. 233.

34 'The Independence of the Judiciary in the 1980s', *Public Law* (hereafter '*PL*'), 44 [1988], 50.

35 J. Steyn, 'The Weakest and Least Dangerous Department of Government', *PL*, 84 [1997], 90 (repr. in *Democracy Through Law* [Aldershot: Ashgate, 2004] 97, pp. 103, 114–15); Lord Steyn, 'The Case for a Supreme Court', *LQR*, 118 (2002), 382 (pp. 387–88).

36 HC Deb., early day motion 961 (11 March 1998).

37 *The Judicial Functions of the House of Lords*, 19 May 1999, pp. 3 (conclusion vii), 15.

38 Diana Woodhouse, *The Office of Lord Chancellor* (Oxford: Hart, 2001), pp. 7, 203, 204, 212. This and the preceding paragraph largely reproduce Bingham, 'The Old Order Changeth', pp. 213–16.

39 'What Do the Top Courts Do?' (London: UCL Constitution Unit, 2000).

40 The present author gave a lecture at Gray's Inn in November 2000, entitled 'The Highest Court in the Land' and – on 1 May 2002 – The Constitution Unit Spring Lecture 2002, 'A New Supreme Court for the United Kingdom', both being sympathetic to the idea of a Supreme Court institutionally and functionally independent of the legislature. Among the publications to appear on the subject were A. Le Sueur, ed., *Building the UK's Supreme Court: National and Comparative Perspectives* (Oxford: Oxford University Press, 2004).

**The Place: Parliament Square**

Acknowledgements: This chapter makes use of research in primary historical sources that was undertaken on behalf of Transport for London (TfL). I am grateful, too, to Roger Hawkins of Hawkins\Brown for permission to reproduce drawings made for that project.

The most comprehensive and accessible guide to the history and architecture of the area is S. Bradley and N. Pevsner, eds, *The Buildings of England: London 6: Westminster* (London and New Haven, Conn.: Yale University Press in association with Penguin, 2005).

1 Quoted in W.F. Moneypenny and G.E. Buckle, *The Life of Benjamin Disraeli*, 6 vols (London: John Murray, 1910–20), III, p. 21.

2 Quoted in K.T. Hoppen, *The Mid-Victorian Generation, 1846–1886*, The New Oxford History of England, gen. ed. J.M. Roberts (Oxford: Oxford University Press, 1998), p. 105.

3 P. Mandler, *The English National Character* (London and New Haven, Conn.: Yale University Press, 2006), pp. 12, 13, 37, 55. See also C. Brooks, *The Gothic Revival* (London: Phaidon, 1999), pp. 40–45, and C. Miele, 'English Antiquity', in *Architecture and Englishness, 1880–1914*, ed. I. Dungavell and D. Crellin (Oxford: The Alder Press for the Society of Architectural Historians, Papers from the 2003 Symposium, 2006), pp. 83–103.

4 C. Thomas, R. Cowie and J. Sidell, *The royal palace, abbey and town of Westminster on Thorney Island*, MoLAS: Archaeological Excavations (1991–98) for the London Underground Limited Jubilee Line Extension Project, 22 (London: Museum of London, 2006), pp. 9–28.

5 Papers and plans relating to this are held at City of Westminster Archives (hereafter 'CWA'); see E 13 (10). See also papers at the National Archives at Kew (hereafter 'TNA', and formerly the Public Record Office) at

MPE 1/489. A plan identifying properties adjacent St Margaret's for clearance can be found at TNA WORK 29/75.

6 H.M. Colvin, ed., *The History of the King's Works*, 6 vols (Oxford: Clarendon Press, 1963–82), V, 428–30.

7 C. Beddington, *Canaletto in England: A Venetian Artist Abroad, 1746–1755*, exhib. cat. (New Haven, Conn., Yale Center for British Art, 2006; London: Dulwich Picture Gallery, 2007), cat. no. 19.

8 CWA Box 64 (25–27).

9 TNA WORK 30/465, 30/467, 30/469 and 30/470.

10 TNA WORK 30/462. A more detailed plan – albeit prepared in 1862 – of the Wyatt layout can be found at WORK 22/43.

11 Colvin, *King's Works*, VI (1973), 504–12, and G. Darley, *John Soane, An Accidental Romantic* (London and New Haven, Conn.: Yale University Press, 1999), pp. 162–63.

12 For the debate that followed on what to do with the site, see C. Miele, 'The Battle for Westminster Hall', *Architectural History*, 41 (1997), 220–44.

13 For the history of the Palace of Westminster, see Christine Riding and Jacqueline Riding, eds, *The Houses of Parliament: History, Art, Architecture* (London: Merrell, 2000). For the involvement of Pugin in the design of the palace, see R. Hill, *God's Architect: Pugin and the Building of Romantic Britain* (London: Allen Lane, 2007), pp. 311–16.

14 The evolution of the design and Barry's plans for a new government quarter are documented in the Rev. A. Barry, *The Life and Works of Sir Charles Barry, RA FRS* (London: John Murray, 1867), which is, however, notoriously unreliable. See, therefore, M.H. Port's article on the architect in the new edition of *The Oxford Dictionary of National Biography* (2004). The responsibility for the design of this building was a point of some dispute between the Rev. Barry and Pugin's son, both of whom published pamphlets in the late 1860s claiming authorship for their respective parents. *The Builder*'s commentary on these proposals can be found in the issue of 29 May 1865.

15 For the background to this plan and the advent of a more interventionist Office of Works, see M.H. Port, *Imperial London: Civil Government Building in London, 1851–1915* (London and New Haven, Conn.: Yale University Press, 1995), pp. 114–137.

16 Port, *Imperial London*, pp. 155–57,

198–99, 237–39. See also TNA WORK 11/9/6, 11/24/10, and 20/28.

17 E.M. Barry gave a good account of the state of play in the square in a lecture delivered to the Royal Institute of British Architects (RIBA) on 1 February 1858. See *Proceedings of the RIBA for 1858*. Barry's explanation of his layout of the square is contained in a letter to the then First Commissioner of Works, Sir William Cowper, dated 30 May 1861, from which this quotation is taken. See TNA WORK 11/22/3.

18 See London Metropolitan Archives (hereafter 'LMA') MCC/CL/L/CC/10/04, and another Office of Works record drawing at TNA WORK 11/56.

19 Parl. Debs. vol. 189, cols 1291–99 (10 August 1867). On the history of displaying sculpture in and around the square, see a recent thesis by Stuart Birch, 'On Stage at the Theatre of State: The Monuments and Memorials of Parliament Square, London' (unpublished doctoral thesis, Nottingham Trent University, 2003).

20 These developments and discussions up to 1939 can be followed at LMA MCC/CL/GP/CER/13 and TNA WORK 16/1440. Other, related documentation survives at TNA WORK 12/718, 16/440 and 16/1939; see also TNA BP 2/55.

21 Perspective views of the initial proposals and Scott's revised Modern Gothic can be found at LMA MCC/CL/GP/CER/13 and LMA MCC/CL/L/CC/10/04 respectively.

22 See TNA WORK 16/1939 for this and much of what follows.

23 These debates of 1946 to 10 November 1949, just prior to Wornum's appointment as landscape architect for the square, can be followed in extensive documentation contained in TNA WORK 16/1937, which provides the source for citations unless otherwise indicated.

24 Press Notice dated 25 November 1949 at TNA WORK 22/170. Further details of the evolution of the Wornum Scheme can be found at TNA WORK 16/1939.

25 TNA PREM 11/2724.

**The Architecture of the Former Middlesex Guildhall**

Acknowledgements: I am especially grateful to Janey Blanchflower, Peter Cormack, Hugh Feilden, Kylie Freeman, Chris Miele, William Palin and Susannah Stone for all their advice and access to relevant research.

1 S. Bradley and N. Pevsner, eds, *The Buildings of England: London 6: Westminster* (London and New

Haven, Conn.: Yale University Press in association with Penguin, 2005), pp. 104–280, especially 271–72; this description is largely based on the first account by Pevsner, published in *The Buildings of England: London: The Cities of London and Westminster* (London: Penguin, 1957).

2 A. Stuart Gray, *Edwardian Architecture: A Biographical Dictionary* (London: Duckworth, 1985).

3 *Opening of the Guildhall Westminster and Unveiling of the Middlesex Memorial to His late Majesty King Edward VII, December 19th, 1913 … Order of Proceedings and Ceremony*, pamphlet printed for 19 December 1913, in the London Metropolitan Archives (hereafter 'LMA') 70.7 MID; the text of the architectural account was clearly supplied by the architect, Gibson himself.

4 Bradley and Pevsner, *London 6: Westminster*, pp. 271–72, and also Feilden+Mawson Architects, 'The UK Supreme Court Conservation Plan: (rev A01)', December 2007, pp. 8–24.

5 C.W. Radcliffe, *Middlesex: The Jubilee of the County Council 1889–1939* (London: Evans Brothers, 1939), pp. 33–41; and *Opening of the Guildhall Westminster*, pp. 8–18.

6 Clare Graham, *Ordering Law: The Architectural and Social History of the English Law Court to 1914* (Aldershot: Ashgate, 2003), talks about 'swagger court' and the 'invention of tradition', and refers to Eric Hobsbawm and Terence Ranger, eds, *The Invention of Tradition* (Cambridge: Cambridge University Press, 1983).

7 Howard Colvin, *Biographical Dictionary of British Architects 1600–1840* (London and New Haven, Conn.: Yale University Press, 2008), pp. 265–66.

8 Minutes of the Middlesex Guildhall Committee, LMA MMC/MIN.

9 *Ibid.*

10 Minutes of the Middlesex Guildhall Committee, LMA MCC/MIN/56/3 (I am grateful to Dr Peter Cormack for drawing my attention to this passage); and also *Opening of the Guildhall Westminster*, pp. 6–7.

11 Serge Chirol and Philippe Seydoux, *The Chateaux of the Loire Valley* (London: Thames & Hudson, 1992); and for Burnet and his French connections, see David Walker, 'Sir John James Burnet, 1857–1938', *Dictionary of Scottish Architects* (2006) at scottisharchitects.org.uk.

12 Minutes of the Middlesex Guildhall Committee, LMA MCC/MIN/56/3.

13 H.V. Lanchester, 'Obituary of

James Glen Sivewright Gibson', *RIBA Journal*, 58 (1951), 332; see also *The Builder*, 180, 11 May 1951, 663.

14 Nikolaus Pevsner, as quoted in *The Guildhall Testimonial* (London: SAVE Britain's Heritage, 2006), p. 6.

15 Gray, *Edwardian Architecture*, pp. 188–89; and see David Walker, 'Frank Peyton Skipwith, 1881–1915', *Dictionary of Scottish Architects* (2006) at scottisharchitects.org.uk.

16 Accounts relating to the opening of the Guildhall appeared in *The Sphere*, 13 September 1913; *The Times*, 13 September 1913, 19 December and 20 December 1913; and *The Graphic*, 20 December 1913.

17 *Academy Architecture*, 1911 (II), vol. 40, frontispiece and p. 15. Peyton Skipwith of the Fine Art Society confirms that the perspectives are the work of William Walcot.

18 Contract drawings in LMA, and reproduced in Feilden+Mawson, 'The UK Supreme Court Conservation Plan', pp. 8–24; and 'Specification of Works to be done and Materials to be used in the rebuilding The Guildhall, Westminster, for the Middlesex County Council', August 1911, pp. 17–30. I am grateful to Feilden+Mawson Architects for the loan of a copy of this document.

19 For Chambord, see Chirol and Seydoux, *The Chateaux of the Loire Valley*, pp. 50–55.

20 *The Builder*, 14 November 1913, 519–21; the effect is especially evident in the floor plans and cross-section (fig. 4).

21 Feilden+Mawson, 'The UK Supreme Court Conservation Plan', pp. 30–31.

22 'Specification of Works', pp. 17–30.

23 *The Builder*, 14 November 1913, 519–21; and also statements by Simon Jervis and John Hardy, both formerly of the Furniture Department of the Victoria and Albert Museum, in *The Guildhall Testimonial*, relating to the debate about the removal of the furniture.

24 *The Builder*, 19 March 1915, 270–71; thanks to Susannah Stone for drawing my attention to this.

25 *Middlesex Guildhall*, undated pamphlet guide, [c. 1970?], LMA P70.7 MID, p. 90.

26 'Specification of Works', p. 2.

27 Feilden+Mawson, 'The UK Supreme Court Conservation Plan', p. 6.

28 'Air Raid Precautions Report', 1938, LMA CE21.

29 *The Builder*, 14 November 1913, 519–20.

30 *The Builder*, 19 September 1913, 287; and Bradley and Pevsner, *London 6: Westminster*, pp. 212–15.

31 *Opening of the Guildhall Westminster*, p. 9.

32 *The Builder*, 19 September 1913, 287.

33 *Daily Mail*, 23 September 1913, quoted in Feilden+Mawson, 'The UK Supreme Court Conservation Plan', p. 35.

34 *British Architect*, 3 January 1913, quoted in Feilden+Mawson, 'The UK Supreme Court Conservation Plan', p. 22.

35 *Opening of the Guildhall Westminster*, p. 12.

36 John Belcher, as quoted in Gray, *Edwardian Architecture*, pp. 103–104.

37 Gavin Stamp, in *The Guildhall Testimonial*, p. 8.

38 J. Parkinson-Bailey, *Manchester: An Architectural History* (Manchester: Manchester University Press, 2000), pp. 121–25.

39 Radcliffe, *Middlesex*, pp. 76–77, gives a list of subjects; and see Peter Cormack's essay in the present volume.

40 Roger Dixon and Stefan Muthesius, *Victorian Architecture* (London: Thames & Hudson, 1985), pp. 155–64.

**Decorative Arts at the Supreme Court of the United Kingdom**
Acknowledgements: I am grateful to Michelle Ault, Tony Benyon, Janey Blanchflower, Sandra Coley, Hugh Feilden, Tim Foster, Kylie Freeman, Martin Harrison, FSA, Luke Hughes, Bruce Jackson (of Lancashire County Record Office), Dr Michael Kerney, FSA, Dr Emmanuel Minne, Jeremy Musson, Dr Pietro di Paola, Susannah Stone and Sara Terreault for advice and help of various kinds.

The full title for this chapter derives from *The Builder*, 7 March 1913, 292: 'It is a long time since an important public building in London has been erected in the Gothic style … But it is certainly Gothic "with a difference" in this case.'

1 *The Times*, 13 September 1913, p. 3.

2 *The Sphere*, 13 September 1913, p. 301.

3 Frank Peyton Skipwith was an acting Major in the 7th Battalion, Royal Scots Fusiliers, when he was killed, aged thirty-four, on the first day of the Battle of Loos on 25 September 1915. During Skipwith's lifetime his name was regularly mis-spelled as 'Skipworth', an error that has sadly been perpetuated on the Loos War Memorial, where he is commemorated among the 'missing'.

4 Sir Charles Nicholson and Charles Spooner, *Recent English Ecclesiastical Architecture* (London: Technical Journals, [1912]).

5 The principal published sources for Fehr are: M.H. Spielmann, *British Sculpture and Sculptors of To-Day* (London: Cassell, 1901),

pp. 138, 139, 157; Kineton Parkes, *Sculpture of Today*, 2 vols (London: Chapman & Hall, 1921), I, *America, Great Britain, Japan* (1921), 81; Edgar A. Hunt, ed., *The Colchester War Memorial Souvenir* (Colchester: Essex Telegraph, 1923), pp. 30–31; Susan Beattie, *The New Sculpture* (New Haven, Conn., and London: Yale University Press, 1983), pp. 131–32; A. Stuart Gray, *Edwardian Architecture: A Biographical Dictionary* (London: Duckworth, 1985), p. 177; Benedict Read and Alexander Kader, *Leighton and His Sculptural Legacy* (London: Joanna Barnes Fine Art, 1996), p. 40.

6 F.H.W. Sheppard, gen. ed., *Survey of London*: 41, *Southern Kensington: Brompton* (London: Athlone Press for the Greater London Council, 1983), p. 103 and plate 55c.

7 Magnoni's words can be translated as 'the execution of all the sculptures of the celebrated Guildhall, a magnificently opulent public building'. His best-known independent commission is the Waggoners' Memorial (1919) at Sledmere, Yorkshire. I am indebted to Dr Pietro di Paola for generously sharing his extensive knowledge of Carlo Magnoni's political background. Magnoni's police file is in the Casellario Politico Centrale of the Archivio Centrale dello Stato, Rome, ref. no. 2932/87542.

8 *The Builder*, 3 March 1911, plates between pp. 272 and 273.

9 Minutes of County Buildings Committee, in the London Metropolitan Archives (hereafter 'LMA') MCC/MIN/6/2, pp. 36–37.

10 *The Builder*, 14 November 1913, plate at p. 519.

11 Minutes of Guildhall Extension Committee, LMA MCC/MIN/6/1, p. 228.

12 Booklet entitled *Laying of Foundation Stone on Thursday May 2nd 1912*, LMA MCC/CL/GP/CER/10, p. 7.

13 *Daily Mail*, 23 September 1913, p.10.

14 *The Sphere*, 13 September 1913, p. 301.

15 Parkes, *Sculpture of Today*, I, 81.

16 The arms of Middlesex, formally granted by the College of Arms on 7 November 1910, are: '*Gules three Seaxes fessewise in pale proper pommelled and hilted Or points to the sinister and cutting edge upwards in chief a Saxon Crown of the last*' (i.e. a red shield with three Saxon curved swords beneath a gold Saxon crown).

17 The principal listings of the east portal sculpture subjects are in *Opening of the Guildhall Westminster and Unveiling of the Middlesex Memorial to His late Majesty King Edward VII, December 19th, 1913*

… *Order of Proceedings and Ceremony*, and another pamphlet, *Middlesex Guildhall* (London: Middlesex County Council [1950s?]).

18 Caroline M. Barron, *The Medieval Guildhall of London* (London: Corporation of London, 1974), p. 27 and plates 9a, 9b and 10.

19 The yale is a supporter in the arms of the Beaufort family and of the Plantagenet Dukes of Bedford. It is not clear why it was specifically chosen for the Guildhall carvings, but several examples are found on the medieval monuments in Westminster Abbey and, coincidentally, it had been a topic of published correspondence when the Guildhall was being designed. See *Archaeological Journal*, 68 (1911), 200–202; and *Nature*, 25 May 1911, 415.

20 Alfred Stevens's lions were removed from the British Museum's railings in 1895, but some remain on the railings outside the Natural History Museum in South Kensington.

21 See *Opening of the Guildhall Westminster*, p. 17.

22 Baker's *King Edward VII* was to launch him on a successful career that brought numerous public commissions (including Huddersfield's Edward VII Memorial) in Britain and in the USA, where he was based from 1916. His most renowned work is the *Pioneer Woman* statue (1930), which is 8.2 metres (27 feet) high, at Ponca City, Oklahoma, where the Marland Mansion Museum now houses the contents of Baker's New York studio. Among American sitters for his portrait sculpture were General John Pershing and five presidents, including John F. Kennedy.

23 Minutes of Furniture & Fittings Committee 1912–13, LMA MCC/MIN/6/12, p. 8.

24 LMA MCC/CL/L/CON/02/1570, 1571 and 1572.

25 Typical examples are illustrated in Charles Tracy, *Continental Church Furniture in England: A Traffic in Piety* (Woodbridge: Antique Collectors' Club, 2002), and in Nicholas Riall, 'The Diffusion of Early Franco-Italian *All'Antica* Ornament: The Renaissance Frieze in the Chapel of the Hospital of St Cross, Winchester, and the Gaillon Stalls, Paris', *Antiquaries Journal*, 88 (2008), 258–307.

26 John H. Harvey, *Henry Yevele c. 1320 to 1400: The Life of an English Architect* (London: Batsford, 1944), pp. 59–60.

27 The archives of Abbott & Co. are held at the Lancashire Record Office (hereafter 'LRO'), Preston, ref. DDAB acc. 8051.

28 *The Builder*, 19 March 1915, 270.

29 LRO, Preston, ref. DDAB acc. 8051: Job No. 7968 in Work Book numbered 7763–7847.

30 Peter Cormack, 'Glazing "with careless care": Charles J. Connick and the Arts & Crafts Philosophy of Stained Glass', *The Journal of Stained Glass*, 28 (2004), 79–94.

31 *The Builder*, 19 March 1915, 270.

32 The types of glass used by Abbott & Co. are described in Arthur Louis Duthie, *Decorative Glass Processes* (London: Constable, 1908), pp. 13–29; some are illustrated in Ralph Mollet, *Leaded Glass Work* (London: Pitman, 1933), pp. 4–18.

33 George P. Bankart, *The Art of the Plasterer* (London: Batsford, 1908).

34 An illustrated advertisement showing James Gibbons's work at the Guildhall is in *The Modern Building Record*, 5 (1914), 168–69. The same volume gives details (pp. 112–113) of all the contractors involved in the decoration of the building.

35 The model for the bronze 'Tommy' figure was Private Robert Ryder, VC (1895–1978), of Harefield, Middlesex, who won his Victoria Cross in September 1916 at Thiepval in the Battle of the Somme.

**Supreme and High Court Architecture**
1 For an account of the problems and abuses under English law in the early years of the colony, see Christopher Munn, 'The Criminal Trial Under Early Colonial Rule', in *Hong Kong's History: State and Society Under Colonial Rule*, ed. Tak-Wing Ngo (London: Routledge, 1999), pp. 46–73.

2 For the imperial overtones of Edwardian Baroque architecture, see Alastair Service, *Edwardian Architecture* (London: Thames & Hudson, 1977), pp. 140–57. As Andrew Saint has shown, it was during this period that architects developed a particular admiration for the works of Sir Christopher Wren. Andrew Saint, 'The Cult of Wren', in *Architecture & Englishness 1880–1914*, ed. David Crellin and Ian Dungavell (London: Society of Architectural Historians of Great Britain, 2006), pp. 37–58.

3 John Brydon in *The Builder*, 2 March 1889, 169.

4 Speech delivered by the chairman of the Hong Kong Jubilee Committee, C.P. Chater, on the occasion of the unveiling of Queen Victoria's statue in Statue Square, 28 May 1896. The National Archives, Kew, Colonial Office Documents 129/272 (Enclosure I), p. 157.

5 *Hongkong Telegraph*, 12 November 1903.

6 *Hongkong Telegraph*, 15 January 1912.

7 Edward McPharland, 'The Early History of James Gandon's Four Courts,' *Burlington Magazine*, 122 (November 1980), 727–35 (pp. 727–28).

8 Murray Fraser, 'Public Building and Colonial Policy in Dublin, 1760–1800', *Architectural History*, 28 (1985), 102–23.

9 Ian Robertson, 'Law Courts', in *Historic Public Buildings of Australia* (Melbourne: National Trust, 1971), pp. 234–41.

10 These were the Court of Queen's Bench at Westminster and the Central Criminal Court; the Lord High Chancellor of England; and for ecclesiastical jurisdiction, in part, the law of the province of Canterbury.

11 Robert Tavernor, *Palladio and Palladianism* (London: Thames & Hudson, 1991), pp. 188–209.

12 Allan Greenberg, *Architecture and Democracy: American Architecture and the Legacy of the Revolution* (New York: Rizzoli, 2006), pp. 86–90.

13 Vincent Scully, *New World Visions of Household Gods and Sacred Places: American Art of the Metropolitan Museum of Art 1650–1914* (Boston: Little, Brown, 1988), pp. 70–71.

14 Quoted in Margaret P. Lord, 'Supreme Courthouse', *Connoisseur*, 214 (1884), 60–67.

15 William J.R. Curtis, *Modern Architecture Since 1900* (London: Phaidon, 1996), p. 293.

16 Allan Greenberg and Stephen Kieran, 'The United States Supreme Court Building, Washington, D.C.', *The Magazine Antiques*, 128 (1985), 760–69 (p. 765).

17 Greenberg, *Architecture and Democracy*, pp. 116–19.

18 Quoted in Bernard Schwartz, *A History of the Supreme Court* (New York: Oxford University Press, 1993), p. 226.

19 Curtis, *Modern Architecture*, p. 293.

20 For the debate surrounding the 'Battle of the Styles', see G. Alex Bremner, 'Nation and Empire in the Government Architecture of Mid-Victorian London: The Foreign and India Office Reconsidered', *Historical Journal*, 48 (2005), 703–42 (pp. 707–16).

21 David Brownlee, *The Law Courts: The Architecture of George Edmund Street* (Cambridge, Mass.: MIT Press, 1984), p. 103. On this point it was stated by A.J.B. Beresford Hope – one of the great champions of the Gothic Revival cause – that 'English Law Courts, built in English architecture, was what English common sense dictated.'

22 Lord Palmerston, then prime minister, forced Scott to rework

this medieval design into an Italianate one, giving us the Foreign and Commonwealth Office we have today. See David Brownlee, 'That "regular mongrel affair": G.G. Scott's Design for the Government Offices', *Architectural History*, 28 (1985), 159–82; and Ian Toplis, *The Foreign Office: An Architectural History* (London: Mansell, 1987), pp. 123–30.

23 For these buildings and their associations, see Harold Kalman, *A History of Canadian Architecture*, 2 vols (Toronto: Oxford University Press, 1994), II (1994), 541. A comparable ensemble of civic Gothic buildings was erected around the same time in Christchurch, New Zealand. Ian Lochhead, *A Dream of Spires: Benjamin Mountfort and the Gothic Revival* (Christchurch: Canterbury University Press, 1999).

24 For the 'Indo-Saracenic' tradition in Anglo-Indian architecture, see Thomas R. Metcalf, *An Imperial Vision: Indian Architecture and Britain's Raj* (London: Faber and Faber, 1989), pp. 55–104; and Philip Davies, *Splendours of the Raj: British Architecture in India 1660–1947* (Harmondsworth: Penguin, 1987), pp. 147–214.

25 The Château-Baronial style arose out of the intersection between commercial interests and a taste for the Scottish Baronial and French Renaissance styles of architecture, later acquiring Canadian nationalist overtones. Rhodri Windsor-Liscombe, 'Nationalism or Cultural Imperialism?: The Château Style in Canada', *Architectural History*, 36 (1993), 127–44.

26 Kenneth Frampton, *Le Corbusier* (London: Thames & Hudson, 2001), pp. 186–87; Curtis, *Modern Architecture*, p. 428.

27 William J.R. Curtis, *Le Corbusier: Ideas and Forms* (London: Phaidon, 1998), pp. 194–95.

28 Vikramaditya Prakash, *Chandigarh's Le Corbusier: The Struggle for Modernity in Postcolonial India* (Seattle: University of Washington Press, 2002), p. 105. For the concept of 'phenomenal transparency' and its relationship to the High Court at Chandigarh, see Colin Rowe and Robert Slutzky (with Bernard Hoesli and Werner Oechslin), *Transparency* (Basel: Birkhäuser, 1997), pp. 22–56, 76–81.

29 Tom Heath, 'High Court of Australia', *Architectural Review*, 169 (1981), 29–35 (p. 30).

30 In fact, the competition brief stated explicitly that locating 'the High Court and the Parliament in proximity to one another ... has strong symbolic significance', as it would represent 'the basis of government and justice at the national level'. Philip Goad, 'Architecture of Court Building', in *The Oxford Companion to the High Court of Australia*, ed. M. Coper, T. Blackshield and G. Williams (Melbourne: Oxford University Press, 2002), p. 27.

31 Paul Katsieris, 'Representations of Justice (Part 2)', *Journal of Social Change and Critical Inquiry*, 1 (1999). See also Hamish Lyon, 'Hassell's Law', *Architecture Australia* (September/October 1999).

32 Michael E.J. Black, 'Representations of Justice (Part 1)', *Journal of Social Change and Critical Inquiry*, 1 (November 1999).

33 Quoted in Federico Freschi, 'Postapartheid Publics and the Politics of Ornament: Nationalism, Identity, and the Rhetoric of Community in the Decorative Program of the New Constitutional Court, Johannesburg', *Africa Today*, 54 (2007), 27–49.

# SELECTED SOURCES

S. Beattie, *The New Sculpture* (New Haven, Conn., and London: Yale University Press, 1983)

W. Besant, *Westminster* (London: Chatto & Windus, 1897)

L. Blom-Cooper and G. Drewry, *Final Appeal: A Study of the House of Lords in Its Judicial Capacity* (Oxford: Oxford University Press, 1972)

L. Blom-Cooper, B. Dickson and G. Drewry, *The Judicial House of Lords 1876–2009* (Oxford: Oxford University Press, 2009)

S. Bradley and N. Pevsner, eds, *The Buildings of England: London 6: Westminster* (London and New Haven, Conn.: Yale University Press in association with Penguin, 2005)

C. Graham, *Ordering Law: The Architectural and Social History of the English Law Court to 1914* (Aldershot: Ashgate, 2003)

*The Guildhall Testimonial* (London: SAVE Britain's Heritage, 2006)

*Laying of Foundation Stone on Thursday May 2nd 1912* (1912), London Metropolitan Archives (hereafter 'LMA') MCC/CL/GP/CER/10

A. Le Sueur, ed., *Building the UK's Supreme Court: National and Comparative Perspectives* (Oxford: Oxford University Press, 2004)

*Opening of the Guildhall Westminster and Unveiling of the Middlesex Memorial to His late Majesty King Edward VII, December 19th, 1913 ... Order of Proceedings and Ceremony* (1913), LMA 70.7 MID

M.H. Port, *Imperial London: Civil Government Building in London, 1851–1915* (London and New Haven, Conn.: Yale University Press, 1995)

C.W. Radcliffe, *Middlesex: The Jubilee of the County Council 1889–1939* (London: Evans Brothers, 1939)

*Royal Westminster*, exhib. cat. by P. Hunting (London: Royal Institute of Chartered Surveyors, centenary exhibition, 1981)

A. Service, *Edwardian Architecture* (London: Thames & Hudson, 1977)

R. Stevens, *Law and Politics: The House of Lords as a Judicial Body, 1800–1976* (London: Weidenfeld & Nicolson, 1979)

A. Stuart Gray, *Edwardian Architecture: A Biographical Dictionary* (London: Duckworth, 1985)

C. Thomas, R. Cowie and J. Sidell, *The royal palace, abbey and town of Westminster on Thorney Island*, MoLAS: Archaeological Excavations (1991–98) for the London Underground Limited Jubilee Line Extension Project, 22 (London: Museum of London, 2006)

D. Woodhouse, *The Office of Lord Chancellor* (Oxford: Hart, 2001)

# CONTRIBUTORS' BIOGRAPHIES

**Tom Bingham (Lord Bingham of Cornhill)** was called to the Bar in 1959, became a QC in 1972, was appointed a High Court Judge in 1980 and was promoted to the Court of Appeal in 1986. He later became Master of the Rolls (1992), Lord Chief Justice of England and Wales (1996) and Senior Law Lord of the United Kingdom (2000), the first person to hold all three offices. On appointment as Lord Chief Justice he became a life peer, as Lord Bingham of Cornhill (in Powys), and was appointed a Knight of the Garter in 2005, the first professional judge to be so honoured. He published a volume of essays, *The Business of Judging*, in 2000, and a further book, *The Rule of Law*, is to be published shortly. He retired in 2008, and in the same year was elected by the Institut de France as the first winner of the Prize for Law awarded by the Alexander S. Onassis Public Benefit Foundation.

**Alex Bremner** is Lecturer in the History of Architecture at the University of Edinburgh. He completed his PhD in the history of Victorian architecture at the University of Cambridge, where he was a Gates Scholar from 2001 to 2004. He has published widely on the relationship between art, architecture and empire in Britain and the British colonial world during the nineteenth and early twentieth centuries. He is currently preparing a book, *Imperial Gothic: Religious Architecture and High Anglican Culture in the British Empire, 1840–70*.

**Peter Cormack** is an art historian with a particular interest in early twentieth-century applied arts. He was formerly Keeper of the William Morris Gallery, London, where he curated many exhibitions on aspects of the Arts and Crafts movement, and is the Honorary Curator of Kelmscott Manor, William Morris's country home in Oxfordshire. He is a Fellow of the Society of Antiquaries, and in 2009 he was appointed MBE for services to Art and to Heritage.

**Fabyan Evans** was called to the Bar in 1969 and has been involved with the criminal justice system for forty years. He practised at the criminal Bar on the South-Eastern Circuit until 1988, when he became a circuit judge. Thereafter he sat in various Crown Courts in the London area until he was appointed Resident Judge at Middlesex Guildhall Crown Court in 1995. He was appointed as chairman of criminal justice committees for London and Surrey. He tried criminal cases at all levels and also periodically sat in the Court of Appeal (Criminal Division). He retired from the bench in 2005, shortly after it had been announced that Middlesex Guildhall would become the home

of the Supreme Court of the United Kingdom. He then became a member of the Parole Board for England and Wales, and is now able to spend more time with his family and indulging his passions for golf, sailing and singing.

**Hugh Feilden** joined King's College, Cambridge, in 1971 and trained at the University School of Architecture. Following practical training, he qualified, and joined the Royal Institute of British Architects in 1981. After working in various small practices in East Anglia he joined Feilden+Mawson, the firm founded by his uncle Sir Bernard Feilden, and became a partner in 1996. He has specialized in work to historic buildings, including Norwich Cathedral, Home House, HM Treasury and the Supreme Court of the United Kingdom. He is interested in the strategic aspects of conservation, and in particular, the concept of long-term beneficial use as a primary means of sustaining cultural value for future generations. Hugh is married, with one son, and lives in Norfolk. His hobbies are sailing, riding and bee-keeping.

**Brenda Hale (Lady Hale of Richmond)** is a Justice of the Supreme Court of the United Kingdom. From Richmond in North Yorkshire, she was educated at Girton College, Cambridge, and called to the Bar by Gray's Inn. She spent the first eighteen years of her career as an academic lawyer at the University of Manchester. She then joined the Law Commission, which promotes the reform of the law. In 1994 she was appointed a High Court judge, the first to have made a career in academic and public life rather than at the Bar. In 1999 she was promoted to the Court of Appeal, and in 2004 she became the first and only woman Lord of Appeal in Ordinary. As a home-maker as well as a judge, she has thoroughly enjoyed helping the team of architects and artists to design a home for the new Supreme Court.

**Chris Miele** was educated at Columbia University and received his doctorate in architectural history from New York University. On settling in London in 1991, he joined English Heritage. Subsequently he retrained as a town planner and is now a Partner at Montagu Evans LLP, chartered surveyors and property consultants. In this capacity he advised Transport for London on the proposed redesign of Parliament Square. Alongside this professional work, Dr Miele continues to engage in historical studies, and has an extensive record of academic and professional publications. His particular interest is in Victorian architecture and the history of the environmental movement. In recognition of this work, he has been elected

a Fellow of the Society of Antiquaries and of the Royal Historical Society. He lives in central London in an Edwardian house he, his wife and their daughter have restored. He commutes by bicycle across Parliament Square every day.

**Jeremy Musson** is an architectural historian and journalist, and author of several books, including *How to Read A Country House* (2006) and *The Country Houses of Sir John Vanbrugh* (2008). A former architectural adviser to the Victorian Society between 1990 and 1992, and an assistant curator for National Trust houses in East Anglia between 1992 and 1995, he was Architectural Editor at *Country Life* magazine from 1998 to 2007 and has written about hundreds of important historic buildings. He has sat on the Council for the Care of Churches and the Pevsner Books Trust. He presented the BBC2 TV series about historic houses, *The Curious House Guest*, screened in 2005 and 2006. Born in London, he now lives in the historic city of Cambridge with his wife and two children. He particularly enjoys looking at fine architecture from his bicycle.

# CREDITS

**Client Team:**

*Programme Senior Responsible Owner:*
Vijay Rangarajan, Ministry of Justice

*Programme Director:*
Stephen Foot, Concerto Consulting Ltd

*Business Implementation Director:*
Charles McCall, Ministry of Justice

*Construction Project Director:*
Alan Sloan, HM Court Service

*Construction Project Sponsor:*
Debbie Ball, HM Court Service

**Programme and Project Teams:**

Feilden+Mawson LLP
– in partnership with Foster+Partners: *Concept and Final Scheme Design*
– *Technical Adviser, Construction and Direct Works*
– *Interior Design*

*Sub-consultants to Feilden+Mawson:*
WSP Group: *M&E, Civil and Structural Engineers*
Gardiner & Theobald: *Quantity Surveyors and Cost Consultants*
Spiers and Major: *Interior Lighting Strategy*
CMS Design Associates: *External Landscape Design*

*Other Team Members:*
Drivers Jonas LLP: *Project Management and Town Planning Consultant*
Bovis Lend Lease: *Technical Project Management*
Malcolm Reading Consultants: *Project Management and Direct Works Project Management*

**Construction Team:**

Kier Property, part of Kier Group plc
Wallis Construction *in partnership with Kier*
Gilmore Hankey Kirke Limited (GHK) architects
  *as principal designer for the construction team*

**Interior Design and Fit-Out:**

*Designers/Artists and Contractors:*
Sir Peter Blake: *carpet*
Andrew Motion: *poem*
Richard Kindersley: *glass, carving*
Bettina Furnée: *glass*
Ian Rank-Broadley: *sculpture*
Luke Hughes & Company: *Library*
Tomoko Azumi (t.n.a. design studio): *furniture*
Timorous Beasties: *fabrics*
Andrew Moor Associates: *glass*
Yvonne Holton: *emblem of the UKSC*
Tom Dixon Studio: *easy chairs in private rooms*
Flexiform: *furniture*
Merson Signs: *signage*

Rapiscan Systems: *security*
William Edwards: *crockery*
David Mellor Design: *cutlery*
Dartington Crystal: *glassware*
Modus Operandi: *public art and building strategy*
MoMart: *fine art handling*
Deirdre Mulley: *fine art conservation*

**Business Implementation Project:**
Redpath Design Ltd: *identity and signage design*
Easy Tiger Creative: *exhibition design*
Logica: *software*
Open Text: *content management systems*
ATOS: *hardware and systems*
Liberata: *payroll and finance systems*
Asysco Systems: *broadcasting and audio*
Aerial Concepts: *digital TV*
RTS Communications: *video conferencing*
XM London: *web design*
Softlink: *library systems*
BT
Dolphin Communications: *telephone systems*

# INDEX

Figures in *italics* refer to illustrations.

**A**

Abbott & Co. 88, 124, *126*, 127, *127*, *129*
Abercrombie, Patrick 61
*Academy Architecture* 80, 81
Act of Establishment (1852) 180
Act of Settlement (1701) 21
Act of Union (1706) 23
Act of Union (1707) 23, 38, *39*
Acts of Parliament
  and European Community law 25
  and European Convention on
    Human Rights 26
Administration of Justice Act (1964)
  19–20
Aethelbert, King of Kent 17
Aethelgoda, Queen of the East
  Saxons 17
Agas, Ralph: *Civitatis Londinium...* 52
Agra, India: Diwan-I-Am, Mughal
  palaces 186
Alexander, Frederick J. 184, *184*
Alexander of Abingdon: *Queen
  Eleanor* (Waltham Cross) *110*
Alexandra, Queen 117
Amboise chateau, Loire, France 79, *79*
Anderson, Robert Rowand 80
'apex court' 21, 22
appellate committee 40–41, 43
Appellate Jurisdiction Act (1876) 40
*Architectural Review* 61, *62*
Arding and Hobbs department store,
  near Clapham Junction 80
art nouveau 96, 111
Arthur of Connaught, Prince 19, *19*,
  75, 101, 117, 137
Arts and Crafts
  movement 101, 127
  style 124, 131, *131*, 134
Assizes 15, 20, 23
Australia, Commonwealth of 188
Australian Constitution 188, 193
Azumi, Tomoko *136*, 137

**B**

Bacon, Henry 180
Bagehot, Walter *42*
  *The English Constitution* 42
Baker, Percy Bryant 84, *84*, 117, *119*
Baldwin, Stanley 60
Ball, Walter 203
Bankart, George 131
Bar Mess 202–203
Baroque style 79, 102, 188
Barry, Reverend Alfred 57
Barry, Sir Charles 24, *24*, 49, 55, *56*,
  57, 77, 93
Barry, E.M. 51, 56–59, *58*, *59*, 61, 64, 70

Basilica Constantine, Rome 186
'Battle of the Styles' 183
Bayeux Tapestry *16*
Bedford, Duke of, Lord Lieutenant
  of Middlesex 81, 86
Belcher, John 95
Bell, E. Ingress *176*, 177, 178
Bentham, Jeremy 42
Beresford-Hope, Alexander 59
Big Ben, Palace of Westminster 201
Bingham of Cornhill, Lord 7, 21, 145,
  148
Binney, Marcus 204
Birch, Nigel 66
bishops 40
Black, Chief Justice Michael E.J. 193
Blackburn, Lord 40
Blake, Sir Henry Arthur 178
Blake, Sir Peter 135, 159, *159*, 171
Blois chateau, Loire, France 79
Blomfield, Arthur 102
Bombay (Mumbai) High Court, India
  184, *185*
Brassington, J.W. *185*
BRE *see* Building Research
  Establishment
BREEAM *see* Building Research
  Establishment Environmental
  Assessment Method
*brise-soleil* screen 187, *188*
*British Architect* 93
British Empire 24, 39, 176, 185
British Museum 114
British Overseas Territories 24
Broad Sanctuary 17, 52, 61, 66, *200*
Brock, Sir Thomas, RA 101
Brougham, Lord 42
Browne-Wilkinson, Sir Nicolas 43
Brunei, Kingdom of 24
Brydon, J.M. 49, 56, 75, 79, *94*, 141, 177
Buccleuch, Duke of 39
Buckingham Palace 16
*Builder, The* 80, 81, *83*, 90, 92–93, 102,
  124, 127
Building Research Establishment
  (BRE) 148
Building Research Establishment
  Environmental Assessment
  Method (BREEAM) 148
Burnet, J.J. 79

**C**

Calcutta, India: High Court buildings
  184
Campbell, Colen 177
Campbell, William 184
Canada, Supreme Court *see* Ottawa
Canaletto
  *Westminster Abbey with the Knights
  Companion of the Order of the Bath

  in Procession, 26 June 1749*
  52–53, *53*
*Westminster Bridge from the North
  with the Lord Mayor's Procession,
  25 May 1750* 52, *53*
Canberra, Australia: High Court of
  Australia 186, 188, *189*, *190*, 191,
  193
Canning, George 55, 57, 58–59, 61,
  155
Canning Green 55, *55*, 58–61, *59*, *60*,
  145, 154
Cardiff City Hall 102
  and Law Courts 79
Care Standards Act (2000) 26
Caribbean countries 24–25
Carmichael, James 81, 92, 119
Cassel, Sir Harold 202
Cenotaph 49, 95
Central Criminal Court (Old Bailey)
  15, 177, *177*, 201, 203, 204
Chambord chateau, Loire, France
  79, 85
Champneys, Basil *94*, 95
Chandigarh, India
  Assembly (Parliament) 186
  Governor's Palace (not built) 186
  High Court buildings 184, *185*,
    186
  Punjab and Haryana High Court
    186–88, *186*, *187*, *188*
  Secretariat 186
Channel Islands 24
Chappel, Alonzo *42*
Chapple, Roger 204
'Château-Baronial' style 184–85
Chater, Catchick P. 178
Chawner, Thomas *54*
Chenonceau chateau, Loire,
  France 79
Chippendale, Thomas 133
Church House *200*
Churchill, Sir Winston 48–49, *49*, 66,
  *66*, 67
Churchill Gardens, Pimlico 64
City of London 15, 18
  Guildhall 111
Clarkson, Derek, QC 204
classicism 176, 177, 183
Cnut, King 17
Cockerell, Samuel Pepys 18, *18*, 53,
  54, 76, 77
Colchester War Memorial, Essex 101
Collcutt, T.E. 79
Collier, Hon. John: *William Regester*
  133
Colonial Office 56, 66, 67
common law 17, 38, 44, 176, 180
Commonwealth 24, 137
Concrete Steel Company Ltd 92

Congrès International de
  l'Architecture Moderne (CIAM)
  Athens Charter (1933) 186
Constitution Unit 43
Constitutional Reform Act (2005) 21,
  23, 39, 44, 141, 151, 159
Cope, Arthur Stockdale *43*
Cormier, Ernest 184, *185*
Cornes, Richard 43
Corsham Bath stone 88
County Aldermen of Middlesex
  102–103
County Buildings Committee 103
county councils, creation of (1888) 18
county courts 23
County of London Plan (1943) *60*, 61
Cour de Cassation, Palais de Justice,
  Paris 182, *182*, 183
Court of Appeal (England and Wales)
  23, 39, 40
Court of Appeal (Northern Ireland) 23
Court of Chancery 38, 43
Court of Session, Edinburgh 23, 38
Court Service 41
  'framework agreement' 141, 143
Courts Act (1971) 20, 203
Crespi, James 203
Cromwell, Oliver 51
Crossrail 71
Crown Court for England and Wales
  20, 23, 140
Crown dependencies 24
Cullen, Gordon 61, *62*, *63*

**D**

DCA *see* Department of
  Constitutional Affairs
de Normann, Sir Eric 61, 64
Dean, Ptolemy 24
Dean's Yard *200*
Debenham and Freebody department
  store, Wigmore Street 80
Delhi, India: Diwan-I-Am, Mughal
  palaces 186
Denison, Neil 201
Department for Culture, Media and
  Sport 68
Department of Constitutional Affairs
  (DCA) 140, 141, 157
Deptford Town Hall 102
Derby, Edward Stanley, 14th Earl of
  58
design of UK Supreme Court
  assessing the results 162–73
  choosing the site 140–41
  a collegiate atmosphere 153
  developing the design 141–48
  equal access for all 149–50
  explaining the law and interpreting
    the building 151

external security 162, *162*
facilities for the legal teams 153–54
a front door 150
integrated art and crafts to match
  the original 154
integrating IT and broadcasting
  151–52
interiors and integrated artwork
  158–59
key ideas 148–49
the Library as a body of knowledge
  152, *152*, 153
a new approach to the historic
  building 154–55
planning approval and listed
  building consent 156–58
procurement and delivery 159–61
refining the design 155–56
restoring the clarity of the original
  building 150–51
security 150, *150*
vertical transportation 151
'devolution cases' 23
Dick, William Reid 60
Diespeker & Co. 92
Disraeli, Benjamin 40, 49–50, 58
dissolution of the monasteries
  (1530s) 18
Doll, Charles Fitzroy 101, *102*
Dominions 24
Downing Street, No. 9 24, *24*, 140, 145
Downing Street, No. 10 150
Dublin
  Castle 179
  Customs House 178, 179
  Four Courts 178–79, *179*
  Royal Exchange 179
Dunstan, St 17

**E**

Easy Tiger Creative 161
Ecclesiastical Commissioners 59
Economic and Social Research
  Council (ESRC) 43
Edgar, King 17, 49
Edward I, King *38*
Edward III, King 120
Edward VII, King 84–85, *84*, 117,
  *119*, 150, *150*, 166
Edward the Confessor, King *16*, 17,
  *17*, 51, 74
Edwardian Baroque 49, 75, 79, 80, 93,
  177, *177*
Edwards Madigan Torzillo & Briggs
  186, *190*
Eldon, Lord 39
Eleanor Crosses 111
Elizabeth I, Queen 52, 120
Elizabeth II, Queen 137, *137*, 161, *161*
  and Acts of Parliament 21

English Heritage 68, 71, 141, 145, 149, 155, 156, 157, 159
Epstein, Jacob 58
ESRC *see* Economic and Social Research Council
European Community law 21, 25, 42
European Convention on Human Rights (1950) 21, 25, 26, 42
Evans, His Honour Fabyan 20

**F**

Falconer of Thoroton, Lord 43, *43*
Fehr, Henry 79, 80, 88, 95, *100*, 101–102, *101*, *102*, 104, 108, *108*, 111, *112–13*, 114, *115*, 117, *117*, 119, 120, *122–23*, 124, *125*, *127*, 128, 131, 157, *163*, 173
  *The Four Winds* 111, *112–13*, 114
  *Perseus Rescuing Andromeda* 101, *101*
  *Virtues* 127, *127*
  *Wars of the Roses* reliefs 102
Feilden, Hugh 31
Feilden+Mawson 49, 140, 143, *149*, 158, 161
Festival of Britain (1951) 64, 65
Fielding, Henry 202
Fielding, Sir John ('The Blind Justice') 202, *203*
figures (statues on the façades of the Middlesex Guildhall)
  *Agricultural Industries* 104
  *Architecture* 108
  *Astronomy* 104, *105*
  *Britannia* 108
  *Classical Architecture* 104
  *Communications* 104
  *Dance* 104
  *Education* 108
  *Engineering* 104
  *Gothic Architecture* 104
  *Government* 108, 114
  *Honesty* 111, *111*
  *Justice* 103, 108, 111, *111*
  *Law* 108
  *Learning* 104
  *Literature* 108
  *Maritime Industries* 104
  *Mechanics* 104
  *Metalwork* 104
  *Music* 108
  *Painting* 104
  *Prudence* 103, 108
  *Sculpture* 104, 108, *110*
  *Shipping* 108
  *Truth* 108, 111, *111*
  *Wisdom* 108
Final Court of Appeal of Hong Kong 40
First Commissioner of Works 60
Flemish Renaissance 79
Flete, John 16
Foreign and Commonwealth Office (previously Government Offices) 51, 56, 66, 93
Foster+Partners 49, 68, *68–69*, 71, 143, 145, 154
Fuller, Lieutenant-Colonel James 185
Furnée, Bettina 134–35, *134*, 159

**G**

Gainsborough, Thomas: *Hugh Percy, 1st Duke of Northumberland 15, 133*, 202
Gandon, James 178, 179, *179*
'gaol delivery' process 201

Garden Square 54, *55*, 57, 58, *58*, 70
Gardiner, Lord 41, 42
General Court Room of the Commonwealth of Virginia 182
George III, King 133
  Royal Arms of *133*
George V, King 60
Gibbons, James 132, *132*
Gibson, James 72, 75–77, *75*, 79–81, 88, 90, 92, 93, 95, 101, 102, 103, 111, 114, 119, 124, *128*, *131*, 173
Gibson, Skipworth & Gordon 80, 93, 103
Gibson and Gibson 80
Gilbert, Alfred 101, 104
Gilbert, Cass *171*, *175*, 180, 182
Gilbert Seale & Son 88, 128, *131*
Gilmore Hankey Kirke 161
GLA *see* Greater London Authority
Gladstone, William 40, 58
Goodhue, Bertram Grosvenor *94*, 95
Gordon, Walter 80
Gothic Revival 75, 77, 79, 81, 93, 95, 96, 183–85, 196
Gothic style 49, 50, 55, *55*, 57, *58*, 70, 72, 74–75, 79, 92–93, 95, 111, 114, 115, 120, 131, 154, 184
Goulden, Richard 134, *134*
Government Buildings *see* Treasury, HM
Government Offices Great George Street (GOGGS) 143
Government Offices Whitehall design (1857) 184
Greater London Authority (GLA) 54, 68, 71
Greater London Council (GLC) 19
Greece, ancient 180
Green Yard 51
Greencoat School 18
Grey, Lady Jane 96, 108, *109*
Griffin, Walter Burley 188
Guildhall Committee 76, 80
Gwynn, John 16

**H**

Hailsham, Lord 204
Haldane, Richard, 1st Viscount 43, *43*
Hale, Lady 155, 158
Hall, Sir Benjamin 56
Hamilton, Alexander *42*
Hampton Court: Great Hall 108, *109*
Harold Harefoot, King 17
Harthacnut 17
Hassell Architects *192*, 193
Hawkins\Brown *50*, 70
Hawksmoor, Nicholas 177
Haytor, George: *The Trial of Queen Caroline 39*
Henry II, King 17
Henry III, King 49, *109*
Henry VIII, King 18, *38*, 120
Herland, Hugh 88
Hicks, Sir Baptist (1st Viscount Campden) *15*, 133
Hicks' Hall 133
High Court 55, 155, 158
  role of 23
High Court Library, Edinburgh 145
High Court of Justiciary (supreme criminal court, Scotland) 23
High Court of Punjab and Haryana, Chandigarh, India 186–88, *186*, *187*, *188*
Holden, Charles 95
Hollar, Wenceslaus 52, *52*

Holton, Yvonne *35*, 134, 159
Hone, Nathaniel *203*
Hong Kong
  Final Court of Appeal of 40
  Supreme Court 176–79, *176*, *178*, 183
Hongkong and Shanghai Banking Corporation (HSBC) 177
Hongkong Club 177
Hopton Wood stone 88
Hotel Russell, Bloomsbury 101, *102*, 124
House of Commons
  and Acts of Parliament 21
  chamber bombed in Second World War 40
  *see also* House of Lords; Houses of Parliament; Palace of Westminster
House of Lords 145
  Appellate Committee 140
  committee rooms 26, 32, *32*, 41, *41*, 140, 148
  as a court of trial 38, *39*
  failure as a judicial tribunal 38
  hereditary peers 22, 39
  King's Robing Room 40
  Law Lords in the Chamber 26, *28–29*, 40, *40*, 149
  life peers 39, 40
  Lords of Appeal *21*
  presence of Law Lords in 21–22, *21*
  reduction of power 96
  working peers 21–22
  *see also* House of Commons; Houses of Parliament; Palace of Westminster
House of Lords Act (1999) 22
Houses of Parliament *48–49*
  burning of (1834) 49, *49*
  Gothic style 93
  location 35
  *see also* House of Commons; House of Lords; Palace of Westminster
HSBC *see* Hongkong and Shanghai Banking Corporation
Huddy, Margaret *26*
Hughes, Judge Bill 203
Hughes, Luke 137, 158, 203
Hull Art School 101–102
Human Rights Act (1998) 21, 25
Hunting Act (2004) 21, *21*, 26
Hyderabad, India: High Court buildings 184

**I**

India Office 56
'Indo-Saracenic' style 184
Institute of Chartered Accountants, City of London 95
Ireland and Maclaren 79
Isle of Man 24, 25
Israel: Supreme Court 145

**J**

Jacobean style 90
JCPC *see* Judicial Committee of the Privy Council
Jefferson, Thomas 180, *180*, 182
Jeffries, Judge 202
Joass, J.J. 79
Johannesburg Fort, South Africa 195
John, King 31, *31*, 96, 108, *109*, 135
John Rylands Library, Manchester *94*, 95
Johnson, A.E. 179, *179*
Johnson, Boris 71

judges
  County Court 202
  district 22
  High Court 204
  office held *quamdiu se bene gesserint* 21
  Resident Judge, Middlesex Guildhall 204
Judicature Commission (1867) 39
Judicial Committee of the Privy Council (JCPC) 23, 24, *24*, 33, 35, 39, 75, 85, *86–87*, 140, *141*, 145, 149, 154, 161
Judiciary Act (1903) 188
Jumièges Abbey, Normandy, France 51
JUSTICE 43
Justices of the Peace 22, 75

**K**

Katsieris, Paul *192*, 193
Kent, William 177
Kent County Council 18
Kier 161
Kindersley, Richard 135, *135*, 137, 159
Knight, John Prescott *56*
Konody, P.G. 93, 104

**L**

Labrouste, Henri 182, *182*
Lanchester, H.V. 80
Lanchester, Stewart and Rickards 79–80, 101
Langdale, Lord, MR 42–43
Late Gothic 75, 76, 79, 93, 95, 101, 120
Law Lords (Lords of Appeal in Ordinary) 21–22
  appointment of 40
  and choosing the Supreme Court site 140, 141
  depoliticized 40
  and developing the Supreme Court design 143, 145
  enhancement of judicial role 42
  number of 40
  reasons for decisions published 33
  Senior Law Lord 41–42
  seniority and rank 42
  shrinking of legislative role 42
  transmuted into Justices of the Supreme Court 44
  visits to Law Courts around the world 145
  *see also under* House of Lords
lay peers 38–39
Le Corbusier 186
Le Sueur, Andrew 43
'lease and lease back' 159
Leonardo da Vinci 85
Leverton, Thomas *54*
Liberty of Westminster 15, 16, 18
Lincoln, Abraham 61, 155
Lincoln Memorial, Washington, DC 180, 182
Lindley, Lord 40
Liverpool Cathedral *94*, 95, 101
Livingstone, Ken 71
Lloyd George, David 117, *117*
Local Government Act (1888) 18
Local Government Act (1963) 19
Loire chateaux, France 79, *79*
London County Council (LCC) 18, 19, 59, *59*, 60, 61, 64
London County Council Hostel for Men, Drury Lane 79

London Mayor 71
London Metropolitan Archives 76, 81
London Quarter Sessions 18
London Underground: Jubilee line extension 51
Lord Chancellor 38, *38*, 41, 42–43, *43*, 141, 204
Lord Chief Justice of England and Wales 41–42
Lord Lieutenants of Middlesex 86, 133
Lords of Appeal in Ordinary *see* Law Lords
Lorimer, Robert 101
Lucius, King 16
Lugard, Sir Frederick 174, 178
Lutyens, Sir Edwin 49, 95, 186

**M**

McAuley, Alistair 135
Macdonald, Margaret 134
Machinery of Government Committee 43
Madigan, Colin 186, *190*
Madras, India: High Court buildings 184
magistrates' courts 22–23
Magna Carta *31*, 96, 108, *109*, *134*, 135, 155, *158*
Magnoni, Carlo Domenico *100*, 101, 102, *102*, 115, 117, *118*
Mance, Lord 155
Mandela, Nelson 58
Marlborough Street Magistrates' Court 204
Martin, Leslie 67
Martyn, H.H., & Co. 88, 119, 131, *132*, 157
Mary Tudor, Queen 120, *120*
Marylebone Magistrates' Court 204
Mauritius 24
Mbeki, Thabo 193
Melbourne, Australia
  Commonwealth Law Courts *192*, 193
  Supreme Court 179–80, *179*
Methodist Central Hall 51, 58, *60*, 66, 80
Metropolitan Board of Works 18, 56
Metropolitan Police 61, 64, 68, 203
Michelangelo: *Dying Slave* 108, *110*
Middlesex, County of
  ceases to exist as an administrative or judicial area 20
  coat of arms *13*, 108, *109*, 111, 115, 131
  county Assizes 15, 20
  map of *14*, 15
  Quarter Sessions 15, 20, 88, 201, 202
  and the Supreme Court building 35
Middlesex County Council 15–20, 59–60, 59, 61, 64, 75, 76, 101, 133
  Guildhall Extension Committee 76
Middlesex County Councillors *201*
Middlesex Guildhall, Parliament Square
  architecture of the former guildhall 72–97
  archive store 92, *93*
  closure of the Crown Court (March 2007) 20
  Committee Rooms 119, 201, *201*
  contract drawings for (1911) 81, *82*
  Council Chamber (later Courtroom 1) 19, 20, *20*, 33, *82*, *83*, 85, 86,

88, *88*, 90, 115, 119, 120, *120*, *121*, *122–23*, 124, *124*, 125, 127, *127*, 131, *131*, 149, *149*, 154, 157, *157*, 171, *199*, 201, *201*, 202, 204, *205*
Council Committee Room 90, *90*
County Engineer, offices of the 90
Court 1 (later the Library) 20, 31, *83*, 84, *84*, 85, 86, 114, 117, *117*, *118*, 119, 127, 128, *130*, 145, 155, 204, *206*, *207*
Court 2 (later Courtroom 3) 85, *86*, *114*, 115, *115*, 119, 131, 201
as a criminal court 198–207
Crown Courts at 12, 15, 19–20, *20*, 141, *143*, 150, 156–57
early site 16, *16*
east front *81*, 103, *103*, *108*
entrance hall 84, *84*
first Guildhall 18, *18*, 19, 76, 77
opening of (1913) 7, 19, *19*, 75, *75*, 76, 96, 101, 137
prison cells 92, *92*
refit and refurbishment (1982–88) 20
second Guildhall *18*, 19, 76, 77
as the third guildhall to have been built on the site 15, 19
tower *81*, *139*
west elevation *95*, 96
Middlesex Guildhall Collection 24, 35, *132–33*, 154, 157, 161
Middlesex Guildhall Collection Trust 154
Middlesex Justices 15, 18, 133
Middlesex lieutenancy and magistracy 19–20
Middlesex Regiment War Memorial 166
Middlesex Sessions House, Clerkenwell Green 15, *15*, 18, 53, 54, *54*, *133*, *133*
Miller, James 79
Ministry of Justice 159–61
Ministry of Transport (MoT) 60, *60*, 64
Ministry of Works 61, 64, 65
Minnesota State Capitol, St Paul 180
Modernist architecture 93, 186
monarchy, power of 38, *38*
monasteries, dissolution of (1530s) 18
Montagu, Ewen, QC 202, *203*
Montesquieu, Charles de Secondat, baron de 42
Mortlock, Ethel: *2nd Duke of Wellington* 133
MoT *see* Ministry of Transport
Motion, Andrew 8, 31, *137*, 162
Mountford, Edward 177, *177*
Moya, Hidalgo 67
Mughal architecture 184
Museum of London Archaeological Service 51, *51*

**N**
National Archives, Kew, Surrey 54
National Portrait Gallery 57
National Society 76
Nehru, Jawaharlal 186
Neoclassical style 53, 76, 90, 178
New Delhi, India
Lutyens's designs for 186
Viceroy's House 186
New Palace Yard 51, 52, *52*, 54, 55, 57, 58, 61
'New Sculpture' movement 101, 104
Newcastle, Dukes of 86

Newcastle, Thomas Pelham-Holles, Duke of *126*
Noble, Matthew 58
Norden, John 52
Northern Ireland: legal system 23
Northern Renaissance 101, 120
Northumberland, Duke of 96
Northumberland, Hugh Percy, 1st Duke of, Lord Lieutenant of the County of Middlesex 15, *15*, 133, *170*, 171, 201–202, *202*
Norwood, Suzanne, Resident Judge 204

**O**
Offa, King of the East Saxons 17
Offa the Great, King of Mercia 17
Office of Works 56, 60
Old Bailey *see* Central Criminal Court
Old Palace Yard 51, 52, *53*, 56, 60, 61
OMM Design Workshop and Urban Solutions 193, *194–95*
Ottawa, Canada
Confederation Building 185
Old Supreme Court building 184, *184*
Parliament Hill precinct *185*
Supreme Court 32, 184–85, *184*, *185*

**P**
Palace of Westminster 17, 21, 74, *74*, 77, 93, 96, *96–97*, 120, 135, 141, 201
before the fire 55, *55*
*see also* House of Commons; House of Lords; Houses of Parliament
Palais de Justice, Paris 183, *183*
Palladian style 54
Palmerston, Henry Temple, 3rd Viscount 58
Parke, Baron 39
Parliament Square *47*, 49
Barry's Parliament Square 55–59
beginnings 50–53
ceremonial routes 49, *50*
a greater Parliament Square? 66–71
lack of architectural co-ordination 49, *50*
the new Sessions House and 'Garden Square' 53–55
the next instalment: public outcry and traffic again 59–66
Parliamentary Works Directorate 68
PDS *see* Private Development Scheme
Peel, Sir Robert 58
peers
hereditary 22, 39
lay 38–39
life 39, 40
working 21–22
Perpendicular Gothic 128
Perpendicular style 85, 95
Pevsner, Nikolaus 75, 79, 96, 111
Phillips of Worth Matravers, The Right Hon. Lord 7, 42
Pilgrim Trust 61
Podmore, David 124
Portland stone 65, 71, *76*, 88, 92
Powell, Sir Philip 67
Pownall, F.H. *18*, 76, *76*, 77
Praya Reclamation Scheme 177
Prior, E.S. 127
Private Development Scheme (PDS) 159
Privy Council 44
appeals to 24, *25*

Judicial Committee *see* Judicial Committee of the Privy Council (JCPC)
premises in Downing Street 24, *24*
role of 24–25
separate from the Supreme Court 24
Pugin, Augustus W.N. *41*, 55, 77, 93, 120, 135, 183

**Q**
Quarter Sessions 15, 20, 23, 76
Queen Elizabeth II Conference Centre *66*, 67, *67*, 203

**R**
Raggi, Mario 58
Rahbula, Ernest 80
Rank-Broadley, Ian 137, *137*
Redpath and Brown of Greenwich 92
Regester, William 103, 133
Register of Historic Parks and Gardens 71
Renaissance style 79, *80*, 101, 104, 137
Reynolds, Sir Joshua: *Earl of Northumberland* 133, *170*, 171, 201–202, *202*
*RIBA Journal* 80
RIBA *see* Royal Institute of British Architects
Richard II, King 115
Richmond, Virginia: Virginia Capitol 180, *180*, 182
RICS *see* Royal Institution of Chartered Surveyors
Roberts-Jones, Ivor 49
Rockefeller Chapel, University of Chicago *94*, 95
Rogers, Thomas 15
Romanticism 93
'Romayne' work 120, *120*
Rome, imperial 180
Royal Commission on the Reform of the House of Lords 42, 43
Royal Courts of Justice, Strand 17, *53*, 55, 145, 150, 162, 183, *183*
Royal Fine Arts Commission 64, 65, 67
Royal Institute of British Architects (RIBA) 64, 65, 80, 95
Royal Institution of Chartered Surveyors (RICS) 19, 61, 66, 75, 76, 156
Royal Naval Hospital, Greenwich 177
Royal Palace 51
Royal Parks Agency 64, 68
Royal Town Planning Institute 64
rule of law 44, 74
Rumsey, Edward 184, *184*
Ruskin, John 183
Russell, S.B. 79, 80
Ryder, Private Robert, VC *134*

**S**
Sachs, Justice Albie 195, 196
Saeberht, King of the East Saxons 17
St Giles's Cathedral, Edinburgh: Thistle Chapel 101
St James's Infirmary, Wandsworth 124
St Margaret's Church, Westminster 52, 54, *54*, 55, 57, 58, 70, 74, *74*, 75, 77, 145, 150
St Paul, Minnesota: State Capitol 180
St Paul's Cathedral 16, 17, 177
St Stephen's Tower, Westminster 57
Saint-Denis basilica, Paris 51

Saint-Gaudens, Augustus 61
Sandys, Duncan 67
SAVE Britain's Heritage 155, 158, 204
Scotland: legal system 23
Scott, Sir George Gilbert 56, 59, *74*, 77, 79, 184
Scott, Sir Giles Gilbert 59, 60, *94*, 95, 101
Scott, William Bell 23
section 106 agreement 157, 159
select committees 39
Senior Courts of England and Wales 39
Sessions House, St John Street 15
Sharpe, Montague 103
Shepherd, Thomas Hosmer 77
Simmons, Paul 135
Singapore Supreme Court 177, *177*
Skipwith, Frank Peyton 80, 101, 102, *103*, 111, 128, 132, *132*
Smith, Alfred Louis 179, *179*
Smuts, Jan Christiaan 58
Snaresbrook Crown Court Centre, 157
Soane, Sir John 24, *24*, 55, *55*, *141*
Solicitor General 39
Somerset House 66
New Wing 140, 141
'Soup List' 203
South Africa
Constitution 193, 195, *196*
Constitutional Court 193, *194–95*, 195–96, *196*, *197*
Stationery Office 66, 67, *67*
Statue Square, Hong Kong: Jubilee Memorial to Queen Victoria 177, *178*
Stephen, King 120
Stevens, Alfred 114
Stone, Chief Justice Harlan 180, 182
Stow, John: *Survey of the Cities of London and Westminster* 52, *52*
Straw, Jack, MP 8, *8*, *9*, 43, *43*
Street, G.E. 183, *183*
Sulcard, monk 16–17
Supreme Court, Auckland, New Zealand 184, *184*
Supreme Court, Parliament Square, Westminster
committee rooms *148*
Courtroom 1 (previously Council Chamber) *32*, 33, *82*, 85, 86, *88–89*, 115, 120, 127, *131*, 149, 156, 157, 171, *172–73*
Courtroom 2 31, *34*, 90, *90–91*, 135, 155, 159, 171, *171*
Courtroom 3 (previously Court 2) 85, *86–87*, *114*, 115, 131, *170*, 171
courtrooms 31–33, *32*, *33*, *34*
Crown Court 2 *148*
design of *see* design of UK Supreme Court
emblem of 2, 35, *35*, 134, 135, 159, *159*
entrance 26, 31, 158–59, *158*, *163*, 166–67
exhibition space 33, 35, 151
exterior stone sculpture 102–114
glass screen 26, *27*
hears appeals 23
hears 'devolution cases' 23
interior sculpture and carvings in stone 114–17, *118*
Justices' accommodation *148*, 149, 150, 153, 156, 166

Justices' sitting-room 90, *90*, 127–28, 153, *167*
lawyers' suite 24
Library (previously Court 1) *30*, 84, *84*, 85, 114, 117, *117*, 118, 128, *130*, 134–35, *134*, 135, 145, 148, *148*, 149–50, 152, *152*, *153*, *154*, 155–59, *156*, 158, 166, 168, 169, 202, 203
light-fittings and metalwork 131–32
and the media 33, 151–52
Middlesex Guildhall Art Collection 132–33
Middlesex Guildhall's decorative scheme and its creators 101–102
newly commissioned furnishings 134–37
opening of building (16 October 2009) 7–9, 137, *137*, 161, *161*
plasterwork and tiling 128–31
role of 25, 43–44, 148
Scottish Advocates' Law Library 154, *167*
separate from the Privy Council 24
stained glass and other glazing 124–28
structure 22–23, *22*
war memorials 133–34
woodcarving and furniture 119–24
Supreme Court of Judicature Act (1873) 39–40
Supreme Courts, worldwide 145
Surrey County Council 18
Surrey Sessions House, Newington 19
Syon House, Middlesex 108

**T**
Thames River 16, 51, 56
Thorney Island 16, 17, 19, 50, 51
Thornycroft, Hamo 51, 95
Three Tunns tavern 18
Timorous Beasties design partnership 135
Tothill Fields prison 18
Trafalgar Square 67, 68, 143
transparency (as a concept for the Supreme Court) 149, 185, 186–88, 196
Transport for London (TfL) 66, 68, 71
Trapnell, Alan 203
Treasury, HM (Government Buildings) 54, 44, 49, 54, 56, 60, 61, 75, 93, *94*, 141, 150–51, 177
tribunals 23
Trinidad and Tobago 25, *25*
Truth and Reconciliation Commission 195
Turner, J.M.W.: *The Burning of the Houses of Lords and Commons, October 16, 1834* 49
Tyburn River 16, 50

**U**
UNESCO 70
United Nations 58
United States
Acts of Congress 26
Constitution 26, 182
United States Custom House, New York City 180
US Capitol: Hall of the People 182
US Supreme Court 26, 32, 175, 180, *181*, 182–83, *182*
Associate Justices 22
Entrance Hall *182*
power of 26

**V**

van Somer, Paul *15*, 133
Vanbrugh, Sir John 177
Vardy, John 52, 55
Victoria, Queen 177, 178, *178*
Victoria and Albert Museum 132
Victoria station 102
Victorian Society 155, 158
Virginia Capitol, Richmond 180, *180*, 182
Vogt Landschaftsarchitekten 70
Vogt–Hawkins\Brown *70–71*
von Herkomer, Sir Hubert: *Ralph Littler* 133

**W**

Wakefield, Yorkshire
    County Hall 102
    West Riding County Hall 79, *80*, 88, 102, 119
Wakeham, Lord 42
Wakelam, H.T. 92
Walcot, William 81, *81*, 102
Wallace, William 23, *23*
Wallace & Gibson 80, *80*
Wallis 161
Walsall, Staffordshire
    municipal buildings 80
    Town Hall 124
war memorials 133–34, *134*, 166
Ward, Frank Dorrington 177, *177*
Warren and Mahoney 193, *193*
Waterhouse, Alfred 75
Watling Street 16
Webb, Sir Aston *176*, 177, 178
Webb, John 177
Wellington, Arthur Wellesley,
    1st Duke of 133
Wellington, Dukes of 86
Wellington, New Zealand: Supreme
    Court of New Zealand 193, *193*, 196
West Hall 17
West Ham Technological College 79
West Minster 17
West Riding County Hall, Wakefield,
    Yorkshire 79, *80*, 88, 102, 119
Westbury, Lord 42
Westmacott, Richard 55
Westminster, abbots of 15
Westminster, City of 50
Westminster Abbey 35, 44, *48–49*, 49, *53*, *60*, 68, *74*, 75, *200*
    Chapter House 56
    founded 49, 74
    Henry III grants charter to 108, *109*
    Henry VII's Chapel 56, 77, 84
    north door 58
    north transept 49, 58, 64
    Old Belfry 17
    rebuilt by Edward the Confessor 17
    right of sanctuary 17
    as St Peter's Church 16–17, *16*
    Sanctuary 92
    Sanctuary Tower 17, *17*, 18, 19, 53
    Tothill Street gatehouse 15
    west front 52, 201
Westminster Archives 92
Westminster Bridewell, near
    Greencoat Place *17*, 18
Westminster Bridge 52, *53*
Westminster Cathedral 18
Westminster City Council 61, 64, 67, 68, 140–41, 155–59, *160*, 161
Westminster Hall 17, *17*, 23, *23*, 49, 51, 52, *52*, *53*, 55, 86, 88, 92, 115, 124

Westminster Hospital *58*, 66, 67, *67*, 75
Westminster House 59, *59*
Westminster market 16, 18, 19
Westminster Real Property Company 59
Westminster School *74*, *200*
Westminster World Heritage Site
    Management Plan 68
Willesden County Court 203
William II, King (Rufus) 17, 51
Wiltshire, Stephen *140*
'World Squares for All' Steering
    Group 67–68, *68*, *69*, 68–71, 143, 145, 156
Wornum, George Grey 31, 64–67, *65*, *67*, *69*, 70, 71, 145, *146–47*, 162
Wren, Sir Christopher 177
Wyatt, James 54–55, *54*, 58, *58*, 70
Wylie & Lochhead 88, 119, 157

**Y**

Yevele, Henry 88
Young, William 79

# PICTURE CREDITS

First published 2010 by

Merrell Publishers Limited
81 Southwark Street
London SE1 0HX

merrellpublishers.com

British Library Cataloguing-in-Publication Data:
The Supreme Court of the United Kingdom: history, art, architecture.
1. Great Britain. Supreme Court of Judicature – History.
2. Courthouses – England – London – Design and construction.
I. Miele, Chris. II. Imrie, Tim.
725.1′5′09421-dc22

ISBN 978-1-8589-4507-1 (hardback)
ISBN 978-1-8589-4508-8 (paperback)


*Produced by* Merrell Publishers Limited
*Designed by* Paul Arnot
*Project-managed by* Lucy Smith
*Indexed by* Diana LeCore

Printed and bound in China


*Front jacket*: photograph by Tim Imrie/Ministry of Justice (see page 78)
*Back jacket*: (top row, left to right) image © The British Library Board (see page 14); photographs by Sandy
Stockwell/Skyscan/Corbis (see page 47); Tim Imrie/Ministry of Justice (see page 139); Tim Imrie/Ministry
of Justice; (centre row, left to right) photographs by Tim Imrie/Ministry of Justice (see page 27); Tim
Imrie/Ministry of Justice (see page 85); © Tim Imrie 2007 (see page 122); Morley von Sternberg; (bottom
row, left to right) photographs by Tim Imrie/Ministry of Justice (see page 84); Tim Imrie/Ministry of Justice
(see page 130)